Mark Wagner and William Wagner (Ed.)

Halfway Up the Mountain

World of Theology Series

Published by the Theological Commission of the World Evangelical Alliance

Volume 18

Vol 1	Thomas K. Johnson: The First Step in Missions Training: How our Neighbors are Wrestling with God's General Revelation
Vol 2	Thomas K. Johnson: Christian Ethics in Secular Cultures
Vol 3	David Parker: Discerning the Obedience of Faith: A Short History of the World Evangelical Alliance Theological Commission
Vol 4	Thomas Schirrmacher (Ed.): William Carey: Theologian – Linguist – Social Reformer
Vol 5	Thomas Schirrmacher: Advocate of Love – Martin Bucer as Theologian and Pastor
Vol 6	Thomas Schirrmacher: Culture of Shame / Culture of Guilt
Vol 7	Thomas Schirrmacher: The Koran and the Bible
Vol 8	Thomas Schirrmacher (Ed.): The Humanisation of Slavery in the Old Testament
Vol 9	Jim Harries: New Foundations for Appreciating Africa: Beyond Religious and Secular Deceptions
Vol 10	Thomas Schirrmacher: Missio Dei – God's Missional Nature
Vol 11	Thomas Schirrmacher: Biblical Foundations for 21st Century World Mission
Vol 12	William Wagner, Mark Wagner: Can Evangelicals Truly Change the World? How Seven Philosophical and Religious Movements Are Growing
Vol 13	Thomas Schirrmacher: Modern Fathers
Vol 14	Jim Harries: Jarida juu ya Maisha ya MwAfrika katika huduma ya Ukristo
Vol 15	Peter Lawrence: Fellow Travellers – A Comparative Study on the Identity Formation of Jesus Followers from Jewish, Christian and Muslim Backgrounds in The Holy Land
Vol 16	William Wagner: From Classroom Dummy to University President – Serving God in the Land of Sound of Music
Vol 17	Thomas K. Johnson, David Parker, Thomas Schirrmacher (ed.): In the Name of the Father, Son, and Holy Spirit – Teaching the Trinity from the Creeds to Modern Discussion
Vol 18	Mark Wagner and William Wagner (Ed.): Halfway Up the Mountain

Mark Wagner and
William Wagner (Ed.)

Halfway Up the Mountain
Restoring God's Purpose in this Chaotic World

Contributors

Jenny Clark
Timothy Goropevek
Thomas K. Johnson
Mary-Catherine McAlvany
Charles Reynolds
Walker Tzeng

Alan Cross
John Langlois
David McAlvany
Timo Plutschinski
Hans-Günter Schmidts

WIPF & STOCK · Eugene, Oregon

Wipf and Stock Publishers
199 W 8th Ave, Suite 3
Eugene, OR 97401

Halfway Up the Mountain
Restoring God's Purpose in this Chaotic World
By Wagner, Mark and Wagner, William
Copyright © 2020 Verlag für Kultur und Wissenschaft Culture and Science Publ.
All rights reserved.
Softcover ISBN-13: 978-1-7252-9444-8
Hardcover ISBN-13: 978-1-7252-9443-1
Publication date 12/4/2020
Previously published by Verlag für Kultur und Wissenschaft Culture and Science Publ., 2020

Contents

Foreword	....Dr. Aiah Foday-Krabenje	7
Preface	....	11
Acknowledgements	....	13
Chapter 1:	**Introduction** ....Dr. Mark Wagner *How Can Evangelicals Transform Society?*	15
Chapter 2:	**Theater and Art** .... Mary-Catherine McAlvany *Regaining Wonder Through the Arts*	37
Chapter 3:	**Business** .... Timo Plutschinski *Influencing the Mountain of Business*	51
Chapter 4:	**Media** ....Timothy Goropevek *The Cultural Mountain of Media: A Global Strategy to Turn the Tide*	71
Chapter 5:	**Education** .... Dr. William Wagner *Changing Education Today*	97
Chapter 6:	**Family** .... David McAlvany *A Basic Building Stone for the Faith*	119
Chapter 7:	**Government** .... Dr. John Langlois *Transforming Government*	139
Chapter 8:	**Military** .... Col. Charles Reynolds *A Strategic Plan for Climbing the Military Mountain*	155
Chapter 9:	**Sports** .... Hans-Günter Schmidts *Sports Today: A World Phenomenon*	183
Chapter 10:	**Technology** .... Dr. Walker Tzeng *A Biblical-Theological Approach to Transforming Technology*	203

Chapter 11: **Religion** .... Dr. Thomas K. Johnson   221
The Word of God and the Mountains of Culture

Chapter 12: **Immigration** .... Alan Cross   239
Receiving Faith: The Hospitality of God Amid the Crisis of Global Migration

Chapter 13: **Christian Education** .... Jenny Clark   255
The Alarming Decline of Christian Theological Education in the UK

Chapter 14: **What Is Next?** .... Dr. William Wagner   289
Creating a Mega Strategy for Christianity

Foreword

Dr. Aiah Foday-Khabenje

Aiah Foday-Khabenje, Sierra Leonean, is the General Secretary of the Association of Evangelicals in Africa (AEA). He previously served in various positions in Sierra Leone. He is the immediate past General Secretary of the Evangelical Fellowship of Sierra Leone, a position he held for ten years, after serving as the founding Coordinator/Principal of REAPS Vocational Institute in the same organization. As General Secretary of EFSL, he was elected Chairperson of the Sierra Leone Association of Non-Governmental Organizations (SLANGO) for two consecutive terms, serving there until his appointment with AEA moved him to Nairobi, Kenya. Other services include Head Optician at the Lunsar Eye Hospital, Proprietor of Fo-Ny Optical Services, Senior Administrative Assistant in the University of Sierra Leone, and an ordained minister of the Presbyterian Church of Sierra Leone.

Aiah holds a D.Min. degree from Asbury Theological Seminary, an M.A. from Wesley

Biblical Seminary in the U.S., BS and an MBA from the University of Sierra Leone. He is a Fellow of the Association of British Dispensing Opticians (FBDO). He is married to Almonda; they have four children. He now lives with his family in Nairobi, Kenya.

Halfway Up the Mountain is a strategic call for evangelicals to finish the task of world evangelization—the only way for the healing and mending of our hurting and broken world. Given the extent of secularism and pluralism of religions in our world today, the Church needs to strategically reposition and engage the world to bring about gospel transformation. Wagner and Wagner correctly posit that it would require strategy at the Mega level to effectively respond to this divine mandate.

God Himself is a master strategist and expects the Church to do no less. The Supreme Communion of Being—The God-head and Holy Trinity, in perichoresis, evokes a sense of innovation, dynamism, and life giving. The Triune God strategically and purposefully created the cosmos and imparted aspects of his creative and moral attributes to a viceroy, at the apex of his creation.

Let us make human beings in our image, to be like us. They will reign over the fish in the sea, the birds in the sky, the livestock, all the wild animals on the earth, and the small animals that scurry along the ground." So, God created human beings in his own image. In the image of God, he created them; male and female he created them. Then God blessed them and said, "Be fruitful and multiply. Fill the earth and govern it. Reign over the fish in the sea, the birds in the sky, and all the animals that scurry along the ground." Then God said, "Look! I have given you every seed-bearing plant throughout the earth and all the fruit trees for your food. And I have given every green plant as food for all the wild animals, the birds in the sky, and the small animals that scurry along the ground—everything that has life." And that is what happened. Then God looked over all he had made, and he saw that it was very good! (Gen. 1:26-31a. NLT).

This is not a myth, even if it does border on the mysterious. This is the origin of human species, uniquely and purposefully made, in the image of God—with aspects of God's attributes for creativity and morale values—wired to care for the rest of the very good world God strategically created. This is how humans can explore the span of the cosmos, from the oceans to the skies, with a small fraction of their brain cells.

That divine privilege was squandered by the first couple with far-reaching consequences for humanity. Humans are estranged from God, with ruptured relationship with one another and the rest of creation. Despite all the industrial and technological advancements, our sin-bound will is not able to love God and our fellow humans, eternally bound, except for the Grace of God. The history of the world reveals its ups and downs as humans mess around with it. It takes humans made in His image and with the ability to pro-create, explore the cosmos in ways that are consistent with God's values and purposes for our own good. We reject this to our peril. Unfortunately, the choice we have made is to reject God's plan and incline our hearts to wickedness. We have kept God out of our lives, and we have opted for secularism.

"But God does not just sweep life away; instead, he devises ways to bring us back when we have been separated from him" (2 Sam. 14:14b). The good and just God, graciously makes a way to fix the brokenness of our world and human depravity for salvation and self-actualization. He has used various strategies to call humans back into himself. He has spoken through the prophets and latterly, He sent His Son. By His death and resurrection, God's love and justice reconciled, and grace extended to lost humanity. Now ascended to heaven, He established His Church as the means to extend His grace to lost humanity. The Church is a community that takes seriously God's special revelation, the Bible. Through the Bible we can know God's mind and through the power of the Holy Spirit and *Imago Dei*, we have the ability to mend and fix God's world. The *Imago Dei*, marred at creation, is enhanced by the Cross of Christ and sealed by the Holy Spirit—the hope of the world, entrusted to the Church.

The Church, no doubt, has done much, but it still has plenty of unfinished tasks. The Church is also experiencing reverses in its gains, even in regions where the church is growing. The growth of the Church appears to be only a numeric and may not seem to match the secularist and other religious agenda. As I write this piece, the world is shaken to the foundation, exposing human deadness, reminding us of our finitude (thanks to COVID19).

Fixing our broken world requires the church's awareness of where the walls are broken and the extent of the problem. Creation or creativity takes intentionality, purposefulness, strategic thinking, and planning. Thus, ten mountains of culture, identified by the editors and the authors and meant to be transformative, are explored in this work. The thesis is that if the church should effectively reach the world and bring about gospel transformation, it needs to do world evangelization differently. The church should seek to engage human culture holistically, inclusive of the ten mountains of culture. To achieve this, a global organization like the World Evangelical Alliance, with structured networks at local, national, regional, and global levels, needs to put in place a Mega strategy.

The Church needs to have a Mega strategy to engage each mountain, speaking life into it, with the hope the Church offers the world, to bring about transformation. Each chapter in this book addresses a different mountain of culture and outlines the current state of affairs and what needs to be included in the Mega plan. Each one of the ten mountains of culture have been addressed by an expert on that mountain of culture, bringing their biblical, theological perspectives and professional experiences to bear on the particular mountain of culture. The particular culture is analyzed, pointing out areas of culture that the transformative impact of the church has been lacking and suggesting ways of engaging them. The underlying secularist culture has real potential to continue to erode the gains the church has made in mending the brokenness of the world. They also highlight themes and outcomes that could be constitute the strategy.

The book illustrates how other organizations who do not necessarily hold biblical values have carved Mega strategies and have implemented these to successfully achieve their goals—somewhat continuing to contribute to the world's messy situation. While the church may have done so much towards achieving its mission, there is still much to do. Metaphorically, the church may have gone only halfway up the mountain. The Church or the evangelical church needs to employ these tools and formulate strategies for engaging these mountains.

I commend this work to the church around the world; it is a great tool to solidify our collaboration and unity in the gospel for the healing of the nations, to the glory of God.

Dr. Aiah Foday-Khabenje

Preface

"Climb every Mountain, search high and low, follow every highway, every path you know, climb every mountain, ford every stream, follow every rainbow, till you find your dream"

– From Sound of Music by Rogers and Hammerstein

If you travel between Munich, Germany, and Salzburg, Austria, you can see a large chain of mountains. At first it appears impossible to cross these majestic peaks. It is only when you get closer that you find the valleys and paths that make it possible to travel down to Italy.

In this book we are discussing the Ten Mountains of Cultures. As Christians we need to discover how we can find the best ways to influence those who live and work under the mountains. It appears that we have been satisfied with doing the same things again and again without realizing that we now have new technologies and tools that we allow us to be far more effective than we have been in the past. It is now our job to explore what we have done in the past and how we can proceed into the future in a way as to make the message of Jesus Christ more assessable to the masses in the world.

It is not easy to climb the mountains of life. Roger Whittaker, famous singer from Kenya, sings the song "Halfway up the Mountain." In it, he says that the hardest part of climbing a mountain is when you are halfway up the mountain. Today it appears as if Christianity is halfway up the mountain. Much good is being done by many people, but much more still needs to be accomplished. When I lived in Innsbruck, Austria, Charles Reynold (one of our authors) was a journeyman missionary working with me. Every day I would get up early in the morning and run up the mountain next to my house, running up five kilometers and then back down for a total of ten. It was very difficult to run up the mountain, and it took me several months of trying before I could run the whole distance without stopping. One day Charlie, who also ran up the mountain, wanted to run with me. I agreed. The run was difficult for me, especially since Charlie, who was younger and ran faster, was with me. At one point, Charlie stated, "We are now halfway up the mountain." At that point I stopped. Only halfway meant that there was still too much to do.

In the church today we still have mountains to climb if we are to carry out the Great Commission. In the past Christians have accomplished much, but we still have more to do. We are only halfway up the mountain. One friend of mine relates the story of the time he and some others were climbing Pike's Peak in Colorado. They had reached the halfway point and were resting when two ladies arrived at the same place. It was apparent that they were both very tired, and one of the ladies, gasping for air, made the statement, "I think the attitude is getting to me." Of course, she meant the altitude, but her first statement was probably also correct: the "attitude was getting to her." We are challenging the church today to change their attitude that often includes accepting the status quo and to attempt new and great things for God.

Today in the church we need to change our attitude and once again go on the offensive in our world. During the decade of 2020s, it is apparent that Christianity, especially in the West, is on the defensive, trying to retain what we have won and trying to ward off the many attempts at intimations that are coming our way.

This book is built on the premise that strategy development can be on three levels: Micro, Meta, and Mega. The church is now doing well at the first two, but not enough is being done at the Mega level. In trying to develop a valid strategy, it will be necessary to break the task down to smaller units; thus, we are looking at the ten mountains of culture. We have been very fortunate to have ten outstanding scholars to write chapters for us. Some of the authors are leaders in their mountain of culture, such as Timo Plutschinsky, who is the leader of the WEA Business Coalition, and Hannes Schmidt, the head of Europe's largest and most influential Christian sports organization. Other authors have gained real experience in the area on which they are writing, such as Dr. John Langlois, who was a member of his country's parliament, and Dr. Thomas Johnson, who leads the Interreligious group of the WEA. Some are old, such as William Wagner, who is 84, and some are young, such as Jenny Clark, who is 35. The authors come from five different countries and three continents; thus, the total approach is both international and multicultural. We have both male and female contributors. All the authors are experts in their fields, and we feel very fortunate to have them work with us as we seek a more effective way to present the Gospel of Jesus Christ to the World of today.

Both editors and each of the authors hope that you enjoy this book and that you will feel more challenged to think about missions on a higher level. We would like to challenge you to start thinking at the Mega level and join us as we seek to change the World for Jesus Christ.

Acknowledgements

Many have helped us in preparing this book. First, we would like to thank the Olive Institute for Global Strategic Studies. This organization has been our operational base, and they have allowed us the necessary time so that this book can be published.

Also we would like to thank Ms. Reta Beall, who has acted as our editor. She has done a monumental job in putting the book together. When you have twelve different writers all with different writing skills, it becomes somewhat difficult to fit it all together. Reta has done a magnificent job in doing just that.

We are also very thankful for the help given us by Dr. Thomas Schirrmacher and Titus Vogt from Culture and Science Publishers. From the very beginning they have shown a willingness to publish this book in order to show the world the need for the Church to create a Mega Strategy for World Evangelization.

Chapter 1: Introduction

Dr. William Mark Wagner

Mark Wagner was born in Albuquerque, New Mexico, in 1964, and grew up as MK in Salzburg, Austria. He studied at Baylor University and Southwestern Baptist Theological Seminary (SWBTS) in Texas, from which he earned a Ph.D in Missions.

He currently lives in Bornheim, Germany, with his wife Carrie Menees, who he married in 1993, and their two daughters, Kate and Natalie.

In 1996 he moved to Europe and served as pastor of the German Baptist Church in Hannover from 1996 to 1999. In 1999 he was appointed by the International Mission Board (IMB) of the Southern Baptist Convention. His assignments have included teaching at Bibleseminar Bonn and at the "Biblisch Theologische Akademie" in Wiedenest, leading the IMB mission work in the German-speaking Europe from 2006—2010, planting two churches, and investing in and equipping young leaders. Since 2017 he has been the director of the Ph.D. Program of the Zinzendorf School of Doctoral Studies at Olivet University. He also serves on the Board of SRS e.V., the main Christian Sports Ministry organization in Germany.

In his free time, he enjoys hiking, running, skiing, and travelling.

How Can Evangelicals Transform Society?

"Where there is no vision from God, the people run wild, but those who adhere to God's instruction know genuine happiness"

Prov. 29:18.

Introduction

Upon reflection on the summer of 2020, I, like many others, have been amazed at the cultural revolution we are witnessing in the U.S. Before our eyes, longstanding values that have defined our nation are being torn down and replaced with new and radical ideas. Who would have ever thought that we would be seriously debating topics such as abolishment of the police force or tearing down statues of our founding fathers? Who could have imagined that we are seriously questioning our 'law and order' society? The death of George Floyd, a linchpin moment, became not only the spring board for racial reform but also the battle cry for a deep-seated change of our society: change in what is accepted and what is rejected, what is considered good and bad, what is desired and what is no longer acceptable. This moment set in motion a change that was decades in the making.

This is how social revolutions and cultural transformations happen. The change process begins with an idea that slowly infiltrates the social and cultural structure of a society. Once it has gained a critical mass, it waits for a linchpin moment to topple the old system and implement the desired change. When we look across history, we can observe this process leading up to significant historical linchpin moments: 1517 Luther and the Reformation-1517; the birth of the United States-1774; the French Revolution-1789; the Revolutions across Europe-1848; the Communist Revolution in Russia-1917; the Rise of power of Adolf Hitler-1933; the Social Revolution in the U.S.—1968; and so on. These, and many others, were historical moments when a society's worldview shifted, new paradigms were introduced, and new values were established. None of these social changes came out of nowhere; they were preceded by a long process that led up to the change. Each change was birthed in the social dissatisfaction and the growing dissonance of the society. The gap between the "haves and have-nots" started to get bigger and more divisive. In the midst of this growing gap, new ideas and new social models emerged. New groups began exploring and trying out these new ways. These new, often radical ideas began gaining acceptance, leading to conflict with the old ideas and systems. The stage was increasingly set for a major clash between the old and new. All these events preceded the linchpin moment.

In many cases, the process was strategically planned and directed, especially with the revolutions of the last centuries. Thinkers, writers, and leaders planted the seeds of change, advanced it, and guided it to its completion. I am thinking here of the Marx, Engels, Lenin connection as it related to the rise of communism. In addition, people like Benjamin Franklin, Thomas Jefferson, George Washington, and others laid the foundation for a new nation. The list goes on. Each revolution/social change has its thinkers and leaders who pave the way. Each transformation is accompanied by a plan, a strategy for change, that serves as a guide for the change process.

Evangelical Christian leaders talk about changing the world, but they seem to always be responding to changes rather than leading the charge for change. It is interesting to note that the current (2020) push for social change in the U.S. is directed against Christians and their cultural influence. Freedom of religion is under full attack, not so much by the government, but by other key forces in society (media, business, Hollywood, etc.). Christian values, like the vow of marriage being between a man and woman, are being redefined as hate speech. The Christian voice is being pushed out of the public arena. The methodology of these forces is social and economic pressures and intimidation. Christianity, especially evangelical Christianity, is on the defensive.

These questions beg to be answered: What should be done? Do we retreat? Do we fight? Do we wait it out? Do we ignore it and do as we always have? Or do we take the initiative and lay the groundwork and develop a plan for transforming the society once again through the Gospel?

Our focus has been on reaching the world for Christ. We have thousands of ideas, plans, and models of how this can be done, yet we are missing a Mega strategy that not only does evangelism, but also leads to social transformation. Our focus has been on Micro and Meta strategies. We have had strategies that reach individuals, people groups, cities and nations, but we have not had any substantial Mega-strategies that focus on societal change. One of the most significant social transformations that took place in world history was the transformation of the Roman society by Christianity. From its inception until A.D. 323, the Christian message and life became an increasing force that challenged the existing power structures and eventually overcame them and reformed them. Even though it did not cumulate in a "moment of change" (unless we consider the conversion of Constantine the linchpin moment), as we study church history, we realize the change came about through a plan initiated by its founder. Is it possible that Christianity can once again reshape our society?

This chapter will explore this idea and ask what a Mega strategy could look like and what we need to do to bring about a Christ-centered social transformation. Through understanding the nature of a society, understanding the spiritual powers behind the existing social structures, knowing the power of the Gospel, and having a plan and strategy of engagement, this type of transformation is possible. The following chapters will look at key areas of culture and will lay out a strategy for reshaping the key mountains of society through the gospel. In order to develop a plan, I will first address the nature of culture and how it shapes, influences, and controls a society. Second, I will look at the process of cultural change and movements as the guide for the transformation process. Based on this, I will lay out the foundation for a Mega strategy for how evangelicals can go on the offensive and restore and reshape society through the Gospel. Just a note, we are not talking about a one- or five-year plan, but a long-term approach that may take years, decades, or longer. We are not seeking to plant and grow an overnight movement, but a transformation that will have a long-lasting effect on this society and the ones to come.

How Does Culture Shape a Society?

Every society has an overriding culture and many sub-cultures. There are different levels of culture, each shaping and influencing the individual and the people of the society. The many definitions of culture all have this one common element: it is a pattern of thinking and behaving that is shared by everyone and which permeates all aspects of life. It is not determinant, but we are conditioned by it. At the core of a culture is its worldview. It is comprised of deeply held core values, premises, and presuppositions, also referred to as themes, that underlie and shape its society. For example, a general concept might be the belief that the world is mechanical and is ruled by the laws of nature or the belief that the world is ruled by spiritual beings.

Another example of a worldview theme is the belief that the world is cyclical or the opposing view that the world is linear. Besides these more general worldview premises, each society also has key premises that are unique to its people. The pursuit of Freedom and Individualism shape American culture. Adherence to a set order is definitive of German society. In Judaism, the Torah is a key concept for all areas of culture. The worldview is formed at the inception of the culture and develops and evolves over the ages.

During the culture change process, these premises and presuppositions are challenged, and new alternative premises are proposed. Usually these new ideas are only a modification or deviation of the original premise. For example, "Freedom of Religion" is replaced by "Freedom from Religion." In most cases, the themes are reformulated and redefined to enable the change to take place. On a rare occasion, the existing worldview is rejected and replaced with a new premise, but for any significant transformation to take place, the core values, premises, and themes of a culture need to be addressed. If we, as evangelical Christians, seek to transform culture, the worldview themes need to be redefined to coincide with God's purpose and original intent. As Jesus said to the Pharisees, "I did not come to abolish the law [worldview theme of Judaism] but to fulfill it." The basic premise here is that these themes are God-given, but in the context of the Gospel, they will be restored to their God-given expression and purpose.

The worldview affects every aspect of one's life. Its importance can't be overstated. It guides and directs everything we do. It explains our world, tells us what is good and bad, and helps us to filter what we experience. It empowers us as well as keeps us from doing things. It defines our relationships, explains why things happen, and determines how we organize and how we relate to one another. Because of our worldview's strong, determinant presence, the themes are intrinsically powerful. Those in power use these themes as tools to gain and solidify their influence and control. If someone can actually reshape or redefine the theme to fit his or her agenda, he or she has tapped into a significant power source for a specific cause. We will follow up on this later in the discussion.

How do these themes express themselves, wield power, or function as a control mechanism over the people? The worldview and its themes are expressed through the different visible structures of its culture. First, the culture and its society are built upon core pillars, or, expressed differently, as mountains of culture. There have been different attempts to define these mountains. In 1975 Bill Bright and Loren Cunningham identified seven mountains of societal influence: religion, family, education, government, media, arts and entertainment, and business. We suggest in this book to expand the list to include military, sports, and technology. Each one of these mountains plays a key role in shaping and maintaining the societal culture.

Their role is to meet the basic needs of a society. An example of the roles of some of the mountains are the following: government is to provide order, media is to communicate and inform, the arts and entertainment are to meet the need for pleasure and creativity, religion is to provide access to the need for transcendence, family is to meet the basic need for relationship, etc. Each of these mountains in its attempt to meet societal needs will be shaped and guided by the existing worldview themes. The theme of freedom will determine how business is conducted. Freedom will influence the way religion is viewed and organized in the culture. The theme of individualism will determine how family relationships are lived out. The mountains meet the basic needs of each society, and they do it within the framework of their worldview.

A healthy mountain is vital to the stability and welfare of a society. If the mountains fail to or only partially meet the needs of the culture, then a growing dissonance develops within the society. For example, if the government fails to govern or fails to provide justice for all and allows for a strong discrepancy between the poor and the wealthy, then this mountain becomes the source and arena of social unrest.

Because of each mountain's key role in society, those who control those mountains have the power. They are the gatekeepers. The gatekeepers can be an individual, an institution, or an organization. It is a concrete entity. They are often the face of the mountain and influence, direct, and control the different entities associated with the mountain. On the media mountain, for instance, there are a number of media outlets, but are only a few of them control the media world. In the U.S., these would be the New York Times, CNN, and Fox News. It really does not matter what the local *Press Democrat* newspaper of Santa Rosa says about national news (which is usually just an extension of what the *New York Times* writes). When there is more than one gatekeeper, there is often an agreement between the parties on how to share the power; however, it can also evolve into a battle for the control of the mountain.

These gatekeepers shape the mountain. They work within the context of the society's worldview. In times of crisis and change, however, these gatekeepers become the vehicle for worldview and societal change, so whenever change is on the horizon, the main focus is on influencing the gatekeepers and getting them on one's side. Without them, transformation is close to impossible. Therefore, whoever controls the gatekeeper controls the society. In other words, the first step in making societal change is to gain control of the gatekeeper. Either the old keepers are persuaded to follow the new path, becoming a vehicle for change, or new gatekeepers emerge that challenge the old gatekeepers and replace them.

The second area in which the worldview expresses itself are the symbols, traditions, and rituals of a society. The key cultural themes of America are found in the Motto (Symbol)– "Life, Liberty, and the Pursuit of Happiness." The homosexuals use the rainbow symbol to express their theme of freedom and diversity. Statues und memorials serve as reminders of what is valuable to the nation and its people. The Fourth of July is a celebration of freedom. Often the symbols are associated with the gatekeepers

How Can Evangelicals Transform Society?

of a mountain. Sometimes, the gatekeepers use the symbols to advance their position and solidify their power. The symbols and rituals unite people, they transmit the core worldview themes (or their redefined understanding of the themes) to the people, and they give people the feeling everything is okay as long as these symbols and rituals are present. As with the mountains, whoever controls the symbols and uses the rituals to their advantage is able to unite the people around their understanding of the worldview themes. The rainbow has become a symbol of a redefined understanding of freedom—a freedom that allows and accepts diverse expressions, a freedom without moral limits.

The new understanding of the worldview themes is wrapped in a symbol or tradition and then becomes the vehicle for identifying with the new message. Every cultural change and the ideas it brings is accompanied by symbols. The Reformation—" Sola Gratia," Communism—the Hammer and Sickle, Nazi Germany—the Swastika, the Homosexual movement—the Rainbow, the current revolution—the "Black Lives Matter" slogan. Sometimes the old symbols are redefined, but usually new symbols are created.

Understanding the place and role of both the gatekeeper and the symbols is vital to any cultural change. Any attempt to make changes needs to direct its attention to influencing the gatekeepers and redefining existing symbols and traditions or creating new ones. If we look back at the history of social transformations, these two features will always be at the center of the conflict.

Before moving on to the process of change and its impact on an evangelical transformation strategy, one more important factor needs to be considered in understanding the worldview, the mountains, gatekeepers, and symbols—the underlying spiritual dimension. As Paul said in his letter to the Ephesians, "For our struggle is not against flesh and blood, but against the rulers, against the authorities, against the powers of this dark world and against the spiritual forces of evil in the heavenly realms" (Eph 6, 12). Further, he said in 2 Corinthians 10,3-5,

> For we live in the world, we do not wage war as the world does. The weapons we fight with are not the weapons of the world. On the contrary, they have divine power to demolish strongholds. We demolish arguments and every pretension that sets itself up against the knowledge of God, and we take captive every thought to make it obedient to Christ.

In reading the Bible, one will quickly learn that there is an entity, Satan, that is opposed to God and his ways—accusing, tempting, and distorting all that God is doing and pulling people and societies away from God. Through sin, we have allowed him to take control of the world and turn it against and away from God. As a result, people are blinded to the things of God (2 Cor 4,4). Of course, we know that through Jesus Christ, the power of Satan has been broken, but he still seeks to deceive and draw people away, so wherever the power is, we find Satan trying to gain control through distortion and deception. If he can distort the worldview themes, gain control of the mountains through its gatekeepers, and redefine symbols and rituals to meet his agenda, he will be able to blind the people and lead the society away from God and its intended purpose Depending on the mountain and the degree of distortion, the process of cultural decay may be slower or faster.

So when one is looking to transform a society and its culture, one needs not only to identify the worldview themes, the gatekeeper, and the symbols, but also to recognize the spiritual powers that pull the strings behind the scene.[1] Once this is understood, then it is also important to understand the cultural change process. Doing so will allow us to then develop a strategic framework for a spiritual social transformation.

A Movement That Leads to Change

Anthony Wallace in his paper "Revitalization Movements"[2] and Luther P. Gerlach and Virginia H. Hines in their book *People, Power, Change: Movements of Social Transformation*[3] provide a road map for the process of a social transformation movement. Their insight will help us later develop our plan and strategy.

The basic premise is that when a society experiences social dissonance, it becomes unstable, leading to social stress. In order to return to stability, one or more movements will emerge that will challenge the existing powers and either replace or reshape the power structures according to a new social vision in order to regain a new stability.

---

[1] This article will not go into more detail on the spiritual dimension and its impact on strategy. For more detail discussion go to my book, Wagner, William Mark. *Spiritual Warfare as an Effective Missionary Method*. Nürnberg: VTR, 2017; or McAlpine, Thomas. *Facing the Powers: What are the Options?* Eugene: Wipf and Stock, 2003.

[2] Anthony F. C. Wallace, "Revitalization Movements," *American Anthropologist*, Vol 58, No 2 (Apr. 1956): 264 – 281

[3] Luther P. Gerlach and Virginia H. Hines, *People, Power, Change: Movements of Social Transformation* (Ann Arbor: Bobbs-Merrills, 1970).

The starting point is a stable society. This means that the worldview meets the needs of a society; each mountain is fulfilling its intended purpose. Even though there may be some social disparity and inequality, it is within an acceptable range. The majority of people are satisfied. The minorities are cared for and have an acceptable status in the society. Even though the society is stable, it is a fluid stability that can quickly lose its balance. Outside or inside forces, events, and situations can quickly lead to cultural stress. Usually it is not one major event, but the accumulation of smaller ones that leads to a rise in inequality. The mountains fail to live up to or deviate from their intended purpose, power abuse increases, and greed and envy reshape the way of life. The gap between the haves and the have nots increase and lead to a dissonance between the cultural ideal of the society and the existing condition.

As the dissatisfaction grows, the yearning for a new order grows. The first voices that speak out are the prophetic ones who point out the situation and warn of the dire consequences if things do not change. Even though these prophets can appear within the context of any of the mountains of culture, they usually first appear in the arts and media community. Sometimes the voices are found in the religious arena. They are the precursor of what is to come. Those who listen will have a head start in dealing with the conflict.

On the heel of the prophetic, new ideas, new approaches, and new strategies to fix the problems emerge. They can range from a complete overhaul of society to minor repairs to the overall system. Often these new ideas include a rethinking and reshaping of key worldview premises. Some ideas are so outlandish that they are quickly dismissed; however, they often become the seed for more reasonable and practical ideas.

As these ideas develop, new leaders emerge who embrace the new ideas. They become the voice and face of a movement for change. Through his or her leadership, the ideas catches fire and people become engaged with the idea. Model sub-cultures are created based on the new approach. They usually function parallel and in contrast to the existing structures. Usually a number of competing groups emerge. As the movement grows stronger, however, they begin to flow together into one movement as they come into conflict with the existing powers.

This process can take years, decades, and sometimes centuries. Often small pockets emerge and challenge the structure, but because the movement is too small or not developed yet, they are suppressed. Looking back at the Reformation, we can notice that there were prophetic voices that spoke out centuries prior to the Reformation. Small sub-cultures developed around key prophetic voices and leaders like John Hus, yet the uprising was quickly subdued. In order for a movement to be successful, it needs to grow and mature and wait for the linchpin moment.

As the movement grows, its ideas come into conflict with the existing power structures. It is usually with the gatekeepers of the different mountains. At first the encounters are isolated and appear harmless. Those in power usually ignore the threat, ridicule it, or quickly isolate it and suppress it. Yet as the movement evolves and the people see the new idea as a means for overcoming the dissonance, the movement gains steam and the encounters increase in volume and in intensity. The encounters usually come by chance, but they are often orchestrated by the leadership of the new movement. If done strategically, these encounters lay the foundation for the linchpin moment.

The existing powers have a number of options to deal with this movement. They can go on as usual, ignoring the call to change; however, when the time comes, the powers have usually weakened and are not able to withstand the force of change. Another approach is to suppress every form of dissent. They persecute and work on cementing their power base. This leads to a dictatorship or a totalitarian regime, but as history shows, the time does come when the dissonance grows unbearable and it leads to a revolt. The most fruitful approach is to engage the new ideas, listen to them, and begin to incorporate them. If done wisely and prudently, this process leads to a peaceful and healthy transformation. In each case, the new challenges the old, and as a result of a linchpin moment, change is implemented. The result is a new normal. A new stability is created, and the process of change begins anew. Those who know how to maneuver through this process are those who will lead the transformation.

How does a movement start? Gerlach and Hines in studying the Pentecostal and the Black Power movements of the 60s showed that five key characteristics are present in all movements. (1) A movement has a clearly defined message. It addresses the core needs, it is simple, and it easy to communicate. The Pentecostal movement—" baptism of the Holy Spirit;" the black Power movement—"black power"; the current movement sweeping the U.S.—Black Lives Matter." (2) The adherents of the movement need to be passionate about the message. There is a willingness to die for the cause. (3) Movements are spread through person-to-person recruitment. Public figures, public events, and good PR will make the movement known, but it is still the personal recruitment that is key in growing the movement. (4) Organization of the movement is decentralized and organic. The organization grows out of the movement. A strong movement has many leaders rather than just one central figure. (5) Movements grow in spite of persecution. Persecution by the existing powers is normal.

We need to keep this process and these characteristics in mind as we look for how to initiate a movement that transforms.

An Evangelical Strategy

Using Wallace's model and Gerlach and Hine's insight on the characteristics of movements, let me propose a plan on how evangelicals can create a strategy to successfully engage and transform a society. I do not intend to create a full-fledged strategy, but rather to provide a framework for such a strategy and establish a basis for further talks and deliberations.

Before we start, let me clarify how the evangelicals relate to social transformation engagement. Many in the evangelical movement hold the view that social transformation is not part of the mission task. They believe the core focus is evangelism and discipleship and that social transformation evolves from effective evangelism and healthy discipleship. Social transformation is desired, but we should not make it our primary focus. I agree that evangelism and discipleship are at the heart of our mission, but it does not exclude targeting social engagement. On the contrary, it is actually an integral part of doing effective evangelism. I believe that social systems play a key role in how open a society and its people are towards the gospel. Social transformation based on biblical principles will open the door for people to hear and understand the gospel.

A corollary to the "only evangelism and discipleship" viewpoint is that social transformation is God's doing. There is no need to target a society; it will happen on its own or it will be brought about by God in his timing. There is nothing that we can or should do. We need to speak out against the ills of the world, but it is not our task to engage and confront the powers who are causing the problems. It is true that this type of change is God's doing; however as with most other things, He uses people and natural processes to bring about change. Just as we plan for evangelism, we should also plan for social engagement.

Not all in the evangelical community hold this view; many are socially active and believe in engaging society on specific issues—abortion, pornography, human trafficking, racism. They seek change and transformation for those issues that do not live up to godly standards, yet there are few who have a comprehensive view of changing the whole of society.

Finally, some are focused on the end times and believe any attempt at social transformation is futile and not worth our time. We adapt to the current context, be it positive or negative, and focus on God. We live in a parallel society, and if our work has a positive effect on society, then that is good; however, we do not seek it out. This view is short sighted.

I truly believe that God wants to see his world transformed and that He is calling His people to step up and become agents of social change. I also believe He will provide and actually has already provided a plan for how we are to proceed. Rather than ignoring or fearing society and its negative change or being defensive in reaction to the increasing anti-Christian sentiment, we should seek out God's plan and then engage society and initiate a transformation process. If we take up the challenge, how do we proceed?

Understanding the Situation

The first step is to understand the current status of the society we are wanting to transform. What is the level of dissonance? What are the core issues affecting the people? What are the prophetic voices saying? What attempts at engagement are currently in progress? Once a clear picture emerges, the next steps will fall into place.

A couple of points are important to consider in this regard. The goal is a stable society, one which is driven by a functional worldview that is aligned with the God-ordained reality and its original God-given purpose. In this stable society, each mountain is led by competent and upright gatekeepers who are properly addressing the needs of the people. The gap between rich and poor, the haves and have nots is minimal. People are free to live and create, order and justice prevail, and people are content. The minorities and sub-groups are free and encouraged to participate in all areas of culture. The established system works for a majority of people. This sounds like utopia, the perfect society. It may be, but it is also a picture of what each society strives for—peaceful stability.

A second point is that societies and their cultures are always in a process of changing and evolving. There is always some level of dissonance between the cultural ideal and the current realities. The smaller the gap between the two, the more stable the society. As the dissonance grows, however, the gap between those that have and those that don't have widens, causing the discontent to grow. The stress on the society will continue to increase, the call for change and transformation will grow stronger, and unless the cause for the dissonance is dealt with, it will at some point explode.

Third, because culture is not static and is constantly evolving and changing, each generation will introduce new technology, develop new ideas, and face new challenges to maintaining stability. Because of this fluidity, one of the dangers and problems with the established powers is that they will stay with what has worked for them in the past, rather than evolving and reinventing themselves to keep up with challenges and changes, thus ensuring the stability of their society, so each generation will face some degree of dissonance and will be challenged to address it.

Fourth, what role do Christians and the Christian church have in society? With whom are they aligned? Are they part of the establishment or are they the voice of change? Are they irrelevant? The Christian message should always be the voice of transformation, a voice leading the people back to God, back to a stable society. Yet too often, the Church has become too strongly tied to the existing powers to exercise its power and influence and has compromised its values and message, so when the disillusioned, the dissatisfied, and those seeking change look for the culprit for the growing dissonance, Christianity and church become the target. As a result, the change process is directed against Christianity. It is important to keep in mind that the core of the gospel message is to transform and restore what is broken; thus, it should always be the voice calling for change and improvement. As we look at the current situation, we need to find out with whom the church is aligned.

So what is the current situation? As we, in America, observe what is happening in our nation, we are faced with a conflict that has reached a boiling point. Two of the themes at the core of the confrontation are freedom and equality for all. The inequality in America is visible in racism and the unequal status of the minority in society. White supremacy is being blamed for the inequality and all the problems associated with it (unequal pay, unequal education, the economic disparity). The redefining of freedom is seen in the idea of diversity, a call for tolerance, and full acceptance of alternative lifestyles such as the LBGTQ movement. Christians have been targeted as those who are intolerant, hateful, and oppressive. Key worldview themes are being used and redefined to establish a new way to deal with long standing issues. At the core of this new agenda is a humanistic, socialist agenda that is setting up a new society devoid of God and biblical values. Those values that coincide with the Bible are being redefined from a humanistic point of view.

Because of prior efforts to influence many of the key gatekeepers from the different mountains of culture for their cause, the movement has gained momentum and has set itself up to succeed. It is to be seen what effect this will have on the U.S. and the rest of the world. It is clear, however, that the new normal will be a far cry from anything that is biblical or Christian based. The result will be a stability built on sand.

As the dust settles and the new normal takes hold of our country, we need to be prepared to initiate a new movement, to restore the worldview themes based on biblical values. We will not be working from a position of power, but from a weakened position. This is to our advantage since God prefers to work through our weakness.

Understanding the situation and context is vital for the next strategic step—developing a relevant, core message.

A Contextualized Message

In order to establish a viable plan, you need to have a revolutionary message that deals with the core issues. Our message is the gospel; however, we have had difficulty in adequately communicating it so that it addresses the felt needs of the times. We need a clear and contextualized gospel message. In order to contextualize, we need to know what the essence of the gospel is. We have been restored to a relationship with God through Jesus Christ who has now been placed over all creation—" Jesus is Lord and Savior." Alan Hirsch, in his book *Forgotten Ways*, states that this message drove the NT church and the subsequent Christian Movement.[4] This gospel is the answer, but it needs to be contextualized to address the specific societal problems. In the current conflict, it needs to show how it leads to ensuring freedom, securing equality, and finding acceptance. It needs to show how it overcomes racism, how it eliminates inequality, how it meets the basic need of the LBGTQ Community for acceptance and incorporation. Our core message is in Christ; all men and women are equal and in Christ we find our identity, acceptance, and true freedom. There are many theological issues that are important, but for a strategy and movement to transform, it needs to be grounded in the simple and clear gospel message that is contextualized and applied to the specific context.

How to contextualize and communicate this message to the people will depend on each context. A general principle is that the message needs to be clear, be able to inspire, and be associated with a symbol or entity. It needs to be clear like the slogan "Black Lives Matter." This caught the attention of people and clearly stated the core purpose of the movement. The people need to become passion about the message. In the 60s, the Black Power Movement inspired the people to believe that they could take back the power that has eluded them for centuries. The message needs to have a symbol, a visual representation of what we are fighting for. The symbolic images are so important that movements will invest exorbitant

---

[4] Alan Hirsch, *Forgotten Ways: Reactivating Apostolic Movements*, 2nd ed. (Grand Rapids: Brazos Press, 2016).

amounts of time and resources to defend their symbols or to discredit the opposition's symbols.

With our message, is it our goal to create a God-centered society? History unfortunately has shown us that theocracies do not fare well and have a tendency to develop into a dictatorship. Let me suggest that the focus should not be the establishment of a God-centered state, but on creating a society in which each mountain is fulfilling their God-given purpose under the leadership of God-centered leaders and gatekeepers. It should be a society in which the gospel can flow freely, and everyone has the chance to hear and choose to accept or reject the gospel of Jesus Christ. The key is to break Satan's blinding stronghold on society and open people's eyes so that they see and understand the truth and then decide. It sounds like a nearly impossible task. It may be, but it is worth fighting for. The United States of America grew out of such an attempt. Throughout its history, it has been a beacon for freedom, equality, and acceptance. It has had its flaws and problems, but at its core, it is based on Christian principles and values; however, this foundation is now being challenged because we have failed to live by the principles and failed to live out our values. Our goal is to expose what is wrong, restore what is broken, and reestablish the core Christian principles in our worldview that guides us.

With a clear and definable message, what is the first point of action?

Prayer

The first action step is prayer. As we look to initiate change, we need to realize that there are two arenas of engagement—the spiritual and the natural dimension. Both need to be understood and dealt with. On the naturel level, we need to engage the mountains and their gatekeepers. On a spiritual level, we need to engage the powers and principalities behind the gatekeepers. Some will engage the spiritual powers directly through binding the powers, exorcising the power, and confronting the powers, while others do not directly engage the powers, but appeal to God to deal with the powers. I believe that we need to engage in prayer directed at God, where we confront the powers through specifically interceding for the society and the people, the specific mountains and the gatekeepers. Through prayer and fasting, God has invited us to take part in the spiritual dimension of the conflict.

Because of the duality of the conflict, any strategic consideration needs to include prayer and fasting. It does not replace action, but it provides covering, guidance, and a reminder that this is not our fight, but God's work and we are part of it. Besides individual prayer, this would include concerts of prayer, 24/7 prayer houses, prayer walking, and prayer demonstrations, to name a few. Any strategy needs to be supported and bathed in prayer.

Creation of Sub-cultures and Infiltration of the Existing Power Structures

In conjunction with prayer, we need to engage in two pivotal actions that will lead us to a movement. The first is to develop a model culture that is centered around the core message. The second is the strategic infiltration of the existing power structures with the message. Both engagements lay the groundwork for the conflict between the old and the new. The goal of the model is to show what is possible, and the goal of the infiltration is to persuade the gatekeepers to be open to, to incorporate, or to adapt the new message. The one seeks to create a new culture with new structures; the other seeks to change the existing culture and structures. Both actions are key for social transformation to succeed.

The first action is to create multiple model cultures. In response to the dissonance, many new ideas are introduced, so either one or more groups emerge where the ideas and the core message are tried and developed. As they are successful and gain a following, they become the model that leads the charge for change. Not all groups will succeed. Several will rise up, but through lack of leadership or infighting, some will fade away. Others will be quickly stopped by the existing powers if they get wind of what is happening. However, through visionary and passionate leadership and a good organic organization, the model will grow and hopefully morph into a movement. Often groups that at first are in competition with each other will unite and expand the movement. As the movement grows, it will begin to interface and clash with the gatekeepers of the old and established system. How the gatekeepers respond will depend on how well the infiltration of the message goes on in the existing power structures.

The second action needed is to make inroads into the existing system with the new ideas and the core message. The basic idea is to engage as many of the gatekeepers with the new message as possible. These gatekeepers are associated with one of the mountains of culture, and through them they exert their control. Behind these gatekeepers there is either a board, a group of people, an individual, or an election process that empowers them. Engaging these people or this process become the focus of this second action. You seek ways to gain access and persuade them. If the gatekeeper is a business, like Apple, Ford, or American Airlines, the gatekeepers are the company's CEOs; however, their power is usually instilled upon them by a board or the company owners. If you can persuade one or more persons on the board or the circle to be your advocate, you can gain influence and ultimately influence the board. Then you either persuade the leaders or install new leaders to become favorable to the new ideas. It will be hard for them to completely change the outlook of the company, but even if they only become favorable, this will be vital when the gatekeepers are challenged by the new movement. The LBGTQs lobby gained their access to gateway companies in the business world and won their support by following this process.[5] This process is key. It is a long-term approach that will take time, will encounter many hurdles, and will experience setbacks and face attacks, yet, if successful, it can open the door for the new message to be positively received.

Once the movement reaches its critical mass and the gatekeepers are successfully engaged, then when the linchpin moment comes, the transformation process can take effect. The new movement will face opposition, but the degree of pushback will be determined by how strong the model cultures are and how well the existing structures have been infiltrated and persuaded.

If we as evangelicals want to initiate such a movement, then we need to rethink how we strategize and where we place our focus. We need to have model communities. Ideally, this should be the church. We need for it to step up and engage culture and provide an alternative, gospel-based approach to dealing with all of society's key concerns. At the same time, we need to engage the gatekeepers and gain access to the inner circle of power with the gospel. When the opportunity arises to gain access, we need to be ready to go. When the doors are closed, we need to mobilize our people to pray, specifically targeting the gatekeepers and their power structures, to pray and fast until the wall of opposition is broken down. But for this to happen we need to have defined strategy and a clear plan.

Once we know what to do, we need to ask the question, who will lead this movement? We need to look to the up and coming generation.

---

[5] I would like to add that they also used the threat of protests and shaming as a secondary means for gaining their support.

The Young Generation Needs To Lead the Way

The key to any societal change is the younger generation. The young people will fuel the movement with their passion and call to action. Each generation will automatically clash with the existing power structures by bringing forth new ideas in an attempt to try to create a better world. These ideas are usually instilled in them during their late teens and early 20s. Where do the ideas come from? They emerge from our educational system. Our universities and secondary education institutions are filled with professors and teachers who were part of previous movements and who are passionately communicating new and often times radical ideas to their students. During these formative years, the future thinkers and leaders of the movement form their views of an ideal society, which then becomes their rallying cry for action. The reality is that those who shape the minds of the students will determine the course of the next societal change.

In order to implement an evangelical strategy, we need to win the upcoming generation. They need to experience a spiritual transformation and discover how "Jesus is Lord" is a revolutionary idea that can best deal with our social issues and problems and realize that this is worth fighting for. Currently, many students stop attending church once they enter university.[6] Those who attend secular universities are daily confronted with a secular and humanistic worldview. It is no wonder that the current movement has become radical and anti-Christian. If we can infiltrate the educational communities and reach these students with a radical, social-transformation oriented gospel, then we will raise up a generation with a Christ-centered DNA. Over the decades, many great ministries like Campus Crusade, Inter Varsity, the Baptist Student Ministry, or the Passion Movement have focused on this task. They have led the way; however, their access and success has been limited. We need to go further and infiltrate the whole educational system with evangelical minded professors, administrators, and presidents. The key is gaining access to the classroom and to the curriculum. The greater the influence, the better prepared the young generation will be to lead.

---

[6] https://lifewayresearch.com/2019/01/15/most-teenagers-drop-out-of-church-as-young-adults/.

What Is the Order of Priority for Engagement?

With the message and an overall strategy in place, what is the priority for engagement? Do we try to deal with all the mountains at once or do we stagger our focus? It is vital that we have a strategy of engagement in place for every one of the mountains of culture; however, the role each mountain plays in the society leads us to prioritize the order of engagement.

Education

Based on the preceding discussion, the realm of education has the highest priority. We have lost our educational system. As stated above, we need evangelical Christian thinkers and educators who can help shift the tide from a secular based education system to an open system that allows and supports Christian values and ideas. The existing system of universities needs to be recovered, while at the same time, new Christian based universities are being created. This is an ongoing principle in engaging the mountains. You engage the existing gatekeepers while creating new gatekeepers who are champions for your agenda. Because we have lost so much ground on this mountain, it will be the hardest to recover. Yet without it, the movement will struggle to succeed.

Family

Strong and healthy families are at the core of each society. The ideal of a traditional family is being replaced by the reality of blended and alternative family structures. Rebuilding the family ideal as found in scripture and helping people reach and live out these ideals is one of two major challenges of this engagement. The other is developing and reintroducing a biblically based view of human sexuality. The key is to reintroduce a biblical family model that will challenge existing models.

Media, Arts, and Entertainment

Both of these areas deal with communication and strongly influence our perception of reality. It is interesting that evangelicals, who were once considered the model of a good citizen, are now despised, considered a hate group, and blamed as the cause for much of the evil in our society. The evangelical movement has not changed, but the perception of the movement has. The news media, Hollywood, the arts, and other communication outlets have reshaped how Christianity is portrayed. In order for the overall movement to gain traction, it needs positive and truthful coverage. It seems everyone is longing for a truthful and unbiased press and a balanced and fair portrayal of all aspects of life in the art world, including Christianity.

Business

The economy is vital to any movement. If people's lives are improved economically, then the movement will thrive. The key here is to create a fair and social economic system that benefits all, not just a few. It is important to infuse the gospel message into the business world to bring about fundamental changes in how businesses run and function. Often many of the ills of society are brought forth by unhealthy business practices. The challenge is to gain the support of the business community while at the same time leading them to change unethical and unhealthy business practices. It is in this arena that a compromise could become fatal to the movement if greed and business interests trump the core message.

Government

The goal for this mountain is to establish a government that will allow the changes to take place. In the past, we have focused extensively on the government to bring about change and have failed or neglected to change the other mountains. The government is important, but it will follow suit as the other mountains change. The initial goal for engaging government is for it to become an enabler for change. Later in the process, it will become the focus of change.

Religion

The goal is two-fold. The first goal is to restore the concept of "freedom of religion," from "freedom from religion." We are not looking to establish evangelical Christianity as a state religion, but to allow for other persuasions to exist and to allow for healthy dialogue that persuades rather than coerces people to follow Christ. The second goal is to strive for spiritual renewal and awakening. Christians and the church are important to the transformation process. A vibrant faith is vital to the movement. The church and its believers should model the transformation that we are looking to introduce into society, so the spiritual renewal of our people and their churches is essential for the transformation process. It is not, however, enough to just have a spiritual awakening. The awakening needs to spill over and affect all other parts of society, as it did in the Second Great Awakening.

Finally, the other mountains of technology, sport and military, will follow. However, more often than not, these three areas are the first to respond to the change, and they can become steppingstones to reaching the other seven mountains.

Once the mountains are engaged, the gatekeepers will either receive the message or fight it. If it turns into a battle, there will be many encounters that will pave the way for a key encounter that usually comes during the linchpin moment. At that time, the new will replace the old, or the new will be combined with the old to create a new approach. In either case, the transformation will occur. The question for us evangelical is, will we be leading the change, or will we once again be bystanders, hoping to be heard as the society transforms and changes?

Where Do We Go from Here?

I want to encourage three practical steps to get the process going.

1. Increase Awareness—It is important that the evangelical world, especially its leadership, become aware of this challenge we face and begin to embrace a Mega strategy vision for transforming our society. We are trying to do this through writing about it and encouraging the dialogue. We are just at the beginning. Much more needs to be done. I hope that this book and future ones will assist in this process.
2. Creating the strategy—A group of visionary evangelical leaders, both young and old, need to work together to map out a course on how to move forward. Maybe multiple groups need to meet. We need leaders from different mountains and from all parts of the world. It should not be a big meeting or large conference, but a small workgroup that will lay the ideological and strategic framework for the strategy.
3. Establishing a Hub—It is important that the strategy has a home where it can be nurtured, developed, and implemented. The organization needs to be global in its focus and big enough to embrace a Mega strategy. It should not be an organization that implements it, but one that empowers others to implement the strategy. The World Evangelical Alliance is best suited for this. If they were willing to provide a home for this, it could provide the communication and logistical support for the movement. Other existing or newly

developed groups may be considered, but by far the best right now is the WEA.

The purpose of this chapter is to make the evangelical movement aware of the need to engage our culture and society and to provide a framework for a strategy to engage society. Even though we are currently in the middle of a significant cultural change around the world, we are at a crossroads in deciding if we as evangelicals will take the lead in initiating the next season of change.

Chapter 2: Theater and Art

Mary-Catherine McAlvany

Mary-Catherine McAlvany's husband calls her a Renaissance woman in modern times. Mary-Catherine began her dance education at age three, visual arts education at age 6, and performing arts education (with Theater Under the Stars' Humphrey's School of Musical Theater in Houston, Texas) at age 8. At age 17, she shared the stage with Kathy Rigby in *South Pacific* and was a TUTS intern during the partnership between TUTS and Disney, culminating in the original musical, *Beauty and the Beast*. She went on to pursue modern and contemporary dance technique at Trinity Laban Conservatoire of Music and Dance (formerly Laban Dance Center) in England, performing pieces for many notable contemporary European choreographers. Alongside earning a BA summa cum laude in philosophy and theology with honors from Boston College, Mary-Catherine attended the Boston Ballet School. She has exhibited her stone sculptures in the U.S. and England, created album covers for Christian bands, contributed to film journals, and has been published in poetry journals. She has worked at the Santa Monica Museum of Art, as well as taught art and dance to all ages in California, Texas, and Colorado. Ms. McAlvany is co-founder and current artistic director of Wildwood Dance Project. A member of Merely Players Theater Company in Durango, CO, she has performed in *Mary Poppins*, *Shrek the Musical*, *A Christmas Carol*, *Sense and Sensibility*, and most recently was the fight scene director and choreographer for *Macbeth*. Mary-Catherine homeschools her four children in the mountains of Colorado, where she passes on to them her deep love for the arts.

Regaining Wonder Through the Arts

> *"The only way to change culture is to create more of it."*[7]
>
> — Andy Crouch

> *"I am afraid that as evangelicals, we think that a work of art only has value if we reduce it to a tract."*[8]
>
> — Francis A. Schaeffer

Prejudices about Art

In approaching this chapter, I was gravely aware that evangelicals are often scared of art. Churches sideline the arts because they are deemed "dangerous." All too often we avoid engagement and choose instead criticism. We choose to believe art exists is the realm of darkness. In so doing, we often forget that God is the greatest artist of all, we were created to be creative, and we are mimicking Him in our creative efforts.

Conversely, we can fall into the erroneous belief that the only art Christians can engage in and with is *realism* (also known as *naturalism*). This belief holds that a subject must be engaged and represented without artistic conventions, truthfully as one sees it with his or her eyes, without implausible, supernatural, sublime, or exotic elements. Ironically enough, this form of art was the only kind allowed under communism. I'm not demeaning *realism* because I think it can be done well and serves its purpose, but I want to caution Christians from believing that realism is the only way of engaging art. Some of the most thought-engaging works of art (whether paintings or plays) leave something to the imagination and create in the viewer a desire for the story.

Imagination and Wonder

We were made to wonder. We were made to stand in awe. We were made to imagine possibilities and ask questions. Though we are born fallen beings, we are created to pursue the true, the good, and the beautiful. After

---

[7] Andy Crouch, *Culture Making: Recovering our Creative Calling* (Downers Grove: IVP Press, 2008), 67.

[8] Francis A. Schaeffer, *Art and the Bible*, 2nd ed. (Downers Grove: IVP Press, 2006), 54.

all, God is truth, goodness, and beauty. He created these things, but He also embodies them. Deep down inside all of us—wherever we were born—we desire truth, goodness, and beauty. When we humans encounter truth, goodness, and beauty through art and creation, our imaginations are sanctified, our souls are awakened to awe and wonder, and we begin to see our creator God and things around us anew. We are experiencing a part of who God is. That experience changes us.

Our imaginations are a gracious gift of the Father as Francis Schaeffer reminds us:

> Christians . . . ought not to be threatened by fantasy and imagination. Great painting is not 'photographic': think of the Old Testament art commanded by God. There were blue pomegranates on the robes of the priest who went into the Holy of Holies. In nature there are no blue pomegranates. Christian artists do not need to be threatened by fantasy and imagination, for they have a basis for knowing the difference between them and the real world 'out there'. The Christian is the really free person--he is free to have imagination. This too is our heritage. The Christian is the one whose imagination should fly beyond the stars.[9]

We have access to the God of all creation. The first Creator. The God of all possibility. We can wake up the world through our artistic endeavors and point towards the true, the good, and the beautiful. We can lead a broken world toward redemption and restoration. When we use our artistic gifts in service to His Kingdom, we become vessels that can speak truths about God and humanity that words alone cannot. Schaeffer says, "An artwork can be a doxology itself."[10] We can draw the world into a profound dialogue. It is in the dialogue that we Christians can have a voice.

In order for evangelicals to develop a Meta strategy by which to share the love of God and make disciples, we need to move beyond our criticism and rejection of the arts and choose instead to speak life into it. Where we as Christians are silent, the void is filled by others. We need to allow room for imagination because when things or ideas become rote and obvious, we humans lose interest in them and cease to wonder at them. The arts can help us teach people to look at something anew, to see God in a new way, to marvel at His creation and His mighty works, to wonder at all there is that we do not know. We may not miraculously deliver someone from physical blindness, but our creative and imaginative works through the

---

[9] Schaeffer, *Art and the Bible*, 61.

[10] Schaeffer, *Art and the Bible*, 18.

Spirit may deliver someone from spiritual blindness. And when that happens, my hope is that the people around us will praise God, as in Luke 5:26 (ESV): "And amazement seized them all, and they glorified God and were filled with awe, saying, 'We have seen extraordinary things today.'"

The Quandary

Life is messy. The Bible makes this clear. Our biblical heroes are all flawed and sinful humans whose faith keeps them seeking God even when their mistakes would ruin them. I often cringe to think of my Sunday school days when I heard edited versions of their lives. Omitted were their sins, and in the omission was inserted their place of perfection in the Bible. After all, they were in the Bible! But this Disneyfied version of the Bible is not truthful. God did not allow their stories in His Word to make them into metahumans that we are all supposed to exalt and emulate. He allowed their stories in His Word because He wants us to identify with their frailties and find hope in their life story of faith, trust, repentance, and redemption. He wants their stories to point beyond them—towards Him.

Christians, evangelical or not, would do well to approach the arts with this same understanding. The job of the arts is not to tidy up the world and therefore make us feel good about what we see. That is not to say that art cannot do these things. Art can exalt us. Art can distract us from the ugliness in the world and place us firmly in pastoral fields where all is made right. This should not, however, be art's chief aim, nor should it always be preferred. Christ came to redeem a fallen and wayward world. Shouldn't good art remind us of this? Shouldn't it remind us of why we need redemption? Art's greatest attribute lies in its ability to confront us, question our deepest desires, and move us towards some thing or some idea. In modern terms, art can be "disruptive." The arts hold this great opportunity to make us pause and consider. They offer up to us humans a reevaluation of what we see around us. Art interrupts and gives us allowance to break and meditate on the state of the world as it is, or how it could be. Christian author Oswald Chambers reminds us, and the artist, that God promises deliverance *in* suffering, not deliverance *from* suffering. Sometimes art portrays the suffering and leaves it at that. Other times, art gives the viewer or hearer assistance in a solution.

I think both can be powerful choices, even for Christian artists. When we Christians police, arrange, and lay out our message too perfectly, the Christian world affirms it and the non-Christian world ignores it. I believe our job as Christians in the arts should not only be to dialogue with the believer but also to extend the dialogue to those outside the faith. The mainstream art world has a deep suspicion and mistrust of Christian artists. Hiring committees of universities and training institutions often pass over applicants whose repertoire of artwork speaks too specifically to their Christian faith. Christian artists who regularly posit explicit faith themes or imagery in their artwork are often turned away and jilted by professional gallery owners. To be a "Christian artist" is a scarlet letter in the Western art world, but to be an artist, who also happens to be a Christian, does not wear the same scarlet letter, so long as the art world does not feel that person's work is proselytizing. What is the Christian artist to do?

We believers in Christ hold out the answer to a hurting world. Our answer does not alleviate the pain the world inflicts, but it does give a way forward towards redemption, healing, and transformation; however, Christians in the arts should be advised not to package the message too explicitly. I like to think about God's temple in the Old Testament. The artistry was excellent, but the symbolism was worthy and pointed to God without writing His name on the wall. God could have just had the craftsmen paint "I AM is the only way to eternal life" all over the wall of the temple. He could have had them paint "YHWH" everywhere. But He did not. He had them paint representations of earthly things that were symbols, and He also instructed them to make representations of non-earthly beings—the angels. My point is that the symbolism was enough to point to Him and to bring Him glory. We Christians should not be uneasy with the symbols and representation. We should not be disquieted to leave people asking questions. We should not be fearful of failing to spell out JESUS all over our artwork. If humans are made in the image of God, we can easily demean our fellow humans by treating them like toddlers and giving them art with all the answers clearly and succinctly attached; when things are too simplistic, we humans become bored and dismissive. Isn't wonder a beautiful and worthy human quality? Should we not give our fellow humans art that encourages questions, wonder, and stirring in their minds and souls? Wouldn't it be lovely if a non-believer was moved in his soul and mind to ask, "What did you mean by that?" instead of turning his head and dismissing the message of the art because it smacks of proselytizing?

Are All Artistic Styles Still Available to Evangelical Christians?

The quandary extends to artistic style and leads to two questions: (1) Does all art made by an evangelical Christian have to conform to a particular style to be acceptable and true? and (2) Is there one style of art that more perfectly portrays the true, the good, and the beautiful?

This question could spark much debate among evangelicals, but Francis Schaeffer speaks well on it in his essay "Perspectives on Art," as presented in Leland Ryken's seminal book *The Christian Imagination*:

> As long as one has a living art, its forms will change. The past art forms, therefore, are not necessarily the right ones for today or tomorrow. To demand the art forms of yesterday in either word systems or art is a bourgeois error. It cannot be assumed that if a Christian painter becomes "more Christian" he will necessarily become more and more like Rembrandt.
>
> This would be like saying that if the preacher really makes it next Sunday morning, he will preach to us in Chaucerian English. Then we'll really listen![11]

At the intersection of Christianity and creativity, style becomes a servant. I say this because, in its simplest form, the grammar of art is visual storytelling. Art tells us a story, and there is a gravitas to stories. Stories shed light on what it is to be human and play a formative role in human becoming. Whether it is a true story or an imagined story, the story will teach us either vices or virtues. These stories can lead us to the true, the good, and the beautiful without being outwardly packaged in realism. Light, shape/form, color, tone, space/depth, line, rhythm, and perspective are all appropriated by the visual and performing artist in service to the story. How those are interpreted by the artist are up to him or her. The style is the servant in telling the story, and even abstract art can tell a story and create conversation and change.

The painting *Guernica*, created in 1937, is one of Picasso's most famous works. It is considered by many to be one of the most powerful anti-war paintings in history, and it has caused almost a century of dialogue and controversy. Though a master trained artist, Picasso did not choose a realistic painting style to convey the brutality and horrors of war. He chose to strip the horrors down to a massive flat monochromatic 2D expanse of agonized humans. Adolf Hitler disliked modern art so much that the official German guidebook for Paris's International Exposition, where *Guernica* was first shown publicly, discouraged its viewing and called it "a hodgepodge of body parts that any four-year-old could have painted." Even if this statement were true, would there be any less validity to the artwork? Does it

---

[11] Francis Schaeffer, "Perspectives on Art," in Leland Ryken, ed., *The Christian Imagination: The Practice of Faith in Literature and Writing* (Colorado Springs: Shaw Publishing, 2002), 41.

create the possibility for a conversation? Furthermore, can an actual four-year-old create art that moves viewers to dialogue and inquiry? Does that art have to look "real"? These are all important questions, especially as we think about the arts and Christianity.

How the Arts Affect Us

Can we see the holy in the mundane? Can controversial art and theater pieces present a truthful depiction of humanity? Can art give us glimpses of the transcendent? Can art deepen and enrich our faith in Christ? My answer to all these questions is a resounding yes!

Art does affect us. All kinds of art affect us. We hate it or we love it. It moves us to catharsis or repulsion or to reevaluate our own lives. It amazes and confounds us. We can stand in awe or revulsion before it. Countless books and articles have been written about the benefits and effects of the arts to the human psyche. The importance of art to humans is undeniable. We are in our very nature, after all, created to be creative. Drawing, dancing, and play acting are all elemental from childhood. Kids all over the world—poor or rich, physically or mentally challenged, schooled or unschooled—engage in these natural human activities. From the earliest adolescence, children are moved to create and be affected by creation.

When I was in India as a young adult, I noticed practically destitute children drawing pictures in the dirt with sticks, and I saw children living in the far out bush and isolated from other people dancing and clapping and singing with carefree abandon. I have seen groups of children on dirt covered streets playing roles as if they were on a stage in a theater—pretending to be someone they are not. Through acting out someone else's life, our empathy can be deepened. Our understanding of the *other* can be challenged.

The creative process is freeing. It offers "play" liberally. Play has become a touchstone in recent years because we workaholic Westerners seem to have forgotten to play. The book *Play* by Stuart Brown is a fabulous book to reawaken our need for play. It reminds me of why God instilled feast days into the calendar year. A feast day is a day of play, of worship, of feasting, of communion with others. It is a day of no work. It is a day set aside for imagination and wonder.

I mention play in relation to the arts because I think if our organizations can begin to see the importance of play and creativity, then we can see how we can use the arts to further God's kingdom, by helping those to whom we minister become whole and healthy creative beings. Art requires creativity. Art requires play.

Know Thy Culture

Fundamentally, Christians engaged in the arts must know their particular culture. American culture is different from the culture of, for example, Honduras or India. The kind of art I would create here in America looks vastly different than what a Christian artist from India might represent to her fellow countrymen. I am not saying that art cannot transcend cultural boundaries because it most certainly can. Truth is universal. However, knowing who my audience is and how to speak most profoundly to them should be a priority as I begin to formulate my art. In India, I might create art—whether plays, paintings, or dance—about the injustices of the caste system, the plight of the untouchables, bride burning, or the utter cultural indifference to severe poverty. In the United States, I might present a photographic exhibition about homelessness, mathematical principles found throughout the natural world, gross overconsumption, or gluttony. I might consider a dance performance with live music about immigration and work, or I might write and stage a play about broken family relationships because of misplaced priorities.

Regardless of where I create art, my Christian worldview will be ripe in all my endeavors. I will be seeing a society's particular culture through a Christian lens, and this will come across in my artwork. It is impossible not to do so. Because of this, I can weave the true, the good, and the beautiful—the story of redemption and restoration—into my play or artwork without beating someone over the head with a Bible.

Ways Forward

We are all missionaries sent out to fulfill the Great Commission. Some of us live in big international cities, some in small rural towns, some in dusty villages in developing countries. Wherever we sojourn in this life, each of us can engage the arts to create dialogue about our world, our spiritual lives, God, the Gospel. We can literally discuss *anything* through art. Anything. Those Ten Mountains of Culture—art and theater, business, education, family, government, media religion, military, sport, technology—can be used to create a profound and life changing dialogue through the arts. If you are an artist, I would like to encourage you to pray for ways in which you can meaningfully create avenues to share the love of God and to create dialogues with others through your art. If you are not an artist and the art world seems very foreign to you, I would like to encourage you to faithfully consider how you might have a part in furthering the arts in your church, town, country, or organization.

Meta Strategy for the Arts and Theater

Looking at a Mega strategy for the arts and theater, larger organizations and denominational conventions need to take a committed role in using the arts to further the gospel. It would be wise for them to create a comprehensive and long-range strategy for integrating the arts into evangelism, not in a trite way, but in a profound way. This is much harder than it may seem. Of all the Ten Mountains of Culture, the arts and theater are the stickiest and most avoided. This stigma is not easy to overcome. We need well-trained thinkers and artists to come alongside the theologians to show them the theology of the arts. These organizations and denominations should consider hiring artists graduating from noted Christian universities and colleges to help them create a Mega strategy. They need to create a whole department dedicated to the arts and Christianity—to missional arts.

Embrace the arts and allow the collaboration of the gospel and the artist to create a voice that can speak to and change culture. Let us create a space in which believers and non-believers alike can experience God through the arts.

Mako Fujimura, a contemporary painter and founder of International Arts Movement, frames why Christians should care about the arts. He says, "The arts are a cup that will carry the water of life to the thirsty."[12] He believes the church needs the arts for the sake of the gospel. What if Christian organizations and denominations allowed for arts conferences in regions or countries, bringing together Christian artists to learn, encourage, and dream of ways to impact and change their culture? What if these same organizations and denominations created online platforms where Christians in the visual and performing arts could place their work and thoughts to impact anyone with inquisitiveness and a computer? If we can begin to think outside the figurative box, I think we Christians can gain a foothold into culture and begin to see how our presence can affect it.

When I started a dance company in my hometown, the founding dancers and I were faced with the grounding question of what kind of dance company we were going to be. Were we going to sell tickets and dance on a proscenium stage? We could not get past the realization that dance is a

---

[12] https://faithandleadership.com/theology-and-arts.

dying art. Fewer and fewer people are willing to pay to watch someone dance on a stage for an hour or longer. We stretched ourselves to think outside the box—outside the literal theater box. Would there be another way forward that would allow us to reach more people beyond the borders of our city? Was there a way forward that would engage viewers who did not think they liked dance? Was there a way to broaden dance and cross-pollinate into the other arts? We alighted on the idea that we would use multi-media and online platforms to build our viewer base, as well as work as collaborators with other visual and performing artists in our region. This would allow us to do site specific performances, stage performances, dance films, short Instagram pieces, and pop-up downtown street performances. We were not bound by the stage itself. We allowed ourselves room to decide what dance would look like and how we could reach the greatest amount of people. Our most recent collaboration was with a local theater company. Numerous audience members approached me after the show to share how our company's dancers added to the play in a profound way and deepened the overall experience.

Where to Begin

The way forward always begins with questions. What is the need where you are? Is it to share stories of hope and healing? Is it to give a path towards forgiveness? Is it to share the Gospel story itself?

I think if I were to start a theater company in Uganda, or Rwanda, or South Africa, a lot of what I would produce (with local African actors) would speak to forgiveness and diversity. I might even set up a theatrical school that could train up the next generation of actors or create free theater camps for children or a touring company that could travel well beyond borders to carry the messages of plays to those who would otherwise not have the opportunity to see live theater. I would need supporters far and wide, and I would need a committed, trained, and passionate staff to begin the process.

If I were to start an art gallery in one of those same countries, I might include works by African artists who are believers in Christ. I might invite local Christians with special talents in the arts to conduct workshops or give demonstrations of their technique. I would dignify their work by dignifying their arts, not the art from my homeland, but from theirs. They can often speak to their own culture much better than we Westerners are able. I might, however, bring in Western Christian artists to create works in collaboration with the local African Christian artists to remind others that we are all brothers and one body in Christ. If I wanted to think on an even more elementary level, I might bring an arts camp to children in a slum area, where they could explore their creativity through painting, sculpting, drawing, acting, dancing, singing, or playing music. Using what is locally accessible to them (such as local clay or local music) might allow them to pursue these activities beyond the camp.

I can imagine the creation of a small dedicated touring theater company in a large international city that brings gospel-infused productions to nursing homes, prisons, institutions, churches, schools, community centers, amphitheaters, and city parks. Perhaps, like at Community First! Village in Austin, Texas, I might open a community art house that would foster healing and creativity for formerly chronically homeless people and support their efforts to earn a dignified income by creating art pieces they could in turn sell to the greater community.

The possibilities for merging the arts into an overall Meta strategy seem endless. Our creativity is our boundary. We must always keep in mind that we begin with questions, and those questions lead to dialogue with the cultures in which we are present or where we intend to minister. Through this dialogue, we will begin to understand the people's needs, their unique attributes, and how they view the arts. We will learn where the demonic spirits are at work. We will discover their family structure, how they experience friendship, and what they think of people of different races.

As I think about ways in which art can dialogue with culture, I am reminded of one of the best monologues of all time—Paul's Areopagus speech to the Greeks in Acts 17:16-34. It was preaching, but it was also theater, rhetoric, dialectic. Paul pierced the Greek's cultural beliefs with truth. Theater can do this. Art can do this. Infused with solid Christian beliefs, art can reach masses of unsaved people in ways that churches cannot.

What Other Religions Are Doing

The arts seem to have escaped most world religions. Fear of freedom of creativity and expression runs deep among the religiously devout. In consequence, I could not find any examples of other religions doing the arts well except the Mormons.

A few months ago, I was in Utah. I turned on the television in my hotel room to find something appropriate for my kids to watch, and I came across BYUtv (part of Brigham Young University). I was dumbfounded; it was amazing. I kept watching. I kept thinking, "Why aren't we doing something like this?" I mean, it was expertly produced, high quality t.v. They did not push the Mormon message. I did not hear one show that talked about Mormon ideas or Mormon books (though I know they do have some LDS programming). It was good, clean, family friendly t.v.

BYUtv is known for its original shows, feature films, nature documentaries, and acquired medical/crime dramas. This channel has won Emmy awards! According to Wikipedia, BYUtv produces shows under several categories: BYU Sports, Campus, Documentary, Faith, Family, Lifestyle, People, and Performing Arts. They even have film agreements with major Hollywood studios. A look at their website, https://www.byutv.org/, is surprising. Evangelicals could be doing this as well. Partnering with one of our own Christian universities (one wanting to build its film and t.v. degree program) or para organizations, we could create a family friendly television station online and on t.v. that could be watched the world over. It would not be filled with Christian talk shows, preaching hours, or terribly produced shows, but well-made shows, documentaries, and films—without a hokey Christian name giveaway like JoyTV, FaithTV or JesusTV. It would be a t.v. station that would draw the world, not just Christians.

Conclusion

We Christians should either do an exceptional job in the arts or give up the arts completely. I think the stakes are too high for us to throw aside our creativity. We must keep our fear of the world out of our artistic endeavors. If perfect love casts out all fear, that is what we need to be sharing with the world through our art. Music, theater, photography, installation art, dance, painting—if we want to use the arts to reach the masses, then all these mediums will require honesty, faithfulness, skill, excellence. No fear. No whitewashing. No editing for sanitization purposes. Our art will require the truth of how the world truly is and what we as Christians really have to offer the world.

The way forward for Christian organizations will include a deep commitment to seeing it through all the ups and downs of starting a new endeavor. Nothing begun is ever easy, but if believers faithfully toil, lives may be changed.

Resources

Art and Theology: https://www.artandtheology.org

Christians in the Visual Arts: http://www.civa.org

Faith and Leadership: https://faithandleadership.com/topics/arts-culture

Christians in Theater Arts: https://cita.org/home

Regaining Wonder Through the Arts

Fuller Theological Seminary's Brehm Center for Worship, Theology and the Arts: https://www.fuller.edu/academics/areas-of-interest/theology-and-the-arts/

International Christian Dance Fellowship, with a list of dance representatives by country: https://icdf.com/

A "How To" Guide on Starting an Art Gallery as Part of Your Worship Arts and Outreach Ministry in Your Church: http://thenewr.org/wp-content/uploads/2017/05/How-to-Start-an-Art-Gallery-in-Your-Church-Christopher-Brewer.pdf

Notable Examples

In this section I want to highlight some organizations that have done well to further God's Kingdom on earth, without compromising artistic and missional integrity. Some are professional companies, and a few are para ministry organizations. I am sure there are untold other groups and organizations working in this same vein of which I am not aware.

AD Players, Houston, TX: www.adplayers.org

The Promise in Glen Rose, Glen Rose, Texas: www.thepromiseglenrose.com

CYT (Christian Youth Theater), locations across US: https://www.cyt.org/

Spring Dance Company, London, England: https://springsdancecompany.org.uk/

Ballet Magnificat, Jackson, Mississippi: https://www.balletmagnificat.com/

Ad Deum Dance Company, Houston, Texas: https://www.addeumdance.org/

Youth With a Mission (YWAM), Kona, Hawaii: https://ywamkona.org/uofn_courses/school-of-dance/, https://ywamkona.org/uofn_courses/school-of-acting-for-the-screen/

Chapter 3: Business

Timo Plutschinski

Timo Plutschinski, an evangelical theologian, is Director of the *World Evangelical Alliance's* Business Coalition and a member of the Wider WEA Leadership. He also serves as pastor of a Baptist Church in Hamburg and as a fellow at the *Olivet Institute for Global Strategic Studies*. Additionally, he is a partner of *MIC Corporate Finances,* which provides inter alia, a global M&A platform.

Timo lives with his wife and their two daughters in Hamburg, Germany. He has published two books in the German language, *Faith in Daily Business Life* and *Political Responsibility of Christians*.

Influencing the Mountain of Business

Analysis

The Meaning of Business

Business is the economic engine of every nation, and business (in a broader sense the workplace) is one of the most important parts of life. So much of our time is spent on this "mountain," many decisions result from it, and business can influence lives for good or for bad.

A lot of material is being written about ministry that expands into the marketplace. Business is not new territory for evangelism, but rather a forgotten territory for discipleship. Unfortunately, this significant mountain is still lacking an orchestrated global mega-strategy to influence the business world; therefore, this chapter should contribute to such a mega-strategy.

The reason that it is a forgotten territory is because Christians have stopped applying biblical theology to business. For too long they have ignored the marketplace and focused on mainly serving on the "church mountain." The marketplace has become reduced to how one earns a paycheck in the secular world and donates it to the church afterwards.

In the past, the relationship between business and church was primarily defined by the provision of financial resources from companies for churches. In recent years the so-called "Business as Mission" model has been frequently discussed. In this model, the company itself is considered a platform for evangelism, discipleship, and Christian mission and is used in a much broader sense. The acceptance and implementation of this new model is desperately required. The fact is very simple and widely known that the traditional church has lost a huge number of members, and many local churches have had to be closed during the past decade. The churches in the United States are currently losing almost 75% of their members in the age group of 18-24-year-olds. Even the Southern Baptists have lost one fourth of their missionary force internationally in the last year. For the first time in history, the number of baptisms is decreasing. In Germany, just last year, more than 400,000 people left both the Evangelical (Evangelische) and the Catholic Church. Currently the institutionalized church is facing difficult times.

A strategic approach in reversing this development is now to train the 97% of Christians working in the marketplace. With all the complications of a post-Christendom society, it is wonderfully true that, globally, in the twenty-first century, the marketplace is the most strategic mission field. Why is this? Because most Christians spend forty to eighty hours a week in the marketplace. It is where life's problems are shared between co-workers. People watch how others work and wonder what makes them tick. Most significantly of all, believers have access to workplaces (and people) where no pastor or professional missionary can even enter. Inevitably, questions of faith will arise.

If we define the traditional church as the only primary arena of spiritual formation and as the only place for using and developing spiritual gifts, the 97% of Christians working in the marketplace cannot make their calling "fit" within the walls of a church and may become dormant and disengaged from church. Accordingly, the current model of church ministry, which consists of getting people involved in church meetings and programs, has to be changed. Paul wrote to slaves in the pagan workplace, "Whatever you do, work at it with all your heart, as working for the Lord, not for men" (Col. 3:23). This verse expresses an enhanced meaning of "church service" in the business world and emphasizes the relevance of faith seven days a week, no matter where you are positioned.

A business leader comments,

> One of the biggest structural questions that I've tried to influence through my leadership is to have the firm not only make money, not only serve customers, not only provide employment — all of which are important, but also to be moral communities for the development and shaping of human character. It's so easy to look at people as just economic animals. But if you step back and say: No, we're also in the process of shaping and developing human character,—then you get into the whole question of what's right, what's wrong. Through business you're touching people in all aspects of life.

Interestingly, it has been during the twenty-first century that many business schools are now offering courses in spirituality, even though the curriculum is pluralistic and sometimes even New Age. People now understand that they take their whole self to work. The primary location for spiritual growth might not be church services, retreats, or even personal devotion, as important as these are, but in the everyday challenges in our places of employment, where we live for most of the week.

Source: RightNow Media 2013

The Spiritual Aspect of Business

Just as starting a church will not get you into heaven, starting a company will not send you to hell! Running a church or a company is spiritually always a matter of purpose. The truth of Jesus Christ does not just save our souls, but entire nations and societies. There is no secular-sacred divide. Truth matters in every way conceivable so that it can be applied to everyday life here on earth. An electrician is not important just because of how much money he makes for the Kingdom, but in how well he lays the electrical lines throughout residential or city property. The electrician gives light, heat, and air to people so that they can perform their jobs, which also matter to God.

In a Christian environment—especially among Evangelicals—business is often seen as slightly immoral, greedy, corrupt, and not as a healthy place for Christian formation. But what is business about? Marketplace activities from Monday to Friday could intrinsically be an expression of God's creativity, emphasizing a holistic worldview and loving service to people. Especially in times of postmodernity and post-Christendom in the Western world, it has the potential to be the future framework for spiritual formation and expression of a "Church at large."

Business itself is able to express various biblical principles:

- Accountability: Business reinforces that in all areas of life we are accountable to a higher authority.
- Trust: Risk-taking helps us learn to step out of our comfort zone.
- Forgiveness: In a failed world forgiveness is offered to those who make mistakes.
- Excellence: The pursuit of excellence motivates people to do better than they have done in the past, and better than others are used to doing.
- Responsibility: Business reinforces that we should work through difficulties to meet obligations and commitments.
- Progress: A business environment stimulates progress and encourages exploration to discover a next level.
- Goodness: Business is doing good for others by providing needed products and services.
- Love: Business forces us to show love and respect to all kind of stakeholders.

Christian-led companies are not simply platforms for proclaiming the gospel. Rather, Christian business leaders see their products or services as a contribution to the Kingdom of God, and they intentionally develop their relationship with employees, suppliers, government, and customers in a way that leads to fruitful conversations about spiritual issues. There are enormous implications for the marketplace, which is now seen not merely as a place to evangelize but as an arena, if not the most strategic one, for the full-orbed mission of God.

Business matters because God cares about all areas of life. He cares about how we go about architecture, engineering, electricity, automobiles, construction, technology, science, industry, agriculture, banking, the housing market, and so much more. The Lord's work is done on farms, in hospitals, at schools, at banks, in retail spaces, and on military bases. The list is endless.

Transforming Business

The idea behind the "business mountain" in the mountain template of discipling nations is that Christians can no longer afford to see business as just a financier of Kingdom work, but rather as Kingdom work itself. Discipleship in business is returning to the theology that business matters for business' sake. The church of Christ is called to review its theology of work and the extent to which it provides a false dichotomy with the implied separation of clergy and laity. In this sense, it is important that the Christian church gives entrepreneurs and business leaders a role in local and global mission that goes far beyond the provision of financial resources.

The Western hemisphere is still suffering from the legacy of pietism and a dichotomized worldview, in which 'ministry' is confined to full-time paid work within the church i.e. as a pastor, evangelist, or missionary. Believe it or not, God did not invent the church to support the clergy. Rather, God gave pastors and teachers to the church in order to equip the saints. People do not go to church on Sundays to support their pastor in his ministry. Rather, the pastor goes to church to support his people in *their* ministry—which is outside the walls of the church, in the world, being salt and light also in the marketplace.

A crucial question needs to be asked of those who seek to follow Jesus in the marketplace: Do you see your work as nothing more than a necessary evil or only as the context for evangelistic opportunities, or do you see it as a means of glorifying God through participating in his purpose for creation and therefore having *intrinsic* value?

We need to remember that business itself can glorify God. Business does not need to be "baptized" by poverty alleviation, church planting, marketplace ministry, workplace evangelism, or missions. These activities are all good things from God, but so is business. By itself! Business is a morally good gift from God. It does not need to be justified by any other non-business or clergy activity.

Business is a high and holy calling from God. We do not have to do business in a cross-cultural context to do business to the glory of God. We can love and honor God in our business itself. Our heart and the way we love people in and through business is infinitely more important than how we label it. Jesus was likely a carpenter. What kind of products did he make? Do we think he made lousy products because he was actually "on a mission"? No! He worked to the glory of God, just as he lived his whole life. Being "on a mission" is no excuse for a poor quality of products or services. It is just the opposite. Great business honors a great God!

Development of The Mega-Strategy: 18 Steps To Climb the Business Mountain

1. Changing the Attitude

As already outlined, the first step up the mountain is simple but essential: change the attitude about business itself! The ability to literally create wealth through ingenuity, enterprise, creativity, and effort is a God-given gift and a universal impulse. The markets and economic systems that emerge whenever people are free to pursue buying and selling become the lifeblood of every nation. These include anything from farms to small businesses to large corporations.

If Christians would consider business with its economic and also spiritual meaning, many more Christians would enter the business arena and many more would pray for spiritual awakening in the marketplace, for prospering Christian-led companies, and for a transfer of wealth into God's kingdom. History is full of dedicated businessmen who were responsible for extraordinary kingdom results:

- Wealthy bankers funded Charles Finney's crusading mission in the 19th century.
- Humphrey Monmouth was an English merchant in London who funded Tyndale's Bible, the first translation of the Bible into English. In addition, he owned a gigantic fleet of ships that were used to transport Tyndale's translation to every corner of the English empire.
- Business tycoons like Sid Richardson funded Billy Graham early in his ministry.
- Today, evangelical business leaders and philanthropists around the globe support numerous parachurch initiatives.

2. Reflecting the Paradigms of Business

In order to see changed behavior in business execution, a changed approach from a Christian point of view is needed to prepare the way for a next kingdom business generation.

Christian universities and business schools need to begin to research and teach the philosophical, theological, and practical aspects of Kingdom business. Unfortunately, business education, if it is offered at all at a Christian educational institution, is usually divorced from the mission education program. This separation between business education and theological training is based on the 200-year-old paradigm that Western missionaries and business students have differing needs and aspirations. Christian business schools are uniquely positioned to equip aspiring Kingdom business professionals and retrain missionaries with the mentality, skills, and tools they need to be effective. Successful business principles mirror the attributes of God, and Christian business schools can be the connection between biblical values, spiritual capital, and business success.

Christians should offer proper business courses (like MBAs) that are rooted in a biblical worldview and include a profound theology of work, of wealth, and of leadership. These courses could cover all parts of business education (incl. bookkeeping etc.), but alternatively they also could be a program focusing on just the ethical themes and topics in addition to the secular University curriculum.

3. Making Use of Business for God's Kingdom

Christians should know business as much as they know charity! Many programs, initiatives, and campaigns can be combined with business endeavors and can be run as profitable sustainable measures. The rise of impact investment—also in the secular environment—is a perfect example of how to combine an ideological approach (be it green or social or feminist—or Christian) with a profitable venture.

There is a saying that a "Donation-Dollar" has just one life—but a "Business-Dollar" has multiple lives! Fundraising is for sure always a very blessed process because it gives wealthy people an opportunity to have a stake in the realization and manifestation of God's kingdom. But a certain investor—rather than a donor—does have the opportunity to get his money back in order to re-invest it into other kingdom projects.

In order to make use of business, the following diagram can help with understanding the ecosystem connecting business and ministry:

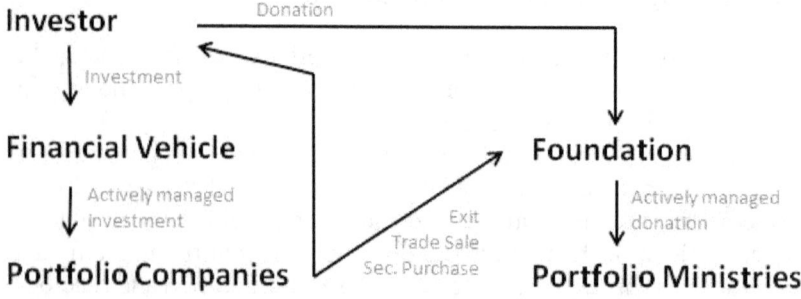

The capital provider (here the investor) has the opportunity to either give a donation to a ministry (probably via a foundation) or to invest money in a Christian-led company (probably via a fund, a bank, or a similar financial vehicle). The advantage of using the business way is that the companies are creating revenues that can either go back to the investor or they can finance (indirectly) other ministries. This principle is like a goose giving golden eggs. As long as you just use the eggs for your daily needs, it remains a sustainable model, but soon as you kill the goose in order to have a one-off benefit, the model crashes.

4. Searching Common Ground

There are many opportunities not just to make use of business vehicles (such as funds) but also to join cooperative projects, especially in areas of sustainability, environment, clean energy, or human rights. In this sense, Christians easily get access to projects on the business mountain and have credibility in many areas. Just the wording could be different. While Christians call it "Creation Care" others talk about "Mother Earth" or "Gaia," but at the end of the day, they run the same projects protecting the creation.

Some years ago, a business conference called "Karma Konsum" took place in Germany. A consortium of different groups invited a group of business people to discuss the conference topic "Empowering a New Spirit in Business." In fact, that is exactly what Christians desire; they also want to empower a new spirit in business—the Holy Spirit (to be more accurate). Unfortunately, no Christian group showed up to co-host this event and a great opportunity to influence a spiritually wide-open audience was missed.

Another example of such an opportunity, a positive one, was a joint event run by a sinologist (in favor for Confucius) and a Christian theologian. They invited quite a large group of business and political leaders to discuss the topic "What leaders can learn from Confucius and Jesus." Because of this event, the Christian theologian had the opportunity to talk (preach) about Jesus in front of people who never would have joined a Sunday service but who nevertheless were spiritually interested. He used this opportunity with its focus on a personal relationship to present a living Jesus, which is the most obvious difference from all other moral teachers, like Confucius, in human history.

5. Fighting for Religious Freedom and the Expression of Faith

The support of religious freedom, which is, of course, valid for each religious group, is definitely common ground. Fighting along with others for more religious freedom will create more opportunities to publicly express the Christian faith in the marketplace. Strategically, it is important to be a pro-active supporter and developer of proper guidelines to guarantee religious freedom and the expression of faith in a business environment.

This focus is more than needed in times of emphasized neutrality in a post-Christian and an irreligious Western society. One of the best driving forces in this matter is *The Religious Freedom & Business Foundation (RFBF)*, which serves as the preeminent organization dedicated to educating the global business community, policymakers, non-government organizations, and consumers about the positive power faith—and religious freedom for all—has on business and the economy. The economic value and social benefits of robust religious diversity and liberty are tremendous. There are many encouraging examples of how a faith-friendly workplace benefits business.

6. Putting Capable People into Top Positions

Every year significant changes occur in those making up leadership teams. Due to expired seat terms, mergers, acquisitions, company growth, and other reasons, new CEOs, CFOs, managing directors, board members, etc. are sought out for responsible and influential positions. If the "business mountain" is to be changed sustainably and to be driven by Christian principles, it is essential to put capable people in these top positions. This endeavor requires three things:

1. To identify capable people among Christian communities
2. To support and encourage these candidates spiritually and free them from other "church jobs"
3. To build vivid networks and foster relationships on a top leader's level in order to drop a certain name at the right moment.

7. Supporting Young Christian Entrepreneurs

Not only the already established large companies are always offering new leadership opportunities, but also the start-up environment provides many opportunities to enter the market with "the next big thing"—whatever it may be. In order to have the next Facebooks, Teslas, and Apples run by Christian believers, it is vital to develop a young entrepreneurs support program providing content, contacts and capital.

A very promising way to support young Christian entrepreneurs is the development of Christian-led business incubators and accelerators. A business incubator consists of a collection of activities designed to help the launch, growth, and ultimate success of business enterprises. Christian-led business incubation has emerged in recent years as a distinct activity aimed at maximizing the success of faith-driven companies. A variety of incubation models support businesses around the world by providing an array of resources and services: facilities, infrastructure, financial capital, mentoring, country analysis, training, business plan development, recruiting, and facilitation of connections with potential partners, including suppliers, distributors, and consumers. Specializations include various geographically focused incubators (e.g. region, country, or city) and those that target a particular client or type of business. In these kinds of incubators and accelerators, Christians should emphasize creativity, collaboration, prayer, and the leadership of the Holy Spirit, alongside delivering an array of high-standard incubation services and resources according to Christian goals and context.

8. Capitalizing Christian-led Start-ups

In regard to the capitalization of Christian-led start-ups, it is desirable to launch a Global Christian Business Fund and have a vivid network of early stage investors who serve as "business angels" by providing capital but also consultancy. "Money makes the world go round" is true on each mountain of culture but especially on the business mountain. This reality means that Christians have to work on proper strategies of wealth creation and wealth allocation. That can be through *Spiritual Venture Funds,* which are financial vehicles to provide financing for spiritual ventures. They operate like venture capital funds but with a primary goal of spiritual rather than financial returns. Spiritual ventures are God revealed and compelled initiatives having the express purpose of multiplying the Gospel through upright enterprises that provide services needed by a community. Led by spiritual leaders, these enterprises will multiply spiritual impact throughout the globe. The fund objective is to advance the Kingdom of God by discovering Christian-led start-ups and raising them up through early-stage investments into freestanding, virally fruitful, spiritual ventures.

9. Considering a Christian World Bank

As the allocation of finances is a major part of a Christian business megastrategy, we could look to secular organizations and financial institutions like the World Bank and probably learn from them. The World Bank describes itself on its website as follows: "The World Bank Group is one of the world's largest sources of funding and knowledge for developing countries. Its five institutions share a commitment to reducing poverty, increasing shared prosperity, and promoting sustainable development." The same is valid in a spiritual way for the desired increase in spiritual prosperity and sustainable development of churches, ministries, and Christian organizations. Every single project could benefit from a globally coordinated financial allocation. An independent financial institution would have the benefit of intentionally financing strategic projects, starting ventures, building alliances, and launching initiatives.

10. Developing a Global Christian M&A Platform

Linked to the idea of a Christian World Bank, another aspect of Christian-led companies is the succession plans of these companies. In many cases Christian owners want to see the kingdom approach and value set sustained, but in case of a sale, that requires a like-minded buyer. A Global Christian Platform for Mergers & Acquisitions (M&A) could exactly match both ends perfectly. In this sense successful companies would not just survive and remain but, because they are built on a common basis, would reach next levels of spiritual impact.

11. Increasing Investments into Christian-led Social Business

Funders, investors, banking leaders, fund managers, etc. can be instrumental in the business arena by providing the needed capital, but Christians are also needed as connectors, supporters, and brokers in order to inform—and probably encourage—potential investors to take a close look at a certain project or company. A great deal could be achieved due to a single connection or a small hint. Christians should also use and further develop global platforms of suitable projects so that initiators, entrepreneurs, and company owners can get promoted widely and connected with potential investors.

A San Francisco venture capitalist refers to these kinds of Christian-led companies as "businesstries." One for which he provided start-up funds is a candle company in Thailand that employs women recovering from sexual abuse. The company offers these women job training and steady employment. He explains, "I require that the businesses be for-profit. It both motivates the workers, and the profits are channeled to support some of the ministries to start [similar] businesses."

His venture is part of a relatively new category for business today, the socially responsible firm. Many of these firms reinvest profits in local communities that produce the commodities sold or donate profits to philanthropic causes. Christian business leaders have taken active roles as founders, directors, and funders of programs that blend business sensibilities with Christian fervor. Most of these are outside traditional church settings and operate instead through special-purpose organizations known as parachurches.

12. Using Communities Economically

Existing trusting relationships among the global Christian community could be used more efficiently. Other communities are more known for the economic support of their members. Chinese business people adhere to this saying: "A single Dollar circles around seven times before this Dollar leaves the community." There are already some examples of Christian inventions, like the cooperatives (Genossenschaften) founded by the German Friedrich-Wilhelm Raiffeisen or the Economy of Community (EoC) founded by the Italian Chiara Lubich and the Focolare movement. It is essential to have the next Raiffeisens and Lubichs in place, people who are able to develop new economic infrastructures in order to serve and strengthen people and communities.

13. Fostering Global Exchange Programs of Students and Expats

In terms of using the global Christian community, it is more than crucial to foster global exchange programs in order to match students and expats with their counterparts in other countries. Doing so has a couple of strategic advantages. First, it helps the companies to find trustworthy people for an internship or a post; second, it widens the horizon and increases the "market value" (also for future positions) of the student or expat himself. Strategically, a coordinated exchange of (young) people (like the Mormons do) would also benefit churches receiving impulses from abroad and would vitalize the global body of Christ.

14. Creating a Culture of Innovation

Unfortunately, in the 21st century Christians are not well known as innovative thinkers. In fact, the most advanced scientists, the most recent inventions, and the highly innovative business ideas do not really come from the Christian community. Thinking in different scenarios, not knowing what comes next and, in some way, living by trial and error is more the opposite of what Christians stand for. They claim to know what is right, what is true, and what has been done for years, decades, and centuries, but in order to climb the business mountain, Christians have to create a culture of innovation and an attitude of being a *frontrunner* rather than a *status keeper*. They are not asked to leave principles of faith and belief but rather to think about next global trends, next levels of business, and new areas of involvement.

15. Launching a Crypto Currency

There are hundreds of areas in the business and finance world worth considering when deliberating on how to make use of most recent trends. One example is the area of crypto currencies, where people still ask, "Is it Bitcoin or Shitcoin?" Why not gather the most advanced financial experts out of the Christian community and launch an exclusive crypto currency to finance mission endeavors? Or at least make use of the block chain technology securing global transactions? Each area offers both risks and opportunities, both threats and benefits. Compared to others, however, Christians have the Holy Spirit and through it, insights into God's wisdom that is not just given for eternal peace and paradise but also to lead people into a just and livable world that expresses characteristics of God right here on earth.

16. Implementing Prophets and Prayer Warriors in and for Companies

Linked to this approach, it is vital to implement internal or external prophets and prayer warriors for business leadership. CEOs, Managing Directors, or Board members need a spiritual backup and support to make the right decisions, to have courage for the next steps, to have patience with others, etc. This initiative has to be part of a global mega-strategy in order to see spiritual change at the top and, as a consequence, a change in leadership behavior followed by transformed companies. It is an opportunity for many workers to organize themselves in prayer groups during the week or have churches praying intensively for company leaders in their neighborhood, cities, or countries.

Especially in the States, we can see a growing movement of corporate chaplaincy taking care of employers and employees in a spiritual way. Christian executives have hired ministers as senior-level consultants. A CEO hired his Presbyterian pastor to help him with special faith-based projects, and another one has been known to fly a noted evangelical business ethics professor to company headquarters several times a year for consultations. Indeed, there is a niche industry of Christian consultants whose clients integrate faith into their business responsibilities—a novel form of executive chaplaincy.

It could also be of great value to pro-actively offer prophetic counsel and spiritual wisdom to secular business and company leaders. They are more than interested in knowing what is going on and increasingly go to esoterics, shamans, freemasons, or other spiritual leaders for council. Prophetic Christians could have a great spiritual impact on top business and political leaders like Joseph did with his economic counsel to the Pharaoh.

17. Branding Christian-led Companies as Pro-City Oriented Companies

Christian-led companies should be known for their "pro-City approach," as Jeremiah 29:7 says, *"Seek the welfare of the city."* Business leaders can play a big part in this endeavor. Christian-led companies should be lighthouses in serving the city well, paying taxes timely and correctly, producing excellent products and services, and treating people and their families to the best of their ability.

It is given that this attitude and correlating behavior will lead to well-respected companies that express God's kingdom to many more people than a single church could do. Having built relationships with local governments, Christians can encourage them to intentionally invite and welcome Christian-led companies into their cities. Local governments have a lot of opportunities to support the settlement of a company or to prevent it; therefore, trustful relationships from local citizens (in the best case also respected local business leaders) are key in order to pave the way for other Christian-led companies.

18. Changing Church Buildings into Local Community Centers

Last but not least, even churches can play a significant role in entering the business mountain. In this sense, important factors and resources are the church buildings and properties themselves. Compared to other religious groups, there is an interesting difference. While church buildings are mainly used for Sunday services and spiritual events, the function of mosques in Islam is much broader than to just offer a place for religious ceremonies. Mosques are community centers with aspects of political debates, exchanging of business ideas, family encounter, and much more. The strategic question for Christian churches is how to make use of their church buildings as service for the neighborhood and cities. The Bible talks about *ekklesia*, which is translated "church," but *ekklesia* means people and not buildings, so the buildings can get used in different ways while the "called people" (*ekklesia*) serve the community in and with these buildings and properties. A certain rent for offering this location for events, meetings, shared desks, etc. could furthermore cover some costs and can be a financial benefit to the church.

Summary

Kingdom business is purpose-driven business. It is business pursued with a goal of achieving spiritual, economic and social transformation in individuals and nations.

The 21st century will see the evolution of Christian investment funds that invest specifically in Kingdom business ventures. The difference from their secular counterparts will be that the financial rate of return on investment, while important, will not be the only measure of success for such firms. Two other criteria, local impact for the gospel (support and growth of the local church) and local economic development (creation of local jobs and financial resources), will be of equal importance to investors. Meaningful metrics need to be devised to measure how well Kingdom business investment funds perform in relation to these objectives.

God's will is an empowering vision that inspires innovation and entrepreneurial activity as it did for Joseph in the book of Genesis. The ability to literally create wealth through ingenuity, enterprise, creativity, and effort is a God-given gift and a universal impulse. The markets and economic systems that emerge whenever people are free to pursue buying and selling become the lifeblood of a nation. This includes anything from farms to small businesses to large corporations.

Of course, this realm is prone to corruption through idolatry, greed, and covetousness. In response, the Church must embrace its responsibility to train up those who are called into the marketplace to manage businesses and provide leadership with integrity and honesty. There are many historical examples of Christians doing business in such a way that people and societies have been transformed and God glorified. This chapter finishes by mentioning just one of them.

Hans Nielsen Hauge was born in Norway in the late 1700's. The country was a poor, underdeveloped agricultural society, with no democracy and limited religious freedom. Hauge traveled extensively throughout Norway and did what we in modern day terminology would call church planting and business as mission. He started 30 businesses, including fishing industries, brickyards, spinning mills, shipping yards, salt and mineral mines, paper mills, and printing plants. He was an entrepreneur and a catalyst. Through his witness, many others were inspired to read the Bible and to meet with other believers for prayer and fellowship, and various businesses were started and developed.

Even secular historians today acknowledge Hauge's legacy and contribution to the development of modern Norway. He is sometimes called "the Father of democracy in Norway." He facilitated equality between men and women, and his work lead to a spiritual awakening and an entrepreneurship movement. Hauge's legacy is thus one of spiritual, economic, and social transformation. He did not use the term of kingdom business, but his life and work illustrate some of the goals, principles, and outcomes.

Resources

Business Ministries & Networks

Name	Country
A Call to Business www.acalltobusiness.co.uk	United Kingdom
Alpha in the Workplace www.alphausa.org/workplace	United Kingdom
BAM Think Tank www.bamthinktank.org	Global
Barnabas Group www.barnabasgroup.org	USA

Business 4 Transformation www.b4t.org	United Kingdom
C12 Group www.c12group.com	USA
Call2Business www.call2business.org	USA
Centurions www.centurionsprogram.org	USA
Christen im Beruf www.christen-im-beruf.de	Germany
Christen in der Wirtschaft Factor C- www.faktor-c.org	Germany
Christian Business Leaders www.christian-business-leaders.co.uk	United Kingdom
Christian Business Men's Committees www.cbmcint.org	USA/Global
Christian Business Networking www.christianbusinessnetworking.com	USA
Christian Financial Advisors www.christianfinancialadvisers.org.uk	United Kingdom
Christian Women in Business www.cwib.co.uk	USA
Christians in Commerce www.christiansincommerce.org	USA
Community Impact Business Network www.cibn.org	USA
Compass Financial Ministries http://compass1.org	USA
Convene www.convenenow.com	USA
Corporate Chaplains of America www.chaplain.org	USA
Crown Companies www.crowncompanies.nl	Netherlands
Crown Financial Ministries www.crown.org	USA
Cypress Leadership Institute http://www.chinacli.com/index-en.php	China

Europartners www.europartners.org	Europe
Excelsis – Chinese Christian Business People http://excelsis.cn/en/	China
FBG – Association for Christian Entrepreneurs www.fbg-eg.de	Germany
Fellowship of Companies for Christ International www.fcci.org	USA/Global
Full Gospel Business Men's Fellowship International (FGBFI) www.fgbmfi.org	USA/Global
Global Advance www.globaladvance.org	USA
Global Women in Leadership Network www.gwlnetwork.com	USA
International Christian Chamber of Commerce (ICCC) http://iccc.net	Sweden/Global
Internationale Vereinigung Christlicher Geschäftsleute (IVCG) www.ivcg.de	Switzerland, Germany, Austria
Kingdom Advisors https://kingdomadvisors.org	USA
Kingdom Business Alliance www.kingdombusinessalliance.com	USA
Krysha Russia https://give.cru.org/2750627	Russia
Lausanne Workplace Network http://www.lausanne.org	Global
Marketplace Ministries www.marketplaceministries.com	USA
Pinnacle Forum www.pinnacleforum.com	USA
The Christian Business Network http://christianbusinessnetwork.com	USA
Theology of Work Project www.theologyofwork.org	USA
Transformational Business Network www.tbnetwork.org	USA
Transformational SME www.transformationalsme.org	USA

Unashamedly Ethical www.tbnetwork.org	South Africa/USA
Worklife www.worklife.org	USA

Further business ministries are listed at http://business.worldea.org/ministries

Books

Baer, Michael R. 2006. *Business as Mission: The Power of Business in the Kingdom of God.* Seattle: YWAM Publishing.

Dickerson, John S. *The Great Evangelical Recession. 6 Factors that will crash the American Church … and how to prepare.* Grand Rapids: Baker Books.

Eldred, Ken. 2005. *God is at work. Transforming People and Nations through Business.* Montrose: Manna Ventures.

Grudem, Wayne. 2003. *Business for the Glory of God: The Bible's Teaching on the Moral Goodness of Business.* Wheaton: Crossway.

Hunter, James D. 2010. *To Change the World. The irony, tragedy & possibility of Christianity in the late modern world.* Oxford: University Press.

Lindsay, D. Michael. 2007. *Faith in the halls of power.* Oxford: University Press.

Rundle, Steve & Steffen, Tom. 2003. *Great Commission Companies: The Emerging Role of Business in Missions.* Downers Grove: InterVarsity Press.

Silvoso, Ed. 2002. *Anointed for Business. How to use your influence in the marketplace to change the world.* Ventura: Regal Books.

Silvoso, Ed. 2007. *Transformation. Change the marketplace and you change the world.* Ventura: Regal Books.

Stevens, R. Paul. 2015. "Christians and the Marketplace", in: Stiller, Brian C. (Hg.). *Christians around the World. A Global Handbook for the 21st Century.* Nashville: Thomas Nelson.

Tunehag, Mats. 2009. "A Global Overview of the Business as Mission Movement: Needs & Gaps," *Lausanne World Pulse.*

Tan, Kim. 2008. *The Jubilee Gospel: The Jubilee, Spirit and the Church.* Milton Keynes: Authentic Media.

Wagner, C. Peter. 2015. *The Great Transfer of Wealth: Financial Release for Advancing God's Kingdom.* New Kensington: Whitaker House.

Further books are listed at http://business.worldea.org/resources

Chapter 4: Media

Timothy Goropevsek

Timothy Kristian Goropevsek has served as Director of Communications and later Chief Communications Officer of the World Evangelical Alliance. He has been part of its Senior Leadership Team since 2012. His passion is at the intersection of faith and communications, seeking to make the world of faith and public engagement understandable to people across nations, cultures, and languages.

An ordained pastor, Timothy holds a BA in Theology and Master of Divinity degree from Olivet University and served in local church settings, in student ministry and as worship leader in his native Switzerland and at events in Europe and beyond. He also gained journalistic experience and insights as Swiss correspondent of U.S.- and UK-based Christian newspapers.

A native German-speaker, Timothy is proficient in English and has acquired a range of language skills, including French, Italian, Slovak, and some Russian. More recently, he is pursuing his PhD in Global Theological Studies at Zinzendorf School of Doctoral Studies with a focus on effective inter-cultural communications in Christian leadership.

Timothy lives in upstate New York together with his wife Rebecca and his two sons, Joseph and Stephen.

The Cultural Mountain of Media: A Global Strategy to Turn the Tide

Introduction

During the first three centuries, any kind of accusation by a fellow citizen could lead to a Christian's arrest, and once in court, there would be few outcomes other than a death sentence for failing to worship the emperor. In those times, Christians were considered a suspicious minority; they were called "atheists" for not believing in a visible god and regarded as "haters of humanity" for not participating in social events like bloody gladiator games or immoral worship ceremonies offered to Roman deities. "They are surprised that you do not join them in their reckless, wild living, and they heap abuse on you," the Apostle Peter commented on the situation of the early believers (1 Peter 4:4). In addition to the risk of becoming victim of rumors and gossip among the common people, many of the intellectual of their time despised Christians for mostly being of the lower class, uneducated, and following what seemed a strange and contradictory belief system. In response, Christians began to logically and systematically respond to misunderstandings and false allegations, with those who defended the faith becoming known as apologists.

The similarities to today seem striking. In an increasingly secular, post-modern world, Bible-believing Christians are frequently depicted as hateful bigots, as anti-society and backward thinking. The LGBT+ issue and abortion are among the most heated topics today where such characterizations have become common whether in news reporting or on social media. The corresponding reaction of Christians varies from angry to dismissive, from fearful to combative, and some seem to have simply resigned from public discourse or prefer to focus on less divisive matters.

The influence of media on the global Church, however, is so immense that it cannot be ignored or dismissed. Not only are Christian views increasingly being marginalized or silenced, but media can also be used to fuel discrimination, anti-Christian sentiments, and even outright persecution—as can be seen in a number of countries in different parts of the world today. Secular media also significantly contributes to the watering down of Biblical values and principles in believers' lives, and it negatively influences the younger generations, leading many of them away from the Church.

Christians should not only consider themselves on the defense. There has never been a greater opportunity to reach the masses with the Gospel than today where media can access almost every part of the planet, even penetrating restricted countries like those in the Middle East. Numerous reports are being made of Christianity spreading rapidly in Iran despite the government's heavy-handed efforts to discourage Muslims to become Christians.[13] This example is one among many.

How then should Christian leaders respond to this challenge and opportunity? What could a global strategy to engage media look like? This chapter seeks to first provide some definition of context to the cultural sphere of media, then outline some essential principles that Christians should follow in their media engagement—whether at the local, national, or global level, and finally, cast a vision for a global center that would feed believers around the world with relevant information, data, and stories on critical issues that they could use in their respective spheres of influence. No single individual, organization, or denomination could tackle the cultural mountain of media on its own. The body of Christ needs to come together just like Jesus prayed in John 17: so that the world may see!

Limitations

The topic of media, including news and social media, is so vast that it could easily fill a book on its own. This chapter will therefore only be able to touch on some of the important issues and not go into much detail or provide many examples. It will also focus more strongly on news media and less on social media, even though many of the principles are the same. It is the author's hope that this chapter will provide some inspiration for Christian leaders to boldly engage with media in a way that is consistent with Biblical values in order to strategically advance God's Kingdom through this cultural mountain.

Background and Definitions

In order to develop a strategy to engage media, it is important to first define what 'media' includes and to consider the diverse global contexts. This first part will therefore briefly review some of the "basics" regarding media that are foundational to any potential media strategy.

---

[13] CBNNews.com Staff Writer, "Christianity Is Rapidly Growing in Iran," *CBNNews.com*, August 15, 2017, accessed August 8, 2020, https://www1.cbn.com/cbnnews/world/2017/august/christianity-is-rapidly-growing-in-iran.

The Culture Mountain of Media—A Definition

One of the definitions of the term *media* describes it as "a channel or system of communication, information, or entertainment."[14] The definition is relatively vague, but essentially the Culture Mountain of Media focuses on the entire area of mass communication: the use of any tool or channel to convey a message to an audience. In today's highly connected world, there are many more media channels to consider than what was available just a few decades ago, especially online.

In order to develop a strategy to engage media, it is important to first define what 'media' includes and consider the diverse global contexts. This first part will therefore briefly review some of the "basics" regarding media that are foundational to any potential media strategy.

It is important not only to know the definition of media itself but also to understand who is involved in the process of communicating the message. Generally, three different groups of people can be distinguished: (1) those who generate original content by speaking or writing, thus creating a message with the intent to convey it to large audiences; (2) media professionals like journalists, editors, and publishers who take such content to produce stories that will be told from their own perspectives to their respective target audiences, and (3) the audience itself that helps spread the message to others, which is especially relevant in the age of social media that allows certain content to "go viral," i.e. gain a lot of attention and online engagement through sharing and comments by a large number of users. The lines between these groups get blurred at times, but it is still helpful to understand the distinction.

Different Media Types

Television, radio, and printed newspapers dominated the news landscape for decades, but this has changed dramatically with the ascent of modern communications technologies. Today, it is almost unimaginable for a printed newspaper not to also have an online version, for a TV channel not to also stream online, for radio not also to be accessible through a mobile app. While more traditional media are generally under some editorial oversight that influences how stories are told, an entirely new space has developed online that is broadly referred to as social media; much of this content is user-driven and only very loosely moderated, if at all.

---

[14] Merriam Webster, *Medium*, accessed August 8, 2020, https://www.merriam-webster.com/dictionary/medium.

The Cultural Mountain of Media: A Global Strategy to Turn the Tide

In addition to today's content-sharing giants of Facebook, Instagram, YouTube and Twitter, there are numerous instant messaging apps, such as WhatsApp, Telegram and Signal, to just name a few. Professional networking apps such as LinkedIn are also considered social media, and many more are coming and going. Each of these channels has its unique audience in terms of geographical spread, generational reach, and different purposes and ways to use them effectively. There is no "one size fits all" approach, so it is important to have a good understanding of the different tools before trying to put them to use to communicate a message. A global strategy to engage the cultural mountain of media should necessarily consider all of these media types in order to be effective.

Different Media Contexts

There is no doubt that media in the United States has an outside influence on the rest of the world. Apart from English being a global language, another reason is the strong emphasis on freedom of speech and freedom of the press that are enshrined in the U.S. Constitution and thus allow media outlets, organizations, and individuals to communicate without government interference. Even though it has become increasingly evident that these freedoms are currently under assault, the U.S. and most of the Western World rank relatively high on the World Press Freedom Index.

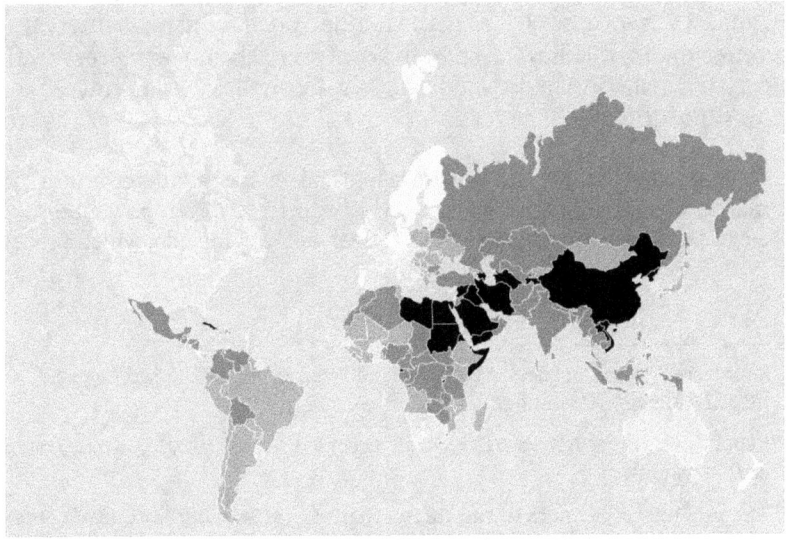

Freedom Index (2020) by Reporters Without Borders.[15]

This freedom stands in stark contrast to other countries, such as in the Middle East and Asia as well as some African and Latin American nations, where governments control the media narrative and routinely censor or crackdown on dissent. Reporters Without Borders states, "At the turn of the 21st century, nearly half of the world population still lacks access to free information.... They are prevented from living in pluralist political systems in which factual truth serves as the basis for individual and collective choices."[16] A global media strategy needs to take into account that getting information into or spreading it within restricted nations can be extremely challenging and may require an entirely different approach.

The Question of Objectivity and Fairness in News Media

The news media continue to have significant influence when it comes to forming public opinion on contemporary issues and developments, which is why it is sometimes referred to as the Fourth Estate or the fourth power in democracies.[17] In a similar way to how political parties and other interest groups seek to increase their representation in government to shape society through legislation, there is a desire to increase influence or even control over the media narrative in order to shape public opinion.

While some media outlets strive to report objectively and truthfully, the reality is that news is always shaped by the narrator's worldview, values, and experience, as well as his or her personal or business interests. In a recent New York Times Op-Ed in the context of the underrepresentation of Black journalists in major media outlets, journalist Wesley Lowery summarizes it well:

> We also know that neutral 'objective journalism' is constructed atop a pyramid of subjective decision-making: which stories to cover, how intensely to cover those stories, which sources to seek out and include, which pieces of

---

[15] Reporters Without Borders, *2020 World Press Freedom Index*, accessed August 8, 2020, https://rsf.org/en/ranking.

[16] Reporters Without Borders, *Our Values*, accessed August 8, 2020, https://rsf.org/en/our-values.

[17] The original term refers to the three other estates in older European contexts, namely the clergy, the nobility, and commoners. Today, the three others include the legislative, executive, and judiciary.

information are highlighted and which are downplayed. No journalistic process is objective. And no individual journalist is objective, because no human being is.[18]

Certain media outlets overtly support conservative or liberal causes and report news accordingly.

The key to effectively influencing public opinion through news media is then to understand how they work, to know what the media landscape looks like locally, nationally, and globally, to be aware of who the influential news outlets, reporters, and editors are, to learn what kind of values they stand for, to whom they speak, and so on. Using this information, a media strategy that builds relationships and trust with the reporters and outlets that align with the desired message and audience can be developed. The more intentional and targeted the approach, the more likely the success of getting into news coverage on relevant issues over time.

Even with the best media strategy, however, it is important to recognize that there is never full control over the narrative when dealing with news media. Generally, conservative media would tend to cover faith-related issues or voices more favorably than their liberal counterparts, who might at times ignore, diminish, or distort them. It might seem safer, therefore, to work with conservative outlets to get the right message across, but even that positive narrative might be picked up and changed by another outlet and presented in a very different light so that the eventual outcome in terms of message reaching various audiences may not fulfill the initial expectations. As an illustration, a conservative news outlet might objectively report on a Christian leader who publicly rejects LGBT-related legislation but strongly emphasizes the importance of loving the person while rejecting the lifestyle. Another LGBT-supportive news outlet might pick up the same story but only highlight the Christian leader's rejection of "inclusive" legislation and present him as a homophobic bigot due to his hateful stance against a discriminated minority. The negative narrative might even end up getting more coverage than the positive. Thus, part of the reality of media engagement is that at times reporting may not be fair.

---

[18] Wesley Lowery, "A Reckoning Over Objectivity, Led by Black Journalists," accessed August 8, 2020, *The New York Times*, June 23, 2020, https://www.nytimes.com/2020/06/23/opinion/objectivity-black-journalists-coronavirus.html.

Christian vs. Secular Media

The news landscape will vary greatly from country-to-country, with some nations relying heavily on secular mainstream or government-funded news media. Other countries may have a much higher share of influential religious or other ideological media. Europe, for example, would offer an abundance of secular media but only very few significant Christian news outlets. In South Korea, on the other hand, there is a strong Christian news presence, including a number of denominations and mega churches that run their own newspapers. Similarly, Christian leaders in some countries in Latin America and Africa have strong media outlets, while the U.S. has a mixture of a variety of secular news outlets but also solid Christian alternatives.

A global strategy needs to take these differences into account, but generally effective media engagement aimed at reaching vast audiences would have to look beyond only Christian media. While Christian media do play an important role and need to be strengthened in their efforts to report on news through the lens of a Biblical worldview, engaging secular news outlets is important in order to reach the wider public beyond the faithful readers of Christian media. Also, the approach, talking points, language, and tone may need to be very different for secular or other non-Christian contexts.

Essential Principles to Engage in Media

Who Should Engage with Media?

The age of social media opens the way for every Christian to become part of a global media strategy. The Apostle Peter reminds believers not to be frightened but to "always be prepared to give an answer to everyone who asks you to give the reason for the hope that you have" (1 Pet. 3:14-15). Social media is mostly a form of communication between ordinary people who share what is on their minds and what they are experiencing. If individual Christians' social media engagement—their words, their behavior, their stories—reflects their faith in Christ, it already becomes a positive contribution to using media to advance God's Kingdom at the grassroots level. The issue is if Christians' online behavior is indistinguishable from secular people, then it can become a stumbling block for others (Matt. 5:13; Rom. 2:24).

Pastors and Christian leaders can serve as role models and encourage their congregation in general and their youth in particular to make every effort to let their online behavior—just like their everyday life—give glory to God by reflecting the fruit of the Spirit: love, joy, peace, patience, kindness, goodness, faithfulness, gentleness and self-control (Gal. 5:22-23). Such social media engagement would be noticeably different over time and become a testimony of God's work in their lives that may lead to opportunities to share the Gospel.

When it comes to news media, not every believer or every Christian leader may feel called to actively engage with reporters or become a journalist. Some vocations will naturally be more prone to media exposure than others, and some organizations may not think of themselves as of interest to journalists. But news does not happen only at national or global levels; it also happens in the neighborhoods. Countless news outlets in cities and towns report on local events and happenings, which influences public opinion at the grassroots level and can be very effective due to the proximity of the audience to the stories. If evangelicals locally were known and valued as a positive influence, a negative narrative from national media would gain significantly less traction. In the spirit of 1 Peter 3:15 and Matthew 5:14-16, every Christian, church, company, and ministry should therefore at least be open and ready—or possibly even proactively seek opportunities—to engage with reporters, neither with fear nor arrogance but with gentleness and respect.

There are those who are ready to speak with national or global media and could become part of a more coordinated media strategy. The following principles may be most relevant to them, but they generally apply to any kind of media engagement from global down to grassroots, even to the point of personal social media use.

Seven Essential Principles

Dealing with news media can be a pleasant experience when a reporter shows interest in someone's work, life, or perspective and wants to share it to enrich the wider public. Even though some people may generally be media-shy, there is nothing really threatening about having a conversation with a friendly journalist. It may become an entirely different story, however, when the topic in question is a hot-button issue, a controversy, or a crisis.

The following seven principles become essential in order to ensure that those engaging media in such contexts do so in a biblically sound and God-honoring way. If every Christian who deals with media were following these principles, the media coverage about God and believers would look very different to what it is today.

Apart from the Bible, a key resource that helped formulate these principles is the book *Missio Politica: The Mission of Church and Politics* by Dr. Johannes Reimer, who serves as Director of Public Engagement at the World Evangelical Alliance and is a member of the Senior Leadership Team. Building on Dr. Reimers decades of experience in community engagement and his personal faith journey that shaped his understanding of the Church and its role in politics, the book offers theological perspectives and practical applications that are equally relevant when working with media.

A Spiritual Battlefield

The first principle is to recognize that engaging with the cultural mountain of media is first and foremost a spiritual battle. It cannot be won with human wisdom and persuasion; instead it requires unceasing prayers. The Apostle Paul concludes his letter to the Ephesians by reminding them, "Our struggle is not against flesh and blood, but against the rulers, against the authorities, against the powers of this dark world and against the spiritual forces of evil in the heavenly realms" (Eph. 6:12). He then urges them to put on the full armor of God and to "pray in the Spirit on all occasions" (v18a). In fact, he mentions the word prayer five times in this section, an emphasis that is also reflected in many of his other letters. Furthermore, media engagement is just one part of the wider effort to fulfill the Great Commission (Matt. 28:18-20). It should not be considered in isolation from the other cultural mountains. As news media and especially social media cover all aspects of life, virtually every other cultural mountain interacts with media and the other way around. One contemporary illustration can be found in the sphere of sports: a Christian basketball player who was the only one standing during the national anthem while all the others kneeled to protest for Black Lives Matter got a chance to share his Christian faith on the liberal CNN network.[19] Such opportunities cannot be orchestrated, but prayer will allow God to move people's hearts and give them courage and the right words at the right time so that they can share their hope in Him.

Prayer is also important as a reminder that it is ultimately God's work and believers are only tools in his hands. Veteran activist and former head of WEA's Nuclear Weapons Task Force Rev. Tyler Wigg-Stevenson wrote

---

[19] Brian Ries and Cesar Marin, "Jonathan Isaac Responds After Being the Lone NBA Player to Stand for National Anthem," *CNN.com*, July 31, 2020, accessed August 8, 2020, https://www.cnn.com/2020/07/31/us/nba-magic-national-anthem-trnd/index.html.

the book *The World Is Not Ours to Save*,[20] in which he reminds believers that it is not through human strength and activism that the world can be changed; it is only when believers are rooted in God and in prayer that they can be used by Him to become change agents— whether in media or any other cultural sphere.

"Who" Before "What"

The second principle is that the person who speaks is at least as important as what the person says. Readers or watchers will consciously or unconsciously ask themselves if the person speaks authentically and whether he or she as well as the group or organization he or she represents is credible. Only if the person is considered authentic and credible will the audience be open to hearing what he or she has to say.

The word *authentic* is commonly defined as "representing one's true nature or beliefs; true to oneself" and "entitled to acceptance or belief . . .; reliable; trustworthy."[21] Speaking authentically then means that what is said by the person is in alignment with who they are; it is not in conflict with past or present behavior or statements and can therefore be accepted as credible. On the other hand, if there are actions or words that are perceived as contradictory to what the person says, the person will not be trusted.

In the Bible, there is a clear contrast between Jesus and the Pharisees and how they are perceived by the people. In describing the Sermon on the Mount where Jesus explains in depth how believers should live according to the highest standards of the Heavenly Kingdom, it says that "the crowds were amazed at his teaching, because he taught as one who had authority, and not as their teachers of the law" (Matt. 7:28-29). Later Jesus points out why the teachers of the law did not teach with authority. He says, "They do not practice what they preach" (Matt. 23:3b) and goes on to warn the people about the hypocrisy of these leaders whose sole motive is for people to see and respect them (verse 5). The entire second chapter of Romans is also very relevant in this context.

---

[20] Tyler Wigg-Stevenson, *The World Is Not Ours to Save: Finding the Freedom to Do Good* (Downers Grove: IVP Books, 2013).

[21] Dictionary.com, s.v. "authentic," accessed August 8, 2020, https://www.dictionary.com/browse/authentic.

For anyone to be perceived as authentic and credible, he or she needs to have lived a life that is worthy of trust. The more a person's life is revealed—his or her history and his or her words and actions in the past and present—and the more this aligns with what the person speaks about or calls for, the more this person will be trusted and listened to. Dr. Reimer observes, "His authority was obviously due to the fact that words and deeds in Jesus' teaching correlated."[22] Leadership expert and author John C. Maxwell also speaks about a similar principle in his book *The 21 Irrefutable Laws of Leadership*,[23] where he explains the "Law of Buy-In." He observes that people buy into the leader first and then the vision. Only if they find the leader to be credible will they at all be open to considering the vision. The same is true for any speaker or writer; the audience first considers his or her credibility and who he or she is and then what he or she has to say.

Hypocrisy—defined as "behavior that contradicts what one claims to believe or feel"[24]—is probably the single greatest threat to Christians' reputation and influence on society. It is also one of the most effective weapons that media can use against them, as a *Huffington Post* contributor suggests with his article titled "Exposing America's Biggest Hypocrites: Evangelical Christians." He then goes on to write, "Ahhh, Christianity in America. Or should I say, the single greatest cause of atheism today. You know who I'm talking about, right? The type of people who acknowledge Jesus with their words and deny him through their lifestyle."[25] These accusations can at times be entirely false or based on a misconstrued image of what they think Christians should speak and how they should act. Numerous examples continue to be found where believers fall short of authentic and credible behavior, which then makes it easy for media and the public to dismiss their views.

How then can someone build up credibility? This will ideally have to start long before a person enters the public view. It will require him or her

---

[22] Johannes Reimer, *Missio Politica: The Mission of Church and Politics* (Carlisle, UK: Langham Global Library, 2017), 116.

[23] John C. Maxwell, *The 21 Irrefutable Laws of Leadership: Follow Them and People Will Follow You (10th Anniversary Edition)* (Nashville: Thomas Nelson, 2007).

[24] Merriam Webster, *Hypocrisy*, accessed August 8, 2020, https://www.merriam-webster.com/dictionary/hypocrisy.

[25] Francis Maxwell, "Exposing America's Biggest Hypocrites: Evangelical Christians," *HuffPost.com*, November 25, 2017, accessed August 8, 2020, https://www.huffpost.com/entry/exposing-americas-biggest-hypocrites-evangelical_b_5a184f0ee4b068a3ca6df7ad.

The Cultural Mountain of Media: A Global Strategy to Turn the Tide

to build a track record of speaking and acting in a way that can serve as a role model for others to follow. Reimer observes, "People will not listen to us, and they will obviously not agree to change their ways of living without trusting us . . .," and adds that "only when basic trust is established, change might be possible. . . ."[26] A good example is Mother Theresa, who spoke out against the violence of abortion at the 1994 National Prayer Breakfast with then-President Clinton and the First Lady sitting next to her unable to say anything.[27] Who would dare to criticize a nun who has lived her entire life sacrificing for the poor and marginalized?

Credibility is also established through a specific personal background that gives the speaker or writer authority because he or she has first-hand experience with the issue. This "personal story" effect is a very powerful tool, especially in the LGBT context where high-profile people "come out" and share how they suffered and were discriminated against all their life and why it is so important to fight for equal rights for all. Similarly, those who suffered because of those who chose this kind of lifestyle can then also speak with credibility. This is what the General Secretary of the Swiss Evangelical Alliance did in an interview conducted by one of the most respected secular newspapers in Switzerland. He was interviewed together with his father who "came out" as homosexual, divorced his wife, and left his family to live with his new partner.[28] The authenticity of the conversation and the visible tension and pain this experience caused made it a powerful witness to how a prominent evangelical leader deals with the issue of homosexuality in a very personal way. The media or public would hardly be able to dismiss him as a hateful bigot knowing what he experienced and that he still loves his father despite disagreeing with his lifestyle.

---

[26] Johannes Reimer, *Missio Politica*, 77.

[27] C-SPAN.org, *User Clip: Mother Teresa Speaks Against Abortion at 1994 National Prayer Breakfast*, September 3, 2016, accessed August 8, 2020. https://www.cspan.org/video/?c4618931/user-clip-mother-teresa-speaks-abortion-1994-national-prayer-breakfast.

[28] Daniel Gerny and Simon Hehli, "Ehre Deinen Vater, Auch Wenn Er Schwul Ist? Ein Prominenter Freikirchler im Gespräch mit Seinem Vater, Der Sich Geoutet Hat" (English: Honor Your Father Even if He is Gay? A Prominent Evangelical in Conversation with His Father Who Came Out), *Neue Zürcher Zeitung*, January 21, 2020, access August 8, 2020, https://www.nzz.ch/schweiz/ein-freikirchler-im-gespraech-mit-seinem-homosexuellen-vater-ld.1534374.

Speaking Truthfully

Another very fundamental principle for media engagement to be effective in the long run is that one must speak truthfully. Speaking the truth should not be difficult in regular conversations or interactions with media; it should be natural for Christians to do so. When debates get heated in a crisis or controversy or if people feel defensive or are afraid their arguments will not be heard, avoiding or bending the truth may be tempting. Some people also hope to get more media attention with stronger, more sensational language. Failing to uphold the truth will always come back to hurt one's credibility, which in turn diminishes the potential influence on public opinion.

Truth is a very important theme in the Bible from Genesis through Revelation, but it is especially prominent in the writings of the Apostle John. Jesus reveals himself as God's Son who speaks the truth (John 8:31-32), which stands in stark contrast with those who follow or teach lies, whom Jesus calls children of Satan (verse 44). John begins his Gospel stating that the Word (Greek: λόγος) is God (John 1:1) and later Jesus says God's Word (λόγος) is truth (John 17:17); therefore, God Himself is truth and whatever is not true is not of God.

The challenge in media engagement is how truth and lie are defined. Where is the line drawn between truth, partial truth, and lie? Sometimes leaving out some facts or overemphasizing only one aspect of the story can twist the truth sufficiently to turn it into a mischaracterization or even a lie. It is notable that even Satan, the father of lies, quoted God's word—the truth—when he tried to tempt Jesus (Matt. 4:6). As an illustration, someone could cynically quote King David as literally saying "There is no God," as he does in Psalm 53:1. The passage in full, however, reads "The fool says in his heart, 'There is no God.'" This example might seem ridiculous, but it is exactly the type of mischaracterization recently used by a prominent CNN reporter on social media.[29] His out-of-context quote was promptly called out as hypocritical, but there are more subtle twists and methods that are commonly used to persuade the public to believe or not believe certain people, which can be frustrating also to Christian leaders if they find themselves or their view portrayed unfairly. It may be tempting to use similar tactics in response, but the Apostle Peter cautions believers to "not repay evil with evil or insult

---

[29] Joseph A. Wulfsohn, "CNN's Jim Acosta Blasted for Taking Kayleigh McEnany Out of Context in Viral Tweet," *FOXNews.com*, July 16, 2020, accessed August 8, 2020, https://www.foxnews.com/media/cnn-jim-acosta-kayleigh-mcenany-science.

with insult" (1 Pet. 3:9a) and to "keep their lips from deceitful speech" (verse 10b).

Christian leaders should hold themselves to a higher standard than people or news outlets in the secular world, especially since evangelicals will be measured against the teachings of the Bible that hold truth in high regard. In order not to be judged and dismissed as unauthentic or hypocritical, it is important to speak as truthfully as possible, presenting facts within a comprehensive picture that addresses important nuances or concerns and responds to valid criticism.

Similarly, Christian leaders should stay away from "ad hominem attacks" that target an opponent's character rather than respond to the actual argument. This rhetoric strategy can at times be effective in the moment by way of diverting attention, but it will increase polarization and sooner or later diminish one's credibility. It is also important to note that ad hominem attacks are usually used by people who lack good arguments and are thus a sign of weakness rather than strength.

When it comes to hot-button issues, speaking truthfully and respectfully may at times be less sensational and thus get less media attention, but doing so will help build up credibility and be more effective over time. It will also give opponents fewer opportunities to criticize Christians as hypocritical—and if they do, it may ultimately backfire to their shame. Like the Apostle Peter says when he urges believers to speak "with gentleness and respect, keeping a clear conscience, so that those who speak maliciously against your good behavior in Christ may be ashamed of their slander" (1 Pet. 3:15b-16).

Speaking Prophetically

A fourth principle for an evangelical approach to media engagement is that they should speak prophetically into a situation. There are two aspects to this, both of which are integral to prophetic speech: judgment and hope. One without the other would either lead to frustration and despair or would cover up the truth of God's holiness and man's sin. It is critically important that believers hold themselves to the same standard and speak prophetically to their own, including when Christians are in positions of power, and not condemn only the sinfulness of the world.

Regarding judgment, Dr Reimer writes, "As God's priest the church will ask God and answer the questions of the people and will speak out whatever judgment God makes over the structures of society and culture. It will never condone those who introduce selfishness and corruption to their people. It will name the unrighteousness and confront injustice."[30] He goes on to say, "It reveals what is wrong, corrupt, sinful, and destructive, acting in bold humility. Nothing else is so much against the prophetic nature of the church as political correctness."[31]

Regarding hope, Dr Reimer states, "Biblical prophecy is a moral voice in the midst of a nation, but prophets were far more than critics only. Pronouncing judgment, they were also announcing ways of repentance and a new beginning. They were messengers of hope and a restored future under God's rule."[32] In media engagement, criticism should always be constructive, and prophetic speaking should always be pointing to hope and restoration.

The Bible emphasizes this aspect when the Apostle Paul—who in his letters frequently pointed out believers' sins in strong terms—talks about "speaking the truth in love" (Eph. 4:15) and says that love "always trusts, always hopes, always perseveres" (1 Cor. 13:7). Even in the Old Testament, the prophets warned of God's imminent judgment but pointed to future hope and restoration, and at times the people responded to the prophets with repentance and God "relented and did not bring on them the destruction he had threatened" (Jonah 3:10). Throughout the Bible, God is revealed as holy and just, but also as loving and forgiving and desiring for mankind to abandon their evil ways and return to him. Prophetic speaking should therefore reflect both sides: criticism where man falls short and the hopeful alternative that God offers when people repent.

Reconciling and Building Peace

The fifth principle of media engagement is that evangelical leaders should seek to reconcile conflicting parties and build lasting peace. This principle applies to society overall but especially to conflict within the Church. Jesus warned that "every kingdom divided against itself will be ruined, and every city or household divided against itself will not stand" (Matt. 12:25). Even though the Church will ultimately prevail (Matt. 16:18), division greatly damages Christians' reputation and makes their witness less effective. Mass media has on many occasions amplified this issue by publicly exposing and further contributing to conflict. Rather than first attempting

---

[30] Reimer, *Missio Politica*, 55.

[31] Ibid., 58.

[32] Ibid.

to solve disagreements in private or small circles as Matthew 18:15-17 suggests, there is a strong temptation today to air frustration and criticism on social media or even in news media.

Here is an illustration of two contrasting approaches. Part of WEA's mission is to speak as a voice on behalf of evangelicals on issues of concern. Naturally, not all evangelicals agree with what the WEA says, and they have the right to hold it accountable. In one instance, a Christian leader made rather lengthy comments in a Christian news outlet and strongly criticized WEA for a possibly ill-formulated statement—though he admitted he wasn't sure if that is what they meant—and then called on WEA to clarify its stance; however, he never contacted WEA, neither before making such public criticism, which would have been appropriate, nor afterwards to find out if he had interpreted the statement correctly. In contrast, the leadership of an organization disagreed with a WEA statement on the Holy Land, but rather than publicly questioning WEA or arguing against its stance, they sent a respectful letter with detailed arguments why they felt WEA's statement may have been problematic. This interaction then allowed WEA to respond with clarifications or express appreciation for the important issues raised.

Conflict occurs naturally between people, and some issues, such as the sanctity of life and protection of the nuclear family, are non-negotiable for evangelicals. But more than irreconcilable disagreements, the lack of listening, respect, and direct engagement between Christians on more complex matters cause conflicts to spill into the media and to become very difficult to resolve. Jesus says that peacemakers will be blessed and called sons of God (Matt. 5:9). He himself came into this world to reconcile man to God (Ephesians 2:16) and break down the barriers between people (verses 14-15), and the Apostle Paul points out that this same ministry of reconciliation was then entrusted to the believers (2 Cor. 5:18-20). But how does reconciliation happen in the midst of or after potentially damaging conflict?

According to Dr. Reimer, it can only begin by both sides admitting their failings and coming together to see the truth beyond their own limited perspectives. Based on his research and his experience of working in the field, he states, "This is the condition of peace building; peace can only be established when the conflicting parties recognize their failure, their sin, and when they understand the consequences and the futility of living in conflict and see the whole and true picture."[33]

---

[33] Ibid., 68.

It can be very challenging to be a peace builder in a highly polarized and politicized atmosphere like the current situation in the United States and many other countries. Whatever is said can easily be misunderstood, mischaracterized, or dismissed. Determination, patience, and humility are required to build trust with both sides, to build bridges, foster understanding among both groups, help both sides see their own limitations or failings, and offer a path forward that could bring all of them together. More unity is critical for effective media engagement, as will be discussed in the next principle.

The Power of Unity

The sixth principle is that media engagement is much more effective when Christians are united. This principle is closely related to the previous one, as unity requires learning to constructively resolve conflict and disagreements. There is good reason why Jesus's last prayer focused strongly on unity: it is the most powerful witness that the Church can offer to the world (John 17:20-23).

Singular voices, especially conflicting voices, can easily be dismissed, but when Christians come together and represent a diversity of age, gender, ethnicity, and denominational background, then their voices can become very strong. This is part of the essence of why WEA has become a desired partner on many issues at the United Nations, and why it can effectively elevate the voice of marginalized or persecuted Christians showing that they belong to a global body of more than 600 million evangelicals.

At the national level, Christians can have greater influence when coming together around critical issues. A recent example took place in Korea when a number of denominational leaders came together to oppose LGBT-legislation and committed to mobilizing their congregations in a joint effort to safeguard the definition of marriage.[34] They realized that no single denomination or organization could do that effectively on their own. Therefore, Christian leaders from local to national and global level should actively look for opportunities to work together and speak up as one on critical issues. Doing so may first require taking the initiative to build re-

---

[34] Daewoong Lee, "차별금지법 입법 반대 ... 소모임 금지는 철회하라" (English: "Opposition of Anti-Discrimination Act ... Withdraw the Ban on Small-Group Gatherings"), *Christian Today Korea*, July 16, 2020, accessed August 8, 2020, https://www.christiantoday.co.kr/news/333160.

lationships and trust between different leaders, churches, and organizations, but the potential difference in outcome is significant enough to justify the effort.

It Takes Time

The seventh and final principle is that media engagement takes time. Public opinion does not change over-night and even individual people do not change easily. The Apostle Peter speaks to this when he says, "The Lord is not slow in keeping his promise, as some understand slowness. Instead he is patient with you, not wanting anyone to perish, but everyone to come to repentance" (2 Pet. 3:9). God waited four thousand years before sending his Son, and even after such a long time of preparation, his own people were still not ready to accept Christ (Matt. 21:37ff). Thus, Christian leaders will need to manage their expectations and ready themselves for a marathon rather than a sprint when seeking to build relationships, establish a reputation of trust and competence, and become influencers in their community and the wider public, from the local to the global level.

One characteristic of the fruit of the Spirit in Galatians 5:22-23 is μακροθυμία, which can be best translated as long-suffering, but also means "waiting sufficient time before expressing anger."[35] Christian leaders can grow tired of fighting for change or going against the mainstream, but the reality is that it took William Wilberforce decades to abolish the slave trade and later slavery as a whole, to give just one example. Similarly, there are leaders today who have worked for decades to raise awareness on and fight to abolish human trafficking, abortion, corruption, and many other evils where media is a critical factor in reaching the public and creating the necessary pressure for change. It is important, therefore, not to expect immediate results but to have a long-term perspective and a strategy that looks at least ten years into the future. The strategy should also expect challenges and setbacks along the way, but God-willing, it will bear fruit if it follows the seven principles above.

One More Thought

One question that has not been addressed by the seven principles is when to speak out publicly and to what extent. In a recent Op-Ed, apologist and

---

[35] Biblehub.com, *3115. Makrothumia*, accessed August 8, 2020, https://biblehub.com/greek/3115.htm.

Christian Post columnist Robin Schumacher reflected on the current atmosphere in the U.S. where people, organizations, and companies are pressured to publicly align themselves with causes or be shamed for standing on the side of injustice. In his column titled "Was Jesus' silence violence?"[36] Schumacher observes that neither Jesus nor his disciples engaged in public advocacy against Roman oppression, the low status of women, or the institution of slavery. He states, "His strategy was a far more effective one than publicly speaking out against the injustices of the first century and bringing down the immediate wrath of the strong-arm government," and adds that Jesus "knew that simply telling bad people to do good is an exercise in futility." He then offers the following conclusion:

> [Jesus] knew that when you change people from the inside out, pretty soon the wrongs that exist in that culture are eradicated in de facto fashion as those people live out their faith. That being true, the most important thing we can do to fight injustice and change the world as Christians is to go beyond just speaking out against evils like abortion, human trafficking, etc., and follow the same strategy as Jesus. Nothing beats the power of the gospel.

Schumacher does not suggest that Christians should never speak out. It is also obvious that the contexts in which believers find themselves vary greatly. Some live under oppression like the early Church while another country's population may have a majority of 90% Christians. Choosing when to speak out and when to remain silent or use other forms of influence is something that Christian leaders should prayerfully consider from case to case. Every day there may be something that could be commented on, but, depending on the mission and capacity of the church or organization, issuing public statements may not always be the most effective strategy. Thus, media engagement has its unique role but also its limits when considered in the wider effort of influencing culture.

The Proposal: A Strategic Global Center

Thousands of individuals, churches, and organizations are actively engaging with or using media locally, nationally, and globally, on a wide variety of issues. They do so with different methods and strategies and varying

---

[36] Robin Schumacher, "Was Jesus' Silence Violence?" *The Christian Post*, July 7, 2020, accessed August 8, 2020, https://www.christianpost.com/news/was-jesus-silence-violence.html.

degrees of success. What is clearly missing, however, is a global strategy to address specific issues that influence culture across geographical boundaries.

An Image Problem

In their book *Can Evangelicals Truly Change the World?* Drs. William and Mark Wagner examine several global movements and to what extent they have a global strategy in place to win people for their faith or ideology. Specifically, the LGBT movement seems a "success story" in how well-defined and effective their global strategy has turned out to be. The Wagners present six strategies developed by Marshall Kirk and Hunter Madsen and used by the LGBT to advance their cause. It is apparent that the basis for the six points is public relations. They want to change the image of the gay and lesbian community.[37]

Looking at these goals and comparing them with societal and legislative changes that have taken place in a range of countries around the world, it is evident that they have accomplished a lot within a relatively short period of time. Evangelicals, on the other hand, have an image problem nowadays due to the negative narrative that has been cultivated among others by the LGBT lobby and liberal media, but also due to the extremely polarized political situation in the U.S. with the often quoted (but actuality somewhat misleading) 81% of White evangelicals voting for President Trump in 2016.[38] This narrative then also spilled over into other countries, creating a rift within evangelicalism where views on U.S. politics have at times become more defining than denominational affiliation or doctrinal matters. There were even meetings where evangelical leaders discussed dropping the "evangelical" label altogether due to its negative connotations, but so far no one has found a better alternative.

In the midst of these challenges, cultural shifts away from Biblical values and internal tensions and divisions within the Church, what could possibly help restore evangelicals' reputation or at least strengthen the influence in the sphere of media to change some of the narrative and negative

---

[37] William and Mark Wagner, *Can Evangelicals Truly Change the World?* WEA World of Theology Series 12 (Bonn, Germany: Culture and Science Publisher, 2019), 74.

[38] Brandon Showalter, "Did 81 Percent of Evangelicals Really Vote for Trump? Not So Fast, Some Say," *The Christian Post,* November 16, 2016, accessed August 8, 2020, https://www.christianpost.com/news/81-percent-evangelicals-vote-trump-eric-teetsel-joe-carter.html.

portrayal of believers? It certainly has to start with prayer and encouraging Christians to follow the above principles could contribute to an improved image and less negativity. Evangelicals also need to be better equipped with information, arguments, illustrations, and stories that will allow them to respond more effectively to cultural issues. This is where this proposal for a global center comes in.

The Need for Strategic Messaging

What is striking about the LGBT movement's strategy is the simplicity of their goals and message: talking about being gay as much and as loudly as possible while emphasizing the clear distinction of and polarization between victimized gays (and their supporters) and the bad and hateful victimizers. Anyone can understand this rhetoric and anyone can participate in supporting these efforts.

The evangelicals' response, on the other hand, is much more fragmented, with some simply calling homosexuals sinners who will go to hell and others trying to be more nuanced by speaking of hating the sin but loving the sinner and emphasizing that the church needs to welcome them rather than reject them. Others again are on the verge of compromise and wonder why this is such a big deal with much more pressing issues like racial divisions and other injustices. And then there are those who prefer to simply avoid this divisive topic or those who have given up altogether on engaging the wider public and instead "hunker down" in their churches, trying not to be defiled by today's fallen society.

Part of the reason for the Church's fragmentation on this and other issues is the lack of a common messaging strategy that is based not only on God and the Bible—whose authority the secular world unequivocally rejects—but also on solid scientific research and data, personal stories, and overall a positive narrative to the extent that this is possible. Even though lot of material is already available on a wide range of issues, it is not centrally and systematically organized and made available to evangelicals around the world. This may be a contributing factor to the insecurity and fear of some or simply ignorance and indifference of other believers who do not feel sufficiently informed and equipped to publicly stand up for what they believe.

Data, Stories, Unity and Solidarity

Four key ingredients to a convincing messaging strategy will be briefly considered here: research and data, personal stories, unity of message, and solidarity among evangelicals.

Research data and statistics can be powerful tools because they can picture a reality that is not based on personal conviction but on fact. It is difficult to argue against data because it is impersonal and ideally independently verifiable. An example of statistics that have been used relatively effectively in the context of abortion is that the rate of Black babies being aborted is disproportionately higher (more than 30%) than the percentage of Black people in the U.S. (16%), which puts in question the pro-abortion argument that it is all about women's health and women's choice.[39] Another example in the context of the LGBT movement is the recent publication in a psychiatric journal of a correction of an earlier study that falsely suggested that surgery improves the mental health of trans individuals. The new evaluation of the data reveals no statistically significant improvement, which means trans surgery is no solution to the mental suffering experienced by those who struggle with their gender identity.[40]

There are a variety of other statistics on this and other issues, and if made available systematically, they could help equip churches and individuals in responding to and countering common arguments. The challenge with research is that it needs to fulfill certain standards to ensure it is trustworthy; methodology, sample-size, peer-review, and other aspects are critical. Using poor or questionable research can backfire and hurt public credibility, so ideally, research should be vetted by experts in the field before being accepted into the pool of resources.

Second, personal stories are essential in an effective media strategy: testimonies from abortion survivors, former members of the LGBT community, a rescued victim of human trafficking, and so on. As mentioned in the principle of "Who Before What," the person's credibility is established

---

[39] Micaiah Bilger, "Black Man Silences #BlackLivesMatter Protesters By Asking: 'Do Aborted Black Babies Matter?'" *LifeNews.com*, June 17, 2020, accessed August 8, 2020, https://www.lifenews.com/2020/06/17/black-man-silences-blacklivesmatter-protesters-by-asking-do-aborted-black-babies-matter/.

[40] Brandon Showalter, "Psychiatry Journal Issues Major Correction to Study on Trans Surgeries Effect on Mental Health," *The Christian Post*, August 6, 2020, accessed August 8, 2020, https://www.christianpost.com/news/trans-surgeries-not-beneficial-for-mental-health-psychiatry-journal-issues-major-correction.html.

by his or her own history and experience, which cannot easily be dismissed by those who do not have that experience. Publicly expressing sympathy for these people and what they went through allows the message to be positive, which is easier to convey than speaking against issues and puts the pressure to speak negatively on the other side. There are many such testimonies available on-line but quality, content, and tone vary greatly, which would make a curated overview of the best stories for each topic a valuable tool.

Unity of message is similar to the earlier principle of "The Power of Unity"; it is relatively easy for news media and the public to dismiss or overpower fragmented voices and arguments, but much more difficult to counter a unified voice and message. The strength of the LGBT movement has been its focus on equal rights and anti-discrimination as a unifying message to achieve marriage equality, discrimination protection in the workplace, and other objectives. As outlined in their goals, they want to make gays appear as victims and those opposing them as bad victimizers. The Church requires a much more unified voice on this and other issues and must keep emphasizing the same message in order to make it more difficult for the media to silence it, but it also needs to be well thought through and persuasive enough to make it understandable not only for Christians but also for the general public. The messaging should then be continuously evaluated and refined based on what is effective in different contexts.

Finally, the witness of evangelicals would be strengthened if they showed more solidarity with each other in cases where they are silenced, discriminated against, or even persecuted. The LGBT community immediately rallies around anyone of their own who appears to have been victimized. Similarly, Muslims are strong in standing in solidarity with each other when there seems to be discrimination against fellow Muslims. Christians, on the other hand, tend to be less likely to publicly stand together in solidarity if other Christians experience some form of negative consequence for what they believe in. Even though some individuals and organizations are very actively speaking up, the indifference by and large makes it easier for media to ignore them, and the media could also perceive it as either a sign of lack of evangelicals' love for each other or a lack of conviction about the issue in question.

A Strategic Global Center

Developing a global strategy with the elements mentioned above on key cultural issues requires a central force that galvanizes the many existing efforts around the world. It would need to include representatives of church networks, subject matter experts, issue-focused organizations, and media professionals who come together not only in a one-time consultation but in an ongoing partnership that would result in concerted efforts to tackle each issue. The platform would need to be recognized as balanced in terms of geographic, denominational, gender, and age representation in order to allow for the broadest possible participation.

Looking at the global landscape of existing evangelical organizations, the World Evangelical Alliance (WEA) would be the most suitable candidate to lead such an initiative due to its structure of regional and national Alliances in more than 130 countries that bring together churches at the grassroots level. It has a long history of addressing global issues, offers a trusted brand that allows it to access the United Nations, governments, and media, and it was established with the very purpose of uniting evangelicals to speak with one voice.

Serving as a strategic global center for hot-button issues, however, would require the WEA to significantly enhance and strengthen its network among subject matter experts, key organizations, and media professionals as well as upgrade its financial and staff capacity. It would also require ownership of such an initiative among its board, leadership, and constituency and realignment of some activities within the organization to fit with such a strategy. While not at all impossible, such an effort would likely take several years to bear fruit.

Alternatively, a Center could be set up independent from but in partnership with the WEA that would provide more flexibility to operate while retaining the benefit of WEA's credibility and network. It would require visionary leadership that could lay out a plan and begin to bring together a first group of leaders and experts around a defined issue in a pilot project; for the longer-term it would need a sustainable funding model to organize consultations and maintain an online resource hub. Global prayer networks could ensure the necessary prayer support that would provide the spiritual strength and protection for an initiative of this scale.

All this is currently only a rough sketch of an idea, but there is no reason to believe such a center could not be established. The potential momentum it could create for positive media engagement is too significant for this vision to be dismissed. Much of the data, information, stories, and even the global network is already available. These resources just need to be put to use in a strategic way by the people God has prepared and called for this task.

Conclusion

Media itself is only a channel of communication, a neutral tool that can be used for good or bad. Over the past years alone, countless people around the world have come to faith or have been strengthened in their faith by messages they received through different kinds of media. However, due to the increasing influence of secularism through media, many believers today may feel insecure, fearful, or disoriented. They wonder if it is still possible to win the cultural battle where they currently see themselves on the losing side facing an overpowering enemy, but as David exclaimed when facing Goliath, "The battle is the Lord's" (1 Sam. 17:47).

Building on a foundation of prayer, equipped with a good understanding of what media is and how it can be used, and following the seven essential principles of media engagement, believers can help turn the tide with their efforts whether they are active locally, nationally, or globally. Their impact could be immensely strengthened if global leaders could come together in forming a strategic center that provides believers with comprehensive and up-to-date information, data, and stories on each of the major issues today. Ultimately, media is only one of the ten mountains of culture, and tackling it requires a comprehensive approach that also takes into consideration the other nine, but a powerful media engagement strategy can help protect and strengthen the Church so it can more effectively engage and advance in other areas.

Chapter 5: Education

Prof. Dr. William Wagner

William Wagner (Th.D., University of South Africa, D. Miss., Fuller Theological Seminary, M.Div., Southwestern Baptist Theological Seminary, B.S., University of New Mexico) is the founding Director of the Olivet Institute for Global Strategic Studies and a professor of Missions at Olivet University. He served for 31 years as a missionary to Europe and the Middle East and has written six books. He helped found two theological seminaries in Europe and one international university. He has taught at seminaries in 35 countries and has been a professor at four seminaries in three countries. He also served Olivet University in many positions including being the President of the University for three years. He was also elected to serve for one year as the Second Vice President of the Southern Baptist Convention. Dr. Wagner was also the Chairman of the Board for the Christian Post for six years. He now lives with his wife Sally in California.

Changing Education Today

Introduction

The Christian Church in the Western World is facing a major crisis with regards to its youth. The Church is losing many of its university age students to the forces of secularism. Not only are contemporary students not ready to be active in church; they are also leaving the faith altogether. It is imperative that we find some way to retain them. One recent study in the U.S. determined that 70 percent of church going young people drop out of church between the ages of 18 to 22, the ages during which many are attending a university. Another study that looked exclusively at young people who were attending college found that they were much less inclined to attend church. The study stated that among incoming freshmen, 43.7 percent said they frequently attended religious services, but by the end of their junior year, attendance was down to 23.4 percent. Another study taken of Southern Baptist students reported that only 4.6 percent of graduating students attended church.[41]

In the elementary and high schools in countries of the West, the problem is just as serious. Secularism seems to have taken over most state sponsored schools. A few years ago, I read a dissertation from a 37-year-old doctoral student who had received permission to return to his old high school to study for a semester. His purpose was to write about the changes in education that had taken place in the past twenty years. The results were eye opening. Among his conclusions was that education was increasingly devoid of any references to faith and concentrated today mostly on science. He also was amazed as to the tremendous advancements being made in teaching methods and how computers are providing advanced ways of making presentations. He also made a study of his old church and its teaching methods. He discovered the same teaching methods, such as using flannel boards and reading from a quarterly, as he had experienced as a child. He mentioned that the average student now spends 32 hours each week in the secular school and only one hour a week learning about his or her faith, so it is no wonder that many of our youth have abandoned the faith. The church has failed to make the necessary strides forward in teaching our children the important basics of the Faith. More and more the church is handing over the job of educating our youth to others. This practice needs to be changed.

---

[41] Thomas Rainer, *Essential Church* (Nashville: B&H, 2008), 31.

A Brief History of Christian Education

The Early Church

King Solomon wrote, "Train a child in the way he should go, and when he is old, he will not turn from it" (Prov. 22:6). For those in the New Testament church, education was a problem. Prior to the birth of the faith, the Jews had synagogue schools that taught both faith and character development to boys, but with the development of the new church, the synagogue education was no longer an option for those of the faith community. The few state-run schools were guided by a different philosophy than what the believing parents desired for their children. In most cases, education was only for the very wealthy, and they provided tutors for their children. Few Christian families could afford them.

Christians also faced intense persecution from many quarters; thus, the education of their children was generally underground and resembled what we now call home schooling. The fathers of the church saw educating their young as a very important task. Origen, one of the well-known fathers of the Faith, observed, "It is appropriate to children that some things should be addressed to them in a manner benefiting their infantile condition, to convert them, as being of very tender age, to a better course of life"[42] As Christian parents tried to find solutions to the lack of education, they needed to be both very careful and very creative.

As the church grew, there was a need to teach the new converts as well as the children the basics of the new faith; thus, there was the development of

Catechetical schools where training was given by the church to all who wanted to know more about Christian beliefs. With time, the catechetical school expanded and began to teach such areas of scholarship as philology, rhetoric, math, and philosophy but with a biblical background. As Christianity became more recognized after the fourth century, these schools formed the basis of higher education, including universities, for the educational systems in the West.

Roman Catholic Missions

Starting around A.D. 300, Christianity became the dominate faith in much of what is now known as Western Europe, but as the Dark Ages befell the

---

[42] Contra Celsus, Chapter XXVI.

continent, the task of education fell mostly on the orders within the Roman Catholic church. Many have said that the monasteries and convents of the time saved the concept of education, and the members of the orders took this task very seriously. During the period beginning about 1500, the Jesuits, the Franciscans, and other orders became very active in mission work, and the Roman Catholic Church saw education and starting schools as a mission endeavor. Part of this program was the founding of an education system to train the new converts, especially in many of the lands conquered by the European colonizing nations. By the middle of the 19th century, the Catholics in large cities in the U.S. had started building their own parochial school system. By this time, the Protestants were leading out in education, and the Catholics felt that if they did not educate their young, many would lose their faith.[43]

It appears as if the Catholics had a Mega strategy in place in that they wanted to protect their children from what they perceived as being false teachings; thus, they built an outstanding school system. By 2010, however, that system had begun experiencing a steady decline in number. From 2000 to 2013, 1755 Catholic schools closed in the U.S.[44] The Mega strategy was successful in the past, but there is now a need for a new plan for Christian education by the Roman Catholic Church, not only in America but possibly for the whole world.

Protestant Schools in America

Protestant schooling is not a recent phenomenon in American education. By the middle decades of the nineteenth century, the spiritual awakenings of the country had spawned new schools. These schools were started out of a desire to train their own young but also because they wanted to see that as many persons as possible had the opportunity to know more about this dynamic faith. James C. Carper writes about this time:

> Throughout these years, Lutherans, Quakers, Presbyterians, Moravians, Mennonites, German and Dutch Reformed, Baptists, Methodists, and Anglicans established elementary schools and academies. Even the so-called town

---

[43] Thomas E. Buckley, "A Mandate for Anti-Catholicism: The Blane Amendment," *America* (September 2004): 18-21.

[44] David O'Reilly, "Closing of Catholic Schools may have long-term effects on faith," *Philadelphia Inquirer*, accessed Nov. 29, 2019, http://www.phillly.com/philly/insisghts/in-the-know/20120116_Closing-of-Catholic-schools-may-have-long-term-effectson-faith.html).

schools of colonial New England and the quasi-public schools and charity schools of the early 1800s were de facto Protestant Schools.[45]

For well over 100 years these religious schools, both Roman Catholic and Protestant, existed side by side but with a decreasing influence in the world of education. By the 1920s, several states had attempted to enact laws to limit or abolish religious schools in favor of public schools. In 1922, the State of Oregon passed a referendum-based law that required children between the ages of eight and sixteen to attend public schools. Three years later, the U.S. Supreme court struck down the law, saying religious schools could co-exist with public schools, but for the past 100 years there has been an increasing emphasis for public schools, even at the expense of all private institutions. Over much of this period, religious educational institutions had limit growth, but by the 1960s, there was a resurgence of interest in Christian education, partially because of the increasing secularization of the public schools. The National Center for Education estimates that between 1960 and 1990, over 10,000 Christian day schools were founded. What will happen in the battle for the existence of the Christian school for the next decades is still up for grabs.

As stated previously, much early Christian education took on the same identity as today's home schools. In recent years, more and more evangelicals as well as others have sought to home school their own children. This movement is a direct reaction to the secularization of many of the public schools. Many of those who strongly support the public education system have been strongly opposed to the home-schooling movement. In Germany, some Russian German Baptists (those Baptists who were brought up in the Soviet Union but allowed to return to Germany after the 1980s) began to home school their children, but the government soon said that it was illegal for children to not go to the public schools. One family fought the government all the way to the top court. A final decision has still not been made. As secularism exerts more influence on the public-school system, more parents will choose to home school their children, which is legal in the United States. There are now several excellent Christian homeschooling programs that can be purchased to help the parents give their children a quality education.

Some of the most prestigious universities in America were started as Protestant schools. Several of them, including Yale, Harvard, Princeton, Brown, and the University of Chicago, were seminaries designed to train

---

[45] James C. Carper, "Colonial and Nineteenth-Century Protestant Schooling, Early Twentieth Century Protestant Schooling," accessed March 20, 2020.

pastors. With time, however, these institutions separated themselves from their Christian heritage and are now leaders in the secular movement. It is important to understand that in education, there is a general tendency for a school to start with a conservative theology but over time, there is a liberalizing action, with end result of the school losing its calling to profess Jesus as Lord. This dynamic has been true with many of the denominal universities in America, both Catholic and Protestant. There are only a few examples of schools becoming liberal and then reverting to conservatism. The two most recent examples are the Southern Baptist seminaries, which took on a more conservative identity after that denomination's conservative resurgence, and Concordia Lutheran Seminary of the Missouri Synod Lutheran denomination.

Mega Strategies Now in Place

Homosexuals (Influence with Teachers)

There have always been homosexuals, but it was only in the 1980s when they developed a full-blown strategy to push for their acceptance as normal. The new strategy came into being when Marshall Kirk and Hunter Madsen, two Harvard professors, published two works designed for gaining public acceptance of homosexuality: *The Overhauling of Straight America* (1987) and *After the Ball* (1989). Both men were highly educated and were well informed about the various social structures in the United States. From these two highly capable men came a plan that is still being used by the LGBT community today.

As we attempt to understand their strategy, it is important to look at the very basis of their argument. In their works, the two men propose a six-point strategy for gaining respect and acceptance:

1. Talk about gays and gayness as often and loudly as possible.
2. Portray gays as victims, not aggressive challengers.
3. Give homosexual protectors a just cause.
4. Make gays look good.
5. Make the victimizer look bad.
6. Solicit funds; the strategy is to get corporate America and major foundations to financially support the homosexual cause.[46]

---

[46] NEA 1999-2000 Resolutions, B-9, "Racism, Sexism, and Sexual Orientation Discrimination," www.nea.org/resulations/99/99b-9.htm.

Changing Education Today

It is apparent that the basis for the six-points program emphasized public relations since they wanted to change the image of the gay and lesbian community. For them, a very important part of changing the views of Americans was to start at the place where people are taught and influenced—the educational structures:

> The first order of business is desensitization of the American public concerning gays and gay rights ... To desensitize the public is to view homosexuality with indifference instead of with keen emotion ... At least in the outset we are seeking public desensitization and nothing more. We do not need and cannot expect a full 'appreciation' or understanding of homosexuality from the average American but if only you can get them to think that it is just another thing ... then your battle for legal and social rights is virtually won.[47]

They determined that it would be better to start at the top of the educational structure and attempt to influence the school administrators and teachers. The one organization that was best represented by both groups was the National Education Association. By 2001 the homosexual movement had already made inroads at the top levels of this association. At their annual convention that year in Los Angeles, a resolution was introduced for consideration. It called for implementing a full-scale indoctrination of children to accept and affirm homosexual behavior. The resolution reads as follows:

A. Development of curriculum and instructional materials and programs designed to meet the needs of gay, lesbian, bisexual, and transgender students.
B. Involvement of gay, lesbian, bisexual, and transgender characters in developing educational materials use in classroom instruction.
C. Dissemination programs that support gay, lesbian, bisexual, transgender, and questing students and address their high dropout rate, suicide rate, and health risk behavior.
D. Recognition of the importance of gay, lesbian, bisexual, transgender, bisexual, and transgender education employees as role models.
E. Accurate portrayal of roles and contributions of gay, lesbian, bisexual, and transgender education employees as role models.

---

[47] Matt Pykeatt, "NEA Task Force Issues Report on Sexual Orientation," CNN News.com. February 13, 2002.

F. Dissemination of programs and information that includes the contributions, heritage, culture, and history of gay, lesbians, bisexual and transgender people.

G. Coordination with gay, lesbian, bisexual and transgender organizations and concerned agencies that promote the contribution, heritage, history, heath and care of gays, lesbian, bisexuals, and transgender people."[48]

When the news of this resolution spread, organizations such as Focus on the Family and others blew the whistle, and the public backlash caused the NEA to table it. A committee was appointed to study the resolution, and the NEA decided to slowly implement this program without the members' approval. Later the NEA, along with the American Academy of Pediatrics, published a booklet entitled "Just the Facts about Sexual Orientation and Youth." This booklet calls for wholehearted encouragement of school children to experiment with homosexuality, and it calls for the censorship of the "religious right" and the censoring of religious speech on the issue.

By 2014 the LGBT community was promoting a nationwide plan for all schools to organize a LGBT History Month. Thirty-one "icons" from the gay community, one for each day of the month, would be studied. Most concerning to parents was the inclusion of CeCe McDonald, who had been released from prison earlier that year after served time in the killing of a man who had insulted her. It was also reported that "works by several of the other induvial included on the list would not be allowed in school, or most homes. For example, a music video of 'icon' John Cameron Mitchell [was] too explicit to be shown on MTV Europe. Comedienne 'icon' Margaret Chol's routines [were] replete with vulgarity and not permitted in schools."[49]

The LGBT strategy to influence the public schools of America has been highly successful. It should be noted that their plan to achieve this goal was a part of a well thought out Mega strategy. Any new plans by evangelicals must include attempts to find ways to make the Christian life an acceptable style that can be promoted in the schools of America. They will continue to work at the local level with the school board, which, in many instances, is the organization that has the responsibility to select the textbooks to be used in the schools. More and more books that do not favor the gay agenda will be set aside for those who do advocate homosexual behavior.

---

[48] Alan Sears and Craig Osten, *The Homosexual Agenda* (Nashville: Broadman and Holman), 48.

[49] Ibid., 34.

Muslims: (Influence at the Local Level)

American schools as well as universities and colleges are prime targets of Islam propaganda. Fatima Mernissi states, "Their main goal is to promote Islamic education in both public schools (from grades to the University level), as well as the mosques and Islamic centers." She goes on to add, "Strong Islamic education and knowledge is the key to both the future of Islam in this country and to attracting the interest of non-Muslims to Islam. One cannot help but notice the sense of Da'wa that motivates then to accomplish such practice."[50] The number of Muslim students at the universities of the world is growing. Approximately 1000 to 1500 international students from 25 Islamic countries are studying in universities in the greater Los Angeles area alone. The majority are affiliated with the Islamic Society of North America and are preparing to work for the establishment of Islamic governments. Muslim alumni who remain in the country seek to evangelize not only American students but also other international students studying at American universities.[51] Several years ago, I was invited to speak at an English class in Morocco. The room was filled with more than 200 young intelligent students. I asked them, "Why do you want to learn English?" One student raised his hand and said that he wanted to learn English to win English speaking students to Islam. I then asked if others felt the same way, and most of them also raised their hands.

A part of their strategy to infiltrate the universities is to use the immense economic strength of Middle Eastern Islamic countries. Financially strapped institutions receive offers to endow a chair of Islamic studies or to build a nice building to house an institute of religion. One report states, "Saudi Arabia has given millions of dollars to Howard University and the University of Arkansas to fund Islamic study centers."[52] Fundamentalist groups with the financial backing of Saudi Arabia send university professors, paid by the sending country, to teach in poorer countries of Africa. The schools are happy to have professors at no cost to them. These "free" professors are often Islamic missionaries. One of the countries that often is visited is Malawi. More than 70% of the population of that country are Christians, but at a recent election, Muslim countries donated millions of

---

[50] Fatema Mernassi, *Islam and Democracy*. (Cambridge, Mass: Perscus 2002), 34.

[51] Marsha S. Haney, *Islam and Protestant African American Churches* (San Francisco International Scholars Publications, 1999), 122.

[52] George Braswell, *What you Need to Know About Islam and Muslims* (Nashville: Broadman and Holman, 2000), 3.

dollars to get a Muslim elected as the president. In the next years, new mosques were built in most of the towns, and in the capital city, a new Islamic high school was established. It was designed to be the best in the country to educate the up and coming political leaders.

As a part of a well-designed strategy to use education to help Islam grow in primary and secondary schools and behind the veil of freedom of speech, they are promoting Islamic instruction. In a California school, exercises in an approved textbook have students role play such activities as wearing Muslim dress, adopting Muslim names, and taking a pilgrimage to Mecca. Most of the school administrators in California received an offer from the state Islamic Speakers Bureau offering to teach Islamic studies as a two-hour room lesson in multiculturalism. One teacher, who was told by the principal to allow this presentation to take place in her class, was amazed that the visiting speaker actively recruited students to come to Islam. This same teacher said that if she mentioned the name of Jesus Christ in her class, she would be fired.

It should also be noted that as a part of their Mega strategy, they are building many Madras schools in countries where Islam is now growing. They see the value of teaching their young about their religion while at the same time doing all possible to negate the influence of Christian schools in the same proximity. Everything they are doing is a part of what they call *Daw'ah*, which when translated into English is our term for missions. Christians can learn from how effective the Muslims have been in the world today as we make plans for a more effective Mega strategy of our own.

Mormons: (Education for Missions)

The Church of Christ of Latter-Day Saints (Mormons) probably have the best thought out Mega strategy in the world. Education is only a part of what they are doing, but it has become a very integral part of their plans. In this section I want to first discuss their philosophy for education and how they desire to implement it. I will then look at the details of their education system for teaching and training in the younger generation, Finally, I will describe how their education philosophy is used to help them be successful in their mission endeavors.

When the Mormon church was founded in the mid 1800s, their children were trained by either home schooling or going to the limited public schools. When Brigham Young led the church out West to Utah, education was of a primary concern. Many felt that they should create their own schools because the public schools were too liberal in their teaching. Brigham Young's philosophy of education was practical and pragmatic. He was not opposed to the more liberal education of the schools but felt that their young people needed a strong influence from the church. Thus, they developed a plan that seems to be prevalent today. The Church has started both elementary and high schools, but only on a limited basis. They report having only 18 elementary and secondary schools, most of which are in mission areas such as in Latin America and the Pacific Islands. Home schooling is used but is not widespread. Their concentration has been on providing an excellent education at the university level in that they have concentrated on building up excellent universities. They now have three universities and one college, all of which are highly accredited. They are leaders in online education for both college level students and for adults who desire to continue their education without attending a university.

Although the Mormons believe they can coexist with the public-school programs present in most states, they also see the need for specific religious education. One of their first steps was to create a religious education program designed for secondary students. These programs, called seminaries, accompany the students who are enrolled in secular schools. These schools consist of one of three options.

The first is a released time program where the students, when allowed by state laws, meet at the school they attend at a time when the school is not in session. A second, and the most popular, method is when they meet In meetinghouses or facilities built specifically for seminary programs, adjacent to public schools. The classes in these forms are generally taught by full time paid teaches. Whether they meet at a public-school building or in another facility, these classes are generally conducted in the early mornings. Depending on the schedule of the school, they may start as early as 5 a.m. but generally start at 6:30 a.m. The third form of training is home-study seminary programs when it is not feasible for the students to attend classes on a regular basis. The teachers for this method are generally volunteer workers. The program is well planned and consists of self-directed programs for all four years. Seminaries are also open to non-Mormon students if they are interested. All Mormon students are encouraged to complete and gradate from seminary. If a young person wants to do the two-year mission program, it is practically a must for him or her to have a degree from a seminary. These seminaries are a successful training system, with the church claiming 342,000 students nationwide currently enrolled in a seminary.[53]

---

[53] In 2000, I was invited to make a visit to the Missionary Training Center in Provo, Utah. Some of the information given was related orally to me during my visit. I was not permitted to take written notes.

Possibly the most effective and successful aspect of the Mormon overall Mega strategy is their emphasis on missions. Most Americans know the Mormons by the two nice looking young men who go from house to house to promote their religion and to make converts. Education plays a very important part in their endeavors. Over the last 150, the Church of Jesus Christ of Latter-Day Saints (Mormons) has grown from a small insignificant sect living in a desert in the United States to one of the most influential religious movements in the world. When a study is made of their theology and their beginnings, it is unimaginable that this growth could happen; thus, the question must be asked, "How did this happen?" I am convinced that it was not their theology or that the Spirit of God led them, but rather it is that they developed a better Mega strategy and have kept to their basic plan. True, they have made some small modifications to this strategy over the years, but they have seldom diverted far from their original plan. Their basic plan is very simple in that they prepare and use university students as their main missionary force.

In 1993, the LDS church reported it had 9,024,569 members worldwide with 47,311 missionaries working in over 300 missions worldwide.[54] By 2015 their membership had grown to 13,372,337 members with over 80,000 missionaries serving in 405 church missions throughout the world. In my discussions with their leadership, they claim that they will have 100,000 missionaries by the year 2020.[55] Many of their missionaries go out to serve for two years when they are between the ages of 18 and 25, but their plans may begin at birth. In Protestant circles when a baby is born, the parents are showered with all kinds of gifts, such as shirts with the words "Grandpa's Little Boy" written on them. In Mormon circles, a saving account is opened for the young boy and instead of giving useless gifts, people begin to give the money that will help finance his eventual missionary work. The education of the young person of elementary school age is done by both the church and the parents. By the high school years, they attend the seminaries. They then are expected to attend the university, and between their sophomore and junior years, they are expected to do their two years of missionary work. After they have completed their missionary service, they are both expected and encouraged to finish their college education.

The missionary experience is a time of learning. The young men are always sent out in pairs. In most cases one of the two has been on the field

---

[54] 1995 Church Handbook, *Church of Jesus Christ Latter Day Saints.*

[55] Information gained at a personal Interview with missionary leadership in 2000.

for a year and has already received both instruction and training from a previous partner. The older person has the task of being a mentor for the younger person. In language situations, the younger member of the pair has an obligation to learn the language, and he spends several hours a day on language training. The older member of the team does all the speaking in the language. After a year, when the older person has completed his tour of duty, then the younger person takes over. By that time, he is fairly fluent in the language and his obligation is to help the new missionary assigned to him in both language learning and discipleship. Discipleship is a key ingredient of their program.

When Mormon young people finish their missionary service, they return to the university to complete their bachelor's degree. Many will go on to graduate studies, but there is also a remarkable phenomenon that takes place. During the latter part of the senior year, large government agencies and private firms will send recruiters to colleges and universities to find the best persons to hire. When they interview a Mormon, they are often impressed that this student has two years of international experience in some important far off country and can speak a foreign language. It is no wonder that a very high percentage of America's FBI and CIA agents ae Mormons. They have been educated for success, but this education has taken many years and has been effective because the leaders of the LDS church have put a complete plan for education in place. They educate their youth with an end purpose in mind—the promotion of their church in the world.

At the turn of the century I put together a plan called the New Antioch, which was designed to be used by Southern Baptists to duplicate some of the more successful aspects of the Mormon plan. I presented this plan to top mission leaders of the SBC only to have the plan rejected. Their reasons were that it would change everything they were doing, and they simply could not see new ideas running parallel to what already was being done. They also said that the best ways to see this plan implemented was to start at the bottom and get a few young people to go on a two-year term of service. One of the problems of trying to implement a Mega strategy is that leaders often can only see something starting from the bottom and going up; they seldom see that they are in a position to develop Mega plans that need to start at the top. Other reasons why the plan was not accepted was that most parents would not allow their young men to leave their studies for two years. The presidents of the Baptist universities were fearful that their student count would go down because their students would leave the school for two years in the middle of their educational program. In the next decade, the Southern Baptists will discover that the Mormons have passed them in the number of members. There is a need for more mega thinkers in the ranks of the leadership of evangelical churches.

Higher Education Today

Universities

From the time described in the book of Acts when Paul challenged the top people in the academic world in Athens until now, there has always been a desire for the more gifted young people to attend school at the university level. As stated earlier, many of America's top universities were started by devout Christians who wanted the best education for their youth. Today in many parts of the world and especially in the U.S., there are numerous Christian universities because many mega thinkers wanted to provide the best education for the future leaders of the church. Many of these schools provide an excellent education; thus, Christianity need not be ashamed of the educational level of its leaders. In the contemporary world, there is a rising need for a quality university education that has the discipling of all nations as a goal. In any strategy, this must be a priority. Let us look at several examples of successful universities that are committed to the concept of proclaiming the Word of God to the world.

Liberty University

Liberty was founded in 1971 in Lynchburg, Virginia, by Rev. Jerry Falwell, the pastor of the Thomas Road Baptist Church. It is an evangelical university with some loose ties to the Southern Baptist Convention. In 2017 it reported to have 15,000 students attending classes on the campus and 94,000 taking online courses. With a total of 110,000 students, it is one of the largest Christian universities in the world. The school has 17 colleges, including a school of medicine and a school of law.

One important aspect of the school is that even with its rapid growth, it retains a conservative lifestyle for both its students and its staff. The honor code prohibits premarital sex, and its leadership is strongly opposed to the homosexual movement. The school is conservative in its belief systems, and it is also very evangelical and missionary in its practice. When studying evangelicalism today, it is common to find leaders who either attended the school or have been influenced by its teachings. The world needs to have more universities like Liberty University.

Olivet University

Olivet University was founded in San Francisco in 2004 by Dr. David Jang. When Dr. Jang was still in Asia, he wanted to find a method that would lead to a growth of the church. Early in his life he determined that he should try to convert the best students to the Christian faith; thus, he went to the most prestigious universities and began two students movements; "Apostolos" was started in most countries of the world and "Young Disciples" was started in China. It was necessary for him to start a different youth organization in China since they would not allow a western organization to come into the country. Both movements were successful, and he felt that the next step would be to create a university so that these new followers could receive the Sprit led training that they needed to carry out the great commission.

In his planning, he felt that in the twenty-first century it was necessary to use technology for the planned outreach. For this reason, he created six well defined colleges. Each one a part of his new plan, and each one was integral to the idea of using the Internet for missions. The colleges were theology, music, Internet technology, art and design, journalism, and business. Each college would give the movement the tools needed to further his plans of a worldwide outreach. With time, other colleges have been added, including engineering, architecture, and language education.

Dr. Jang was also aware of the Stanford experiment, which recommends the academic world partnering with the business world. The success of this plan is seen in the creation of what is known as Silicon Valley. Dr. Jang felt that the creation of businesses, with most of them being Internet based, could be used both to help finance the growing university and to make the proclamation of a risen Lord more acceptable. The plan was for an international university that would start in America but eventually reach the nations for Christ. His plan is one of the best thought out Mega strategies in the realm of education.

Today, sixteen years later, the university has over 2000 students studying on 10 campuses in three countries, and it appears as if they have only started. They have created over 300 businesses, each of which is independent of the school, but the leaders of these business feel not only a direct responsibility to support the school but are also committed to the basic evangelical goal. Two internet businesses that were birthed early are the *Christian Post* and the *International Business Times*. Both have received high marks in their areas of expertise for quality reporting. The IBT has even able to purchase the well-known magazine *Newsweek*.

An important aspect of the school is their Zinzendorf School of Doctoral Studies. It has two accredited doctoral programs, the Doctor of Ministry and the PhD in Global Studies. From its very inception, the goal has been to offer the highest education possible. In the ten years that the doctoral program has been in existence, they have trained almost 100 students at the doctoral level, many of whom are serving in various countries of Asia. They have a faculty of outstanding International professors from over twelve countries.

Again, it should be stated that the goal of the school has always been deeply rooted In the missionary message of presenting the Gospel to the world. Olivet University is a good example of strategic thinking, mega planning, and practical application.

Baylor University

In the United States, there are many denominational universities with a Christian heritage. Some have retained their identity as a Christian school while other have, with time, slowly become more liberal in their theological position. It seems that the bigger and more famous a school becomes, the more it tends towards a secular position. One exception is Baylor University, a Southern Baptist school, located in Waco, Texas. This school is a private Christian university that is recognized as a nationally ranked research institution. Chartered in 1845, it is the oldest continuously operating university in Texas. With over 1,000 acres of campus, it is the largest Baptist university in the world. It has numerous colleges, and three of them, the College of Law, the Business School, and the George W. Truett Theological Seminary, have very high national ratings. In describing their student activities, they emphasize such activities as Faith in Practice, Global Missions, and Serving Christ in the Waco area. It is good to see such a prestigious institute retain its commitment to the Gospel.

Other Universities

The United States is blessed to have many other schools that are considered to be Christian. Some are Christian in name only, but a large number are very dedicated to giving their students an awareness of the need for world evangelization as well as giving them a strong positive value system. In recent years many new college level schools have been started. Several of these are in the process of receiving accreditation from the Association of Biblical Higher Education, an official accrediting agency recognized by the government.

Recommendations for a Mega Strategy

In the U.S

Education at the Elementary and Secondary Levels

To develop a working strategy for influencing the present-day educational structure for Christ, we need to begin at the elementary and secondary levels. We recognize that much is already being done on these levels, but these recommendations are intended to expand our vision and to create a Mega strategy that does not replace what is being done on the Micro and Meta levels but enables us to do even bigger tasks in order to better implement our dreams. Following are some recommendations:

1. Become more aware of the importance of local school boards, which are generally made up of locally elected members. Every state should have one fully paid person whose job is to promote believing Christians who are running for these offices. Often other groups such as the homosexuals are far better at the local level than are Christians ones. It is the local board who generally makes decisions on which textbooks to use and gives the whole local system its identity.
2. Work together with those working on the Sports Mountain to find ways to use sports to make the faith more acceptable in the high schools.
3. Encourage the existence of Christian schools now operating at this level and attempt to establish more. Since doing this is generally more of a funding problem and one of finding qualified leaders, there should be more correspondence with the Business Mountain so that financially strong groups can be aware of the needs in this area of life.
4. Encourage and work with the excellent Christian organizations that are advocating for home schooling.
5. Work with those in the Government Mountain as they continue to challenge legal threats to the rights of Christians in schools. This is important since Mega groups such as the ACLU continue to attempt to deprive faith-based groups their legal rights.
6. Form a nationwide committee to identify where Christian teachers are now functioning and see if believing teachers can be encouraged to resettle in areas where few, if any, Christians are working in the schools.

University Level Education

1. Seek to find interested parachurch organizations as well as denominations to develop a larger plan for using university students in mission work for two years between their sophomore and junior years of college. This plan would be like what the Mormons are doing but would have important changes to fit it into evangelical settings. There could be a meeting of Christian university presidents, mission, and denominational leaders.
2. Make a study to determine the number of students who are graduating from the Christian universities in the field of education. There needs to be plan where universities see the great importance of more believing teachers so that they can have the most influence in the educational systems.
3. Encourage Christian universities to invest in the development of doctoral programs. Dr. Cal Guy, the man who possibly trained more missionaries than any man in the last two centuries, told me that he once believed that doctoral studies were useless and that those wanting to study further should go out into the mission fields as soon as possible. He later changed his mind and began to encourage qualified students to do PhD. work because the world listens to those who have this advanced degree. In the world today, we need a plan for getting more dedicated believers to obtain the highest possible terminal degree.[56]

International Education:

In the early days of the modern missionary movement, the building of schools was very important in the spread of the faith. Both the Roman Catholics and the Protestants saw this as an important aspect of their work. Today, however, with the limited funding that most missionary sending organizations are experiencing, there is a tendency to stop building and funding institutions. Both hospitals and schools seem effected. There needs to be a revival of the placement of well thought out schools in many of the developing countries of the world. Here are a few suggestions:

1. Encourage Christian universities to place missionary professors in selected secular universities and colleges in the developing world.

---

[56] Information gained at a personal Interview with Missionary leadership in 2000.

This is a great need today, particularly in Africa. This offer can be made to national universities. Some excellent organizations are already doing some of this work, especially in China, but it is still limited in scope and effectiveness.
2. Locate both financing and leadership to build at least one top-tier, highly recognized Christian high school in each of the capital cities of developing nations with the expressed purpose of training the next generation of political leaders of the country. Some mission organizations might be challenged to see this need.
3. Encourage mission organizations not to close schools but to help them find ways to locate adequate financing in order to continue their needed service, particularly at the primary school level.
4. Create a topflight university in all the major areas of the world that can offer a quality education, including doctoral studies, to promising students who are indigenous to the area. We need to get away from the idea that the best students need to come to the West to get a quality education. This often robs the area of their best students. In many areas of the world, this can be combined with Christian schools that already exist but that need to see their potential to reach out to larger population.

Conclusion

As already stated, it is extremely important that a Mega strategy be developed in the area of education in order to give future generations a solid foundation from which to work for God, but education is not an end in itself nor does it stand alone. As Mega strategies ae developed in other cultural areas, it is important to see the need to join thinking and implementation. Some cultural areas, such as business, sports, art and theater, government, and family, need to contribute to educating our youth for future work. To accomplish this, five overarching proposals need to be made:

1. We must be aware of the need to provide Christian education for five levels of Christian workers. Dr. Donald McGavran of Fuller Theological Seminary defines the five types of leaders who need to be trained:
   - Type 1 leaders. Unpaid volunteers who mainly work in the church. These are Sunday school teachers, deacons, church treasurers, etc.
   - Type 2 leaders. Unpaid leaders who are in the local church but who work outside of the church. These are leaders such as those

who go to the local jails or work with the city's homeless population.

- Type 3 leaders. Unpaid volunteers or partially paid leaders who work from the church but are full time in a ministry supported by the church. These are those working as leaders in missions supported by the church.
- Type 4 leaders. These are generally fully paid pastors or full-time denominational leaders who are generally seminary trained.
- Type 5 leaders. These are full time international leaders who know several languages and represent the church at major global conferences.[57] (It should be added that Mega thinking leaders generally come from this group.)

In any Mega plan, care must be taken to provide a plan for an expanded system of education for all five types of leaders in the church.

2. As Mega thinkers we need to see the global situation and realize that in our plans we must take into account the differences in various cultures and must not plan only for the Western world but must consider the needs of the developing world as well. This means that any planning for a larger strategy needs to include top tier leaders from various areas of the world. Today we are privileged to have such leaders in most countries of the world. They need to be both identified and challenged.

3. Much is being done by Christians and churches on the local level, thus our main task needs to be looking at how we can influence major educational organizations such as National Education Association and the National Association of Teachers. Only a concerted effort by the larger church can adequately address this challenge.

4. We need to locate outstanding leaders from different denominations who can be challenged to be a part of the development and implementation of a Mega strategy. In my contact with many national leaders, I have found many who see the need but have not yet

---

[57] Discussion with Dr. Cal Guy, long time Professor of Missions at Southwestern Baptist Theological Seminary. In a private discussion with Dr. Donald McGavran of Fuller Seminary, Dr Guy was mentioned and Dr. McGavran stated that "this man had trained more missionaries than any man in the last 200 years."

been given the tools or the information they need to work on the Mega level to change the world.

5. We need to recognize that there are many working at both the Micro and Meta levels whose work is excellent, and they need to be brought into the conversation so that the effectiveness of what they are already doing can be elevated.

The purpose of this chapter is to help the reader see the importance of promoting more and better Christian education in the world to develop future leaders. Education is only one of the ten mountains of culture covered in this book, but it is one that is very essential if success is to be obtained. As nonevangelical and non-Christian religions, sects, and cults continue to grow and expand, it is time for us in the church to rethink our strategy, especially in a world that now employs rapidly advancing technologies that are changing the way man communications with man. Let us spend the necessary time and energy rethinking our strategy to use education as a path to make disciples of all nations for Jesus Christ.

Chapter 6: Family

David McAlvany

David McAlvany is a well-respected expert on the global economy and author of *The Intentional Legacy*, his thoughtful memoir and musings on the power of legacy and what it means to create a meaningful family culture. McAlvany graduated from Biola, served as wealth manager at Morgan Stanley, and is the second-generation CEO of the McAlvany Financial Companies. He has been a featured guest on national television programs, including CNBC, Fox News, Fox Business News, and Bloomberg as well as financial seminars around the world. After leaving Biola, David met his wife, Mary Catherine, an accomplished ballerina, sculptor, and student of philosophy. Together, they are the parents of four children with a very active family culture characterized by home schooling, community theater, daily readings, hiking, skiing, cooking, church life, and priority on togetherness.

A Basic Building Stone for the Faith

Does the Family Have a Significant Impact on Society?

Family is foundational to many of the other subjects in this book, such as education, sports, government, and business. Family is the basis of personal identity, emotional development, spiritual growth, and inter-relational dynamism. Within a healthy family, we nurture the capacities hard-coded into our design for love and connection. When families fail to live out an ethic of redemption informed by the love and mercy of God, great damage is done, not only within the family unit, but by extension to wherever broken and wounded people find themselves acting out of pain.

Broken people, debilitated to one degree or another, can miss their greater developmental potential and neglect the full impact they could have for the kingdom in other spheres simply by remaining hurt or wounded. If we multiply those wounds exponentially, our present crisis emerges. The third decade of the 21st century may be remembered as a season of unprecedented cultural desperation. Not as evident is the reality that many of the headline crises in our culture are directly traceable to unresolved issues of deteriorating family life in America and elsewhere.

We see the symptoms: the exponential rise in violence, bullying, entitlement, and abusive behavior between the genders, coinciding with the decline of civil discourse, work ethic, and the personal and public virtues long recognized as a bulwark of any free society. None of these issues emerged in a vacuum. They were nurtured by decades in which family life was redefined in terms of bad parenting choices, changing social mores, absentee fathers, high divorce rates, and the transfer of family culture to social media. The result is millions who remain deeply wounded and unclear of their own identity. That distraction often prevents a far-reaching internal transformation, critical to kingdom architecture, and the role of Christ followers guiding the ascent into the other nine mountains.

There is an open door for Christ followers to demonstrate the power of the Gospel in human relationships and display lives of wholeness, beauty, hope and restoration. Heroic individuals and families have pursued and will continue to pursue obedience to God's designs both in terms of structure and practice even as external cultural pressures increase.

In 1949, China was overtaken by a communist regime. Over the next 10 years, the Christian church was put under greater and greater pressure, until in 1966 the only remaining churches were state controlled and atheist. Social dynamics like this, on the surface, appeared bleak—even hopeless. This pressure, however, was sufficient to recreate first-century cultural dynamics: Christianity flourished as stress intensified and as the essence of Christian community was distilled. The Spirit of God moved mightily. The outcome was not bleak but brilliant, serving as a reminder of how we should engage a crisis, seeing the end from the beginning through a lens of hope and faith. In China, the estimated number of Christ-followers grew from 5 million to 50 million in just a few decades. The Gospel is more alive today in China than at any time in the last century, a fact that would have been difficult to predict one generation ago.

Any strategy for the family begins with intentionality—the commitment to be purposeful about family culture and the vision for future generations. A family Mega-strategy begins with a vision of hundreds of millions of families across the globe living out the simple truths of scripture, where love serves as a cornerstone and grace received becomes grace conveyed to all. This strategy requires us to imagine a revolution like that of the first century, where caring communities conveyed incarnational truth to a world full of pre-judgement, cynicism, and brokenness. Family is a cornerstone for society. When family life is deeply flawed, or worse, does not exist in a traditional nuclear form, the impact on society can be felt everywhere. The strength of the family unit is critical to establishing a healthy trajectory for the family and each individual in it. Families in aggregate, on a healthy trajectory, make for a profoundly different community, nation, and world. When grace pervades a life, and in turn the lives of a community of people—a family—there is a compelling testimony to the power of God, not in pretense or perfectionism, but in the basic appeal that speaks to the inner depth of every person.

Our social and spiritual paradigm is formed in our youth. If we care about the priorities of our politicians, the ethics of our business leaders, and the worldviews of our teachers (and all the other mountains), we are wise to engage with those people in their formative years, around the dinner table, long before they grow up and move out of our homes. Tomorrow's leaders are today's children, and they need to know the Gospel, experience our love and guidance, and be adequately prepared to wrestle with the big questions of the day.

Developing depth takes time. Maturity is not an accident of circumstance but directly corelates to time and particular choices. So what are the circumstances, prayerfully curated, that bring us into a depth of maturity and enable us to grow and flourish? M. Scott Peck, in his book *The Road Less Traveled*, notes, "Some even believe that by imitation they have really become saints and prophets, and are unable to acknowledge that they are still children and face the painful fact that they must start at the beginning and go through the middle."[58]

We journey with our family, with our children, from the beginning through the middle. There is no shortcut to maturity. There is, however, the possibility of an abiding presence and a guiding hand from parent to child, and within an extended family of grandparents and aunts and uncles to children as well.

We demonstrate in real time, as we learn ourselves, about the redemption that takes place after we are saved. This redemptive process is critical to keep on display as a foundation stone for world evangelism and for *evangelism in our homes*. Propositional truths can be parroted and maintained largely as a religious or idealistic façade. Our children, however, can judge best if those truths are penetrating to the core, and transforming us, and informing our functional life choices. Authenticity is something even a young child can discern.

World evangelism in the first century grew out of personal transformation, growth, and relational connection. As Michael Green describes in his book *Evangelism in the Early Church*, the spiritual upheaval of the first century "was in reality accomplished by means of informal missionaries ... not through formal preaching, but informal ... in homes and wine shops, on walks, and around market stalls.... They did it naturally, enthusiastically ... Having found treasure, they meant to share it with others, to the limit of their ability."[59]

What Is Being Done for the Family Today?

Many organizations have been created to support family life and practice. The Family Research Council, Focus on the Family, and the American Family Association all support a biblical approach to marriage and family. These groups focus primarily on US domestic policies and are by and large partisan in their efforts. The International Organization for the Family, or IOF, and the World Congress of Families have both focused efforts on defining a traditional family structure within the context of the UN's Universal Declaration of Human Rights, article 16.

---

[58] M. Scott Peck, The Road Less Traveled (New York: Simon and Schuster, 1978), 77.

[59] Michael Green, *Evangelism in the Early Church*, 2nd ed. (Grand Rapids: Eerdmans, 2003), 243-244.

In both cases, these organizations are fighting for family structure and political representation. There are other valuable efforts as well. The practical and yet profound influence of sound household financial management is championed globally by Crown Financial Ministries. Joyce and Cliff Penner have traveled the globe, bringing insight and nuance to healthy sexual relations in marriage. Dozens of authors, including Gary Chapman, Gary Smalley, John Trent, Henry Cloud, John Townsend, and others, have written books on communication and relationship dynamics; they are designed to help the reader understand how to more skillfully engage a spouse or family member.

Other religious groups, such as Muslims and Mormons, also place a critical emphasis on family, with more energy focused on defending traditional roles and encouraging scale. The Mormon community has proactively engaged culture through television and film and continues to make a broad appeal through stories that showcase the importance of family and faith. A non-religious group that has taken the lead and successfully redefined family in the 21st century is the LGBTQ community, which has targeted educators and media in an effort to normalize same sex relationships and move past the traditional definition of marriage as between one woman and one man. Normalization has been the key tactic. To depict characters as funny, likable, and relatable and to have the narratives seem as normal has moved the general public's view on family structure very far away from its traditional moorings in a very short period of time. Attempts to capture the high ground of science to buttress the social mood of support have also been a key strategy. In the process the lines between genetic determinism and psych biographical preference have been blurred.

A Mega Focus

Our Mega-strategy needs to distill the essence of transformation and growth within a stable environment, with less emphasis on structure and size (we can still assume the importance of these things) and more emphasis on the qualitative aspects that a spirit-filled family can manifest and bear witness to.

The revolutionary aspects of family life, such as forgiveness and loyalty, are qualitative in nature. They assume the stability that comes from having a father and mother (traditional structure) present in the home. Building on that biblical team dynamic to create an environment for development, flourishing, and sanctification is the critical distinctive between the Christ-centered approach to a family Mega-strategy and any other approach. For the world to encounter Christians who are alive in

Christ and being transformed through daily encounters of love, grace, and guidance within the home opens the possibility of *evidential evangelism*, where the beauty of a changed and maturing life compliments propositional truths. There is no greater apologetic than functional and mature believers overflowing with the Holy Spirit and living out the effects of being incubated in an environment of love and redemption.

The world is not lacking in the quantity of people who claim to follow Christ; rather the world is lacking in the quality or maturity of those people. Maturity in Christian communities is often thought of as spiritual maturity only, driven off of a reading and structured study of God's word. This Enlightenment influence (leaving out other equally important contributing factors) emphasizes study and reflection and assumes objectivity and accessibility. It is an incomplete process that leads to a shallow and merely stylistic expression of spiritual maturity.

If the psychological aspects of maturity are neglected, neurosis can run in a parallel track with spiritual growth, ultimately acting to sabotage relationships and preventing true and comprehensive maturity of spirit. The importance of family relationships and healthy family dynamics to the emotional aspects of the human growth and development is immense. Relationships with father and mother, in particular, inform our most basic understanding of the heart of God. We directly encounter love or a lack of love or a brand of love, and that imprint dwells in our noetic structures as we grow in faith. Thus, the experience we have of Christ is overshadowed by the childhood formational encounters within the home.

My parents work at an orphanage in the Philippines. The universal question from the abandoned children they work with is "Why?" "Why is my father gone?" "Why does he not care?" "Why did he leave?" Clearly, a mother's role is critical; however, it is fascinating to listen to the deepest cry of the heart as these children struggle for an identity and seek to understand "why" their father is not present.

This is not the first time the family has come under attack. In fact, there has been a battle for the family since Satan declared war on it in Genesis. We can expect a struggle for control in any arena where power and influence guide and inform cultural norms. Each of the cultural mountains of influence discussed throughout this book holds the possibility of good and of evil. A spiritual battle rages for dominance in each of these spheres. Family is no exception. From the first idea of spiritual rebellion, a supernatural struggle has existed for control of a central cosmic narrative. The echo of "hath God said?" whispered to Eve in the Garden can be heard down through the ages, with a nuanced iteration in each of the 10 mountains expressing doubts about the veracity and goodness of our Creator's intentions. It is not enough to affirm the propositional truths of God's goodness; we are partnered with those truths through praxis (action). Therefore, the family must be a living expression of God's design both in its structure and in the redemptive activities we map out and engage in.

What Are the Weaknesses in the Family?

Family is a critical cultural mountain. Imbedded in the experience of family life is the potential weakness of this particular mountain. To look at the weaknesses, let's explore the mountain analogy further. **Are you fit for the ascent?** To reference a mountain—any one of the ten here in discussion—suggests that we are fit to ascend and claim that ground. What makes the peaks so accessible? Nothing. Mountains are not friendly places, and the effort required to climb them presumes preparation and a certain kind of "fitness." Most people engage mountains via a postcard or coffee table book, and while they remain inspired by beauty and grandeur, they never directly encounter the thrills, challenges, and even terror that are a part of the landscape. On a good day there is delight. On a bad day there is dread and desperation. As long as the sun shines, we ascend without complication. But who are we and how do we handle treacherous terrain when weather develops, and storms roll in?

There are qualitative requirements to be a good alpinist. Training and experience start somewhere. Similarly, family is the intended starting point for all mentorship and life preparation, regardless of the mountains its members will climb—hence the priority of family as a launching point for many of the other mountains. Rarely is anyone fully prepared for the challenges to be faced in life, but the context of family life serves as a training ground.

Each mountain in this book requires engagement from a thoughtful and skilled practitioner—a person who is not afraid of hard labor or remote places—and an awareness that a misstep is quite consequential. The kind of person someone is as he or she ascends the mountain of government, business, or the arts is critical to the journey, so I argue that family is a starting point for all other ascents. It ties directly to our being and becoming. What we bring to bear on the other nine mountains begins with *who we are*.

Who we are is in large part an origin's story? Out of a family we emerge with more or less developed minds, hearts, and purpose. We discover early on what our unique bent is and where our lives can be effectively focused, combining practical observation and prayerful consideration of calling and divine purpose.

Family is the place where we discover who we are for the first time. It is the place where we forge our ideals and where character building starts. Family is the first place we encounter relationship and trust. We begin to learn listening and communication skills. We learn conflict resolution and a host of other skills that set the stage for fellowship and the interpersonal growth we will experience during the rest of our lives. Without a healthy family life, we are like the mountaineer headed out with a twisted limb or chronic pain, a detriment to ourselves and others, most noticeably when the grade is steep, the journey arduous, or the conditions unfriendly. In addition to preexisting conditions we may bring on our journey, as we noted earlier, a misstep in the high country is highly consequential. Our mistakes (sins) impact all those around us.

Human relationship is fragile because we are dealing with incomplete contributions. For our understanding, relationship is the stuff between two people, and it has its own personality dynamics, and energy. A relationship can be fed or starved by either of the two external contributors. As imperfect people, prone to selfishness and easily given to offense, we often perpetuate an imperfect world by introducing our flaws into the *in between. The love that exists between two people can grow and strengthen or diminish and disappear, resulting in either resilient and robust relationships or broken hearts and broken relationships.*

Relationships have a unique existence separate from who we are and yet dependent on what we contribute to them. Augustine describes the relationship within the Trinity by analogy to the lover, the beloved, and the love that exists between them. The Holy Spirit being situated between Father and Son, according to Augustine's *De Trinitate*, captures the existence of a unique third person *in between*. If we are honest, the factors that create weakness in the family are often what we bring into relationships.

If you have ever clung to the side of a mountain with someone (literally or figuratively), you clearly see the qualitative aspects of their development, and often times you can also see where development was arrested and weakness or wounding remains. Many dangers exist on a mountain ascent, even more so when the people you depend on are nursing unhealed wounds or are not adequately trained for the task. Would you choose to venture out on a great trek or expedition knowing that your companions were walking on splinted legs or unable to carry their own pack? What if the walking wounded is you? Are you fit for the ascent?

Think again of the people who occupy the ten mountains. *Who are they and how did they grow and develop?* We either grow into the fullness of God's design or we do not. Imbedded in the experience of family life is the potential weakness of this particular mountain. Not all experience is created equal. Not all love is given freely. Not all family culture is free from the toxicity of control and conditional love. Certainly, that process of growing into the fullness of God's design extends beyond the short years we have at home, yet those short years can cast a long shadow into the rest of our lives, for better or worse. The health of our relationships or the burdens we bear from those relationships with fathers, mothers, sisters, and brothers are woven into our personal narratives and have a lingering impact on all we do and who we become.

What Are the Inroads for Christians To Impact This Mountain?

This is our mountain if we can do it well.

Our first inroad is to display the fruit of God working in our lives. How powerful is a life well lived? Tying together the richness of a well-lived family life and the impact it can have on others, be they neighbors, colleagues, friends or children, is the phrase "if you live it, they will love it." When we live out a story of redemption and love as testimony to what God has woven into our being, the family becomes something that shines like a beacon on a hill.

When we formulate a strategy for healthy family dynamics, it has to be with an appreciation for livability, or, as 1 Corinthians 14:1 describes it, "the way of love."

The spirit of a family is reflected in how family life is arranged. You could say that lifestyle informs the identity (shared identity) of the family. Our shared experiences define the memories and future reflection on the value of life together. This can be an accidental outcome or an intentional process. Pew Research found, in a 27-country study, that six in ten people believe family ties have grown weaker over the last 20 years.[60] Many of the social troubles of our day relate to this familial disconnect and unraveling of family ties. Reversal of that trend will require a thoughtful appraisal of how we spend time together and how valuable those experiences are perceived to be by each member of the family.

The incubator for transformation, growth, and identity formation is the family. The process of transformation and maturity within the family is driven by practical choices, arranged into the fabric our daily lives. The

---

[60] Pew Research Center, https://www.pewresearch.org/global/2019/04/22/how-people-around-the-world-view-family-ties-in-their-countries/.

order and structure of our lives speak to our priorities and the treasure we seek, the values we elevate. As we grow up and grow into our unique identity, these values and choices propel us towards Christ's particular calling for each of us. Through that distinctive calling, we extend his healing and redemption into the world. The impact of family life on the rest of the world builds from the foundational development of identity and the core role that close relationships play in the transformation of the individual through love, friendship, and mentoring.

The second inroad for influencing family combines vision and planning. The co-creative process is one of grace-laden curatorial effort. Matching up ends (the visional aspect) and means, we prepare our children—body, mind, and spirit—for an encounter with the world, equipping them to be salt and light. Think of the team that shows up on the field to demonstrate months of discipline and hard work, ready for game day. There is a regimen, a lifestyle, that serves as preparation. How can we expect our children to flourish without proper coaching, guidance, and discipline? *What begins with intentionality leans heavily on our choices and the interplay of those choices with God's grace.* John 8:12 reminds us, "Whoever follows me will never walk in darkness but will have the light of life." The disciples followed Christ in a way of life. They lived the life He lived, they watched Him, they imitated Him, and He demonstrated what a life of service looks like. We must do the same, demonstrating to our children what life in Christ looks like.

What Are Some Well-Defined Activities That Can Be Accomplished Now to Help Us in the Development of a Mega-Strategy?

What Families Can Do

The trickiest part of this chapter is separating the Macro or Mega strategy from the Micro initiatives that are paramount for progress. The inroads can be organized from a top down perspective, encouraged by Church initiatives (seminars and sermons), college curriculums (classes that open and deepen the heart and mind), men's groups (that remind us how to better define success), home groups (where we live out truths and encourage one another with other families), and educational resources (books, courses, mentorship), which together better enable families to grasp the scope and importance of life together as a living expression of the Gospel. But the most important aspect of this Mega-strategy is getting the little things right. The inroads need to start from the grass roots or from the bottom up. You could describe this as a family liturgy, the organization of service. You could also explain it as a journey or a trek.

Family Culture Map

A road trip these days does not require much planning. You pack and you leave. The journey is defined by your onboard mapping system or an app on your phone that tells you when you will arrive and where you can fill up with gas along the way. Preparation is minimal. Forethought is hardly necessary. Not that many years ago, an actual map was a part of the process of planning. Imagine a long family trip, but rather than one that passes through towns and geographical places, imagine instead a journey of the heart, mind, and spirit: a family culture map would be invaluable. Where are you going? What resources do you need to get there?

Curating life together through a series of intentionally chosen experiences requires a refinement of what is most important to us. There are things to which you say yes and things to which you say no. To say yes to generosity and philanthropy may translate into a regular commitment to serve together as a family at a local soup kitchen. To develop better listening skills may be to set guidelines for how the flow of conversation goes at the dinner table. To encourage an ethos of comradery and joy may include a weekly game night. Your family culture map aids in lining out all the possibilities of activities and conversations, books and poetry, events and trips that promote maturity, generosity, and others-centeredness.

Are families assuming that an app or onboard mapping system will get them where they want to go throughout their lives together? Has legacy planning changed from an intentional effort to something determined by an algorithm? These days it is easy to arrive at a destination without much intentional planning. Are families getting to where they could be with a little more intentional thought and prayer? Auto pilot is not an answer. This is a bottom-up approach for each family to engage in.

There is a prequel to the family story we create. This is where a significant Mega-strategy effort can be forged from a top down perspective. Who we are prior to marriage leads into who we are in the midst of marriage? There is an instructive role for the Church, the Christian college or university, and for media and technology to play in getting families on an improved trajectory.

What Churches Can Do

There is a great need for resources and training of young adults prior to marriage. While there is no lack of resources for making a marriage better, wouldn't all marriages be better if they were between people of improved compatibility, possessing the abilities needed to engage in a relationship with excellent communication and conflict resolution skills and a shared vision of a legacy journey prior to embarking on it?

On a trip to Hawaii, the Caribbean, or some other seaside destination, tourists can indulge in scuba diving though they have no previous training or exposure. The "resort course" gives you the basics in a matter of hours so that, at a depth of 20-40 feet, you are less likely to die. Of course, trained divers who have spent weeks in class and years improving their skills are in a much better position to deal with crisis when submerged at any depth. Marriage and pre-marital counseling are a little like the resort course; very little preparation and training are involved prior to jumping into one of life's most important decisions. Vows *may be* adequate to keep a marriage together, but rarely are they sufficient for a flourishing relationship. When we count the value of the family, we must consider the steps necessary to get it off to a great start.

In the 12th century, monks tried to figure out how to improve life together, given their differences in personalities. The Enneagram[61] is one of many personality studies that exists (like the Myers Briggs). From the 12th century forward, it has been refined to show not only a biblically informed path towards personal transformation and spiritual growth, but also a path towards deeper relational integration.

Can we improve the quantity of successful marriages as well as the quality of those families by a deeper level of training and preparation prior to the tying of the knot? I believe so. Accepting our differences can be a means to extending grace and supporting the collective family efforts towards peace, cohesion, and a vibrant life together. You don't get this in a "resort course." Many of the failures in marriage occur when people who should not have married in the first place (lacking sufficient compatibility) are stuck between the realities of a challenging personality mix (never fully appreciating their hardcoded differences in temperament) and the vows they have taken to stay together. Were they *compatible* from the start or primarily *combustible*?

---

[61] Richard Rohr, *The Enneagram: A Christian Perspective* (Spring Valley: Crossroads, 2001).

The church has an existing organizational structure that allows it to facilitate studies, retreats, and dialog on the key areas of personal growth and formation that makes for an improved "sum of the parts" contribution in the family. Materials can be created for Bible study and discussion of family culture, the role of father and mother, and in particular an in-depth look, for singles at what is required for a healthy marriage. Additional course work and discussion on financial stewardship is also critical, as conflict over finances remains a key contributor to divorce. Creating a universal framework for marriage preparation is critical for the church's contribution to this Mega-strategy.

What about the church leadership itself? They should start at home, literally, and extend out from there. Leaders in the church can start by maintaining a focus on family as a first expression of ministry. It is not enough to create a myopic world of serving the needs of others, only to overlook the needs of those closest to you.

Having graduated from a Christian university, anecdotally I can say that the students who consistently struggled with their faith were missionary kids and pastors' kids. There may be a variety of reasons for this, but "the ministry first" as a focus often left kids feeling passed over.

While the Church's role is key, there are limitations to the depth and specificity of conversation that can occur in a big group. There are very neglected conversations on sex, finances, personality conflict resolution, and a host of other topics that require a different environment for exploration, candor, and accountability.

What Colleges Can Do

The Christian college or university is in an excellent position to teach and even require an in-depth study on relationships and personal soul formation. What are the tools that someone needs to engage with fatherhood, motherhood, and marriage? What are the ways we can appreciate personality differences and, through an improved understanding, extend more grace? In the absence of adequate mentorship, how does someone become ready to be a servant leader to his or her family? The Christian college can engage soul growth from a biblically based, psychologically sound, and practically implementable standpoint. What if every graduate from a Christian college understood his or her own strengths and weaknesses and was prepared with communication and life skills that enabled deeper relational engagement and facilitated intergenerational maturity?

Trustees and university leaders can begin by discussing the balance between academic excellence and wholistic development of mature individuals. Where in the college life or curriculum is there a priority placed on the character of the person being educated? Is there a dimension of this that fits as an integration of personal maturity within each field of study? Is there a specific regimen or course to augment every major? This is more than, for example, an ethics class for a business major. Rather this is the integration of personal maturity with one's field of study. This might be accomplished through a senior thesis or other customized project directed and guided by a thesis director. There is a dual integration, first of faith into one's field of study and second the purposeful development of the interior life of the student.

Most colleges have an incoming orientation that lays out college life and reveals the landscape of engagements an incoming freshman might consider. I would also suggest an exit orientation where the landscape of life after college is mapped out and legacy objectives are discussed that reinforce the meaning and kingdom contribution of what has been learned. In that context, an introduction to family life and a framework for thinking about the visional aspects of family leadership and ministry can be explored.

What Can Men's Groups Do?

YPO (Young Presidents Organization) is a group of executives who gather routinely to share experiences in business and learn from each other. With 29,000 members and 430 chapters in 130 countries, representing nine trillion dollars in annual revenue, this is an amazing network of leaders, isolated at the top of industry and in need of fellowship. YPO members join to "become better leaders and better people through peer learning and exceptional experiences in an inclusive community of open sharing and trust." For many young executives, there is no routine outlet for feedback and executive guidance, so this trusted group of peers is invaluable. There is a sense of not being alone in one's struggles, and a comfort that others are there to help when it is needed. We must facilitate this same openness and resource-rich environment for men, both in full time ministry and laity. When I wrote the book *The Intentional Legacy*, the overwhelming and consistent request for practical materials for further group discussion and study was from men's groups.

Promise Keepers is a movement that reminds men of the role they play as agents of change within their families if they will commit to living with integrity. The church is the sum of its parts, and a critical part is the role men play in contributing both to the family and to the larger church body. A Mega-strategy for family must fully engage the needs of men for peer-to-peer learning and development.

What stands out in the quote about YPO? "Better leaders," "better people," "peer learning," "exceptional experiences," "community of open sharing and trust." Men's groups may promote a variety of things, but these aspects of relationship and growth are vital to thriving masculinity, emboldening maturity and Christ-inspired leadership. John Donne reminds us, "No man is an island, Entire of itself, Every man is a piece of the continent, A part of the main."

Men are generally very focused. Providing specific questions for men to consider that jumpstart their conversations and point them towards candid and constructive dialogs with their trusted peers would be revolutionary. There has to be a theoretical and theological basis for these practical questions; it could be a series of books on the masculine journey: "Everyman's guide to ... true wealth ... deep friendship ... great sex ... being a better dad." Taking those books as a starting point and then building out study guides and journals to compliment the more theoretical resource, you end with the questions that are less formal and geared for two to five people to banter about.

As noted earlier, the cry of the orphan heart is for a father's presence, love, and affirmation. The enemy understands the importance of the father's role in a family and has stopped at nothing to upset God's design. A family Mega-strategy requires a winsome approach to the development of the masculine servant leader, a leader who is well supported by a community of men walking a similar path.

What Can Business and Military Leadership Do?

There are generational differences in how a work-life balance is struck. Business and military leaders can set the stage for family, maintaining its priority by the cultural tone they set as their subordinates organize their personal lives. The expectations of leadership are a key variable in the equation of work-life balance.

The workforce continues to evolve in the ways an employee is compensated and the types of benefits available. This can be an avenue that conveys support to families and reinforces a value system that prioritizes a work-life balance within the military or business communities. If benefits are not codified, then economic and cultural barriers to more family time remain firmly in place. The default mode will tend to be deprioritizing family time even when it is most needed with the risk of being passed over for a promotion or raise.

Is it possible to influence the ethos of the businesses and military to elevate the family unit? It is far more likely if the costs associated with being family-friendly are mitigated. There are public policy options for consideration here, as well as private market solutions. Perhaps the workplace has experienced a beneficial form of catastrophism with Covid-19. Work from a remote location, whether home or elsewhere, is more feasible than ever before.

HR departments seeking a holistic offering of benefits would be wise to care for the persons in their employ, as well as their families. A 2014 Department of Labor study looking at highly educated professional fathers in the U.S. found that "nine of out ten reported that it would be important when looking for a new job that the employer offered paid parental leave, and six out of ten considered it very or extremely important."[62] The primary question for leaders in these spheres of influence is a cultural one: How do our policies and procedures reflect the priority of family life and health?

The Role of Media and Technology

Sometimes we just need to see something (or hear it said a different way) for it to make perfect sense to us. Story telling has always been a powerful teaching tool. Now, as technology changes the distribution channels for all things, including radio, television, and film, there is an opportunity for showing and demonstrating the "how" of family culture and ethos through multiple outlets. As I discussed earlier, the Mormon Church has successfully engaged in television and film productions that depict the role of family as something dignified and worthwhile. The Mormon example is useful. These mediums convey values implicitly and could be used equally well to display in narrative form the ideas and beauty of the Gospel message.

Movies like *Same Kind of Different as Me* and *To End all Wars* recount how real people have made vital choices and impacted the lives of others. True stories and narratives are just one example of what film can explore. Fiction is equally powerful. Other media is available to make messaging more cost effective than ever before.

We live in an age of You Tube "do it yourself" learning, where any question you might ask has an answer (not always the best!) and a video that

---

[62] www.dol.gov/sites/dolgov/files/OASP/legacy/files/PaternityBrief.pdf.

provides specific instructions. We are not always asking questions and seeking answers, but when we need an answer, the binge search and engagement begins. Such is the age in which we live, of search engines and direct access to helpful information.

Technology provides us with both the means of production as well as the means of distribution for content that can serve as a "how to" for so many aspects of family life. The fact that production costs are as low as they are means that any college, church, or parachurch organization can create meaningful curated content and distribute it at virtually no cost.

Media and technology are powerful tools for a family mega-strategy. The continuum of opportunities ranges from high-budget blockbuster movie production to virtually free low-fidelity podcasts and YouTube channels. The audience for content created and distributed via the internet is global. The opportunity to routinely engage an audience and provide interaction through the digital landscape is profound. A study of social media best practices, digital audience engagement, and a strategic plan for artistic and thoughtful content creation are a starting point.

Family Can Be a Vital Contributor to World Evangelization

Family evangelism starts at the table. We share life together around the table. As we talk and listen and explore both the exterior world of current events and the interior world of thoughts and feelings, people are appreciated and dignified. We learn from each other. We connect. We are valued and treasured. We become known. Doing this well as a family is a stepping-stone to hospitality where others are included in the rhythms of our daily and weekly lives and are equally valued, loved, and celebrated.

Tim Keller describes it this way:

> It is informal but sustained relationships and conversation that will become more important in our increasingly secular world, as many Christian beliefs are highly offensive to people, as was the case in the first century. Now, as then, most people won't show up to hear Christian public speakers. Movement toward Christian belief will have to be personal, organic, and incremental.[63]

Hospitality allows others outside the family to share the internal family dynamic of time spent and relational connection. Evangelism starts at the

---

[63] https://www.redeemer.com/redeemer-report/article/evangelism_in_the_early_church

table when we allow the stranger into our homes and lives. A Gospel invitation is an invitation to life. Yes, eternal life, but also abundant life where our souls and our bodies are fed. Our neighbor or the stranger is welcomed into that experience. Relationship is the defining factor for family as well as the defining factor in world evangelization. Bob Goff reminds us, "No one leads people to Jesus. He leads people to Himself. All the pressure's off. All we have to do is give away all the love He's poured into us. Give of yourself without an agenda, and His love will speak for itself."[64]

To bring someone into your home requires transparency. There are no perfect families just as there are no perfect people, so when someone sits with you, observes and listens, and takes note of the undercurrents in a home, it is revealing. Are we ready for what is revealed?

Hospitality is humbling, but people seeing us as we truly are, with our imperfections, is important because perfection is not a prerequisite for God's love, nor should it be for ours. We need not be perfect prior to the practice of hospitality; all we need is Christ's love flowing through us. When we open our hearts and we invite others to spend time with us, there is an opportunity to know someone and to serve and honor them, beginning the process of friendship.

The practice of hospitality highlights an application of being salt and light. There are thoughtful treatments of this idea that reinforce the key notion that family and a shared table can be the centerpiece for a particular kind of evangelism.[65] Who is your neighbor? Everyone. It has been said that the most powerful word in any language is a person's name. Do you know your neighbor's name (who they are and what makes them tick)? This is not just the person living adjacent to you. It is your coworker. It is the panhandler on the street corner. It is your brother and sister.

Conclusion

Family is essential to a healthy functioning society. Family is the cornerstone of social construction and is the life force of a community. Broken families draw down the collective potential of a people group, which is why the family has been and will always be under spiritual attack. Destroy

---

[64] Bob Goff, *Live in Grace, Walk in Love: a 365-day Journey* (Nashville: Thomas Nelson, 2019), 414.

[65] Rosaria Butterfield, The *Gospel Comes with a House Key* (Wheaton: Crossway, 2018); Lonni Collins Pratt and Father Daniel Homan, *Radical Hospitality: Benedict's Way of Love*, 3rd ed. (Paraclete Press, 2011).

the structure that is responsible for our initial growth and adaptation and you will have sapped the strength of a nation and altered its trajectory. Alternatively, if you elevate and by God's grace perfect the form and function of the family unit, you will find a spiritual force and social structure of immeasurable potency. The proper strategy is not defensive but one of substantive counterattack. Positive actions are the defining elements of family life, bringing health to the family unit and the larger community. This chapter has explored the spheres where positive action can be encouraged and facilitated with the intention of tying together who we are as created by God and how we live into our full potential.

We can see God's kingdom work established through family formation and the transformative relationships that emerge from it. How different does the world look when individuals seek healing and transformation, and through the elements of grace, love, and forgiveness learn to model on the Micro scale of family life, what the world so desperately needs at the Macro level? As Francis De Sales reminds us in his *Introduction to the Devout Life*, "The soul that rises from sin to devotion may be compared to the dawning of the day, which at its approach does not expel the darkness instantaneously but only little by little."[66] Such is the Mega-strategy for family, which requires attention to the little details to unleash the fullness and beauty of God's design.

---

[66] Francis de Sales, *Introduction to the Devout Life* (Garden City: Doubleday, 1957), 43-44.

CHAPTER 7: GOVERNMENT

John Langlois

John Langlois, lives in Guernsey, Channel Islands, with his wife, Patricia. He was called as an Advocate to the Guernsey Bar in 1971 and has now retired from the professions. As well as graduating in Law in 1969, he graduated in theology at the London Bible College, England. Since his graduation from LBC, he has worked with the World Evangelical Alliance and has served on its International Council since 1980 and still serves on the Council as Member Emeritus. In 1969 he met Dr. Ralph Winter who encouraged him to promote Theological Education by Extension around the world. Shortly afterwards he went to India and Singapore where he helped establish TEE in Asia and then in Africa. For his international work, Olivet University awarded him an honorary Doctorate of Christian Ministry degree.

In 1980 John was elected to the legislature of the island of Guernsey on which he served for 24 years until 2001. During his 22 years of service in that position, he held multiple ministerial portfolios including that of deputy chief minister for six year. Upon retirement from politics he was granted the rare honor of being appointed Officer of the Order of the British Empire" (COBE) by Her Majesty Queen Elizabeth II for his services to the community as well as for his worldwide work. The Channel Islands are internally self-governing democracies which have never been part of the United Kingdom or European Union. Their external relations are handled by the Crown through Her Majesty's government at Westminster.

Transforming Government

Introduction

Some years ago, I visited the Colosseum in Rome. Most people walked around it in silence. The whole edifice was a gruesome reminder of what happened there on the Roman equivalent of a Saturday afternoon football game, when the stands were packed with cheering and jeering spectators watching gladiators as they sliced into each other until death or defeat. If the loser was spared death by the victor, he would look up to the emperor for his decision: thumb up, let him live; thumb down, finish him off. The emperor did not usually make the decision unguided. He normally turned to the crowd for their verdict, a vote by acclamation indicating live or die, a gruesome way of ending a Saturday afternoon sports match.

More gruesome yet was the spectacle of defenseless families of Christian men, women, and children dragged into the arena to be eaten by ravenously hungry lions. Such was the weekend enjoyment of the crowds. How could it happen that the populace was so desensitized to such savagery?

Even worse atrocities were perpetrated in the twentieth century when millions of Jews, gypsies, homosexuals, and others were disposed of in gas chambers in a brutally efficient industrial-scale machinery of death. How was it that so-called civilized peoples were so desensitized to a culture of torment that they allowed their leaders to carry out their evil schemes? The evidence shows that in most cases, leaders cannot do so without the explicit or implicit support of the people.

Adolf Hitler argues in Mein Kampf (1924), "If propaganda has imbued a whole people with an idea, the organization can draw the consequences with a handful of men. Propaganda and organization—in other words, supporters, and members—thus stand in a certain mutual relation. The better the propaganda has worked, the smaller the organization can be."[67]

In the Roman period, Christians were thrown to the lions with the enthusiastic consent of the people because in their eyes the Christians were denigrating and denying their pagan gods—a religious justification worthy of death. In the twentieth century, science, or more properly pseudo-science, provided that basis. Charles Darwin claimed that he had proved that human beings were descended from lower links in the evolutionary chain,

---

[67] https://fcit.usf.edu/holocaust/resource/document/DocPropa.htm.

latterly apes, so human beings were just more evolved creatures in the animal chain. He discarded the divine source of human and animal life. His teachings led to Social Darwinism, which took root with the eugenics movement in the United States, advocating forced sterilization and selective human breeding that later led to organized genocide in Nazi Germany. In the twenty-first century, advocates of so-called "reproductive health" are now pushing their culture of death through the United Nations, demanding that all countries submit to uncontrolled abortion on demand, the killing of babies even at full-term, through persistent propaganda and organization, as described by Adolf Hitler.

The Italian Marxist political scientist Antonio Gramsci (1891-1937), a contemporary of Hitler, argued that the Left did not have to win election after election. Instead it only needed to take over all the key institutions of the state and then indoctrinate the people, which is what the LGBT groups have done in relation to sexual ethics.

How Can This Be Changed?

As I approached the exit at the end of my visit to the Colosseum, my eye was drawn to a small plaque on the wall; it read "The Games ended in AD 423, the citizens of Rome having become Christians." That is how it happened. The key institutions of state changed when the people embraced Judeo-Christian values.

Changing values is our essential task today. Christians need to live out the biblical values they profess. When I visited Iran some years ago, I asked why Armenians were not hated and persecuted by Muslims. I was told by Muslims that it was because Armenians were good people. They went about doing good things, both to their fellow Christians and to Muslims.

In rebuilding our foundations for civilized values, which in turn will result in our governments advocating civilized values, we are aided by the fact that these values are not narrow Judeo-Christian values. These are values that God instilled into the heart of humankind by Creation. For example, the Ten Commandments are primarily values for the good of all mankind, not just for Jews and Christians. The Ten Commandments go even further than that; they are also good for the animal world and the environment. As a result of the innate values imbued in them by their Creator, people know what is right, even if they do otherwise.

Knowing what is right should make it easy for us to advocate values that are good for society and for the environment; they are instinctive. But that is not the case. We run into opposition. As Antonio Gramsci would have put it, we have seen how illiberal progressives (who are far from "liberal") have achieved cultural hegemony by taking over all the key institutions of the state and then indoctrinated the people through their claim of victimization, leading to discrimination of others.[68] They do not respect diversity. We are faced by an illiberal demand to "endorse, accept and acclaim" all illiberal progressive values as superior to the traditional morals of human communities, which have been the bedrock of society through millennia. It is an attempt to turn the world order upside down. The early Christians were accused of turning the world upside down (Acts 17:6), but what they were doing was in fact seeking to restore the true world order, setting it the right way up, which is what needs to be done in the twenty-first century.

That task is not as formidable as it may at first appear. You can fool some of the people some of the time but not all the people all the time. That is what we have seen in the first two decades of the twenty-first century. There is an increasing backlash against illiberal progressivism through the ballot box, where ordinary people are now seeing through the extraordinary illiberal reconstruction of societal values that are contrary to science, reason, and experience. For example, the people are told that gender is not static, and that one can choose one's own gender without any reference to irrefutable scientific facts. The people are revolting against this nonsensical pseudoscience.

Our first step in making the needed changes is to reaffirm the accumulated wisdom, the body of fundamental values, that human communities have developed and lived by through six thousand years of recorded human history. It is the bedrock of societal well-being that enriches families, communities, and nations. This bedrock is grounded in the belief that the basic building block of society is the nuclear family, a nucleus of spouses, father, mother, children, and grandchildren. The family is bound by ties of blood and marriage and by family community values that promote human flourishing, including security from physical violence, financial security, protection from mental stress, health, education, and overall wellbeing.

Our task is to bring the need for a change of values to center-stage in politics and government. We shall have to point out the countless occasions when the illiberal, radical, progressive, pontificating "emperors" have no clothes and when what they are trying to have us believe is nonsense. Take, for example, transgenderism, a new concept that has been

---

[68] https://en.wikipedia.org/wiki/Cultural_hegemony.

around for less than ten years; remarkably, human society did not recognize it for the previous six millennia! Transgenderism is a mental construct, an illusion. There is no scientific evidence for the concept. That house of cards will collapse when enough psychologists, psychiatrists, physicians, and other scientists are brave enough to tell the scientific truth. A historical example is Germany in the 1930s and 1940s, when all the professors in university science faculties asserted the allegedly scientific fact of the pre-eminence of the Aryan race. Then suddenly, on May 9, 1945, they all admitted that it was scientific nonsense. They had to admit that the emperor had no clothes.

Christians must clearly and fearlessly endorse the truth of the distilled wisdom of past generations until falsehood is exposed, the false indoctrination of the people is reversed, and government reflects the communal values of the people.

Getting from A to B, Preparing the Ground

For more than a century, indeed probably since 1870, Christians with biblical values have vacated the public square, leaving "progressives" to trample down the values that had guided societies, both Christian and otherwise, through the centuries. The two last decades of the nineteenth century saw the rise in 'progressive' human breeding, resulting in euthanasia, abortion, and sterilization, leading to the attempted extermination of gypsies, Jews, and other peoples unwanted by the elite as well as discrimination against homosexual people. The 1980s saw a reaction by homosexuals, who started new movements to gain acceptance into society, which has led to increasing diversions into bisexual, transsexual, and transgender claims. Currently there are claimed to be seventy-two genders, and that number is increasing, quite contrary to the evidence of science.

Not only do we need to find a road through the swamp of unscientific irrationality; we also have to re-construct the foundations on which a road can be securely laid to carry society to the enlightened values that are necessary for human communities to flourish. These values are democracy, individual liberty, the rule of law, and mutual respect and tolerance of those with different views. These are the gold standard of human societal values, yet in practice they are neutered by those who preach diversity but lack respect and tolerance for others and really want uniformity.

Laying the Foundations of Flourishing Human Society

The past fifty years have been dominated by 'progressive,' originally 'liberal' but now illiberal, ideas whereby the metropolitan elite have trampled on the people's rights as human beings. Those rights are endowed by their Creator, not by the International Declaration of Human Rights, the European Convention on Human Rights, the Constitution of the United States, or any other constitution. Those rights are innate and inalienable. They simply need to be reasserted.

Democracy is the mechanism through which the will of the people should be exercised. That will should be ascertained at regular elections by the demos. The liberal metropolitan elite, who often despise the communal views of the ordinary people, will do all they can to ensure the people "vote the right way." This is the modus operandi that the unelected governing classes of the European Union in Brussels followed when the people voted "the wrong way" in a referendum in Ireland in 2008. Since the Irish people had voted the "wrong way," they were asked to vote again; in the eyes of the EU Commission, they got it right that time, so a third vote was not required. The elite said the wrong vote in the first referendum was the result of an "unspeakable" and "ignorant" mass of people who should have been "swatted away by the forces of the establishment." One Brussels official described them as "ungrateful bastards," blaming "populist demagogues." Three years earlier, in 2005, when in a referendum French and Dutch voters rejected the new European constitution, it was said to be a "triumph of ignorance" by an "odd bunch of racists, xenophobes, nationalists, communists—the plebs." The same happened when the British voted for Brexit in 2016—except that the stubbornly independent British refused to be cajoled. The high-sounding virtue of democracy of the people can so easily be highjacked by elites who know better. Free elections must reflect the free will of the people.

Individual liberty or freedom (that is, the right of the individual to believe, act, and express oneself freely) sounds good, but in a world where human society is created in the context of families, communities, and society, individual freedom can be a way of opting out of society itself. If individual freedom becomes too individualistic, it will weaken communities. Individual freedom is often illusory. Our freedom to vote in exercise of our democratic rights is limited in practice by the availability of candidates who espouse our values. Our freedom to buy as consumers is similarly limited by the power of the markets against individuals. In the same way, we are dependent on the services available within our communities for education, health, and employment. Individual freedom is largely an illusion in human society. A good community is based on mutually beneficial interdependability and inter-accountability.

In a similar way we see the limitations of the rule of law, which is the principle that all people and institutions, including government, are subject to and accountable to laws enacted by representatives of the people. They should be impartially applied and enforced by the rules of by law, not by the dictate of rulers or privileged elites. The rule of law is widely regarded as essential to avoid discrimination, prejudice, favor, and the arbitrary use of force. But how does this work out in practice in the face of the poverty of the many and the huge economic muscle of the few? The inequality of poverty and wealth in the legal system results in inequity, especially in relation to one of the core ideals of the rule of law—that people should be treated equally and impartially by the law and by those responsible for its implementation. Ordinary people seeking to sue a pharmaceutical company for personal injuries would find themselves fighting against a team of highly paid lawyers who are highly literate in the technicalities of the law. In such circumstances, the rule of law is inevitably biased in favor of the rich and powerful.

The rule of law should refer to the application of laws reflecting the will of the majority, passed by legislatures elected by the people, which in turn are interpreted and applied by courts and tribunals. Too often, however, interventionist judges, who are more social scientists than professional lawyers, seek to 'modernize' laws which they regard as not sufficiently progressive. Modernizing the law is the prerogative of the elected representatives of the people, not unelected judges. The fundamental principle must be the Rule of Law, not the Rule of Lawyers.

Naturally, the application of laws reflecting the will of the majority requires respect and tolerance towards those in the minority, whether they are those of minority faiths or none or those with minority lifestyles. In fact, all members of society have different characteristics from one another, such as age, culture, ethnicity, family structure, gender, marital status, national origin, political persuasion, race, religion, sexual orientation, and socio-economic status as well as personal beliefs and values. For human society to flourish, all these diverse characteristics must be respected. There must be a proper regard for the dignity of the person.

Whereas it should be a foregone conclusion that the principle of mutual respect and tolerance is fundamental to civilized society, experience demonstrates how brittle it is. As soon as the demands for equality by illiberal activists had been accepted by society and laws passed to normalize their behavior and prevent victimization, they immediately began a campaign of disrespect and intolerance against all who disagreed with their views, including alleged "hate" speech, in order to victimize, silence, and remove the majority from the public square. A minority of 4.6% foisted their practice and beliefs on the other 95.4%. Such behavior has to be quashed so that civilized respect and tolerance for all can be reinstated in society.

The Experience of History

History gives us cause for optimism. Often in history, peoples mired in degradation have had leaders to show them the way ahead to higher ideals; those principled individuals led the way by their forethought, perseverance, and conduct. One such person, well known across the world, is William Wilberforce, the social reformer who for decades in the 19th century fought a lonely battle in England to change government policy and public morals. On October 28, 1787, he wrote in his diary, "God Almighty has set before me two great objects, the suppression of the Slave Trade and the reformation of manners."[69] At the time, English society was decadent, with unrestrained drunkenness leading to mass poverty, child labor, and a high crime rate that resulted in many criminals being hanged. The established church was little better; the upper classes were irreligious and corrupt. Political corruption was endemic. Wilberforce labored to change the moral climate and make goodness fashionable. His small book, *A Practical View of Christianity*, describing what genuine Christian faith really is, became a best-seller.

At twenty-eight years of age Wilberforce was already a member of the British Parliament but was uninfluential. He was confronted by a corrupt and self-serving Establishment. Slavery was hugely profitable enterprise for the country, with many vested interests. The country's social conditions were deplorable. He was on a mission against all the odds. He labored for no less than 46 years after he wrote those words in his diary. Just three days before he died on July 29, 1833, the Slavery Abolition Act was passed by parliament, abolishing slavery throughout the entire British Empire. The act for the abolition of the slave trade, that is the trading and transportation of slaves, had been passed 26 years earlier in 1807.

In 1996, Wilberforce's biographer, John Pollock, gave a lecture in which he stated the seven principles that Wilberforce followed, which we would do well to note in our search for changing government:

---

[69] https://christianhistoryinstitute.org/study/module/wilberforce.

1. Wilberforce's whole life was animated by a deeply held, personal faith in Jesus Christ. It was his belief that Jesus Christ, who had died on the Cross to save humankind from depravity, could save and transform depraved English society in the 19th century.
2. He had a deep sense of calling that grew into the conviction that he was to exercise his spiritual purpose in the realm of his secular responsibility. He had a holistic view of the sacred and the secular. Indeed, he had to. The established Church of England was deeply entrenched with financial investments in the slave trade.
3. Wilberforce was committed to the strategic importance of a band of like-minded friends devoted to working together in chosen ventures. His team of like-minded reformers, known as the "Clapham Sect," were disdained by the elite but they persevered. The loneliness of his position was mitigated by his caring supporters.
4. He believed deeply in the power of ideas and moral beliefs to change culture through a campaign of sustained public persuasion. He mobilized the public to support him, presenting to Parliament petitions with hundreds of thousands of signatories. He was not a one-man band. He spoke for millions and Parliament had to take notice.
5. He was willing to pay a steep cost for his courageous public stands and was remarkably persistent in pursuing his life task. For almost half a century he was despised and derided by his contemporaries at Westminster, impacting severely on his health, but he never gave up. On his deathbed he was applauded as the person who had been the agent for the abolition of slavery and the reformation of manners. He was a man who changed his times.
6. His labors and faith were grounded in a genuine humanity rather than blind fanaticism. He lived out his faith as an expression of his gratitude to Christ who through redemption had secured his own freedom from the slavery of sin.
7. He forged strategic partnerships for the common good irrespective of differences over methods, ideology, or religious beliefs. He maintained his own strong principles yet working with many others who differed from him as long as their motivation and objectives were the same."[70]

---

[70] https://www.worldcat.org/title/william-wilberforce-a-man-who-changed-his-times/oclc/45083603.

Wilberforce's principles were deeply rooted in scripture. He was one of the founders of the British and Foreign Bible Society and a founder of many others, especially for the alleviation of poverty, the promotion of education, and the welfare of animals. The encouragement and opportunity through literacy of the masses to read the Bible and the consequential increasing development of a Christian social conscience had a marked impact on attitudes toward morals, justice, and character in an era of the social ills resulting from the world's first industrial revolution. The reading, understanding, and application of scripture was foundational.

In the years after William Wilberforce's death, his influence persisted. There was a revival of virtue and goodness. Public life emphasized morals, integrity, character, and justice. He made a difference. By God's grace we can do the same if we are faithful to our calling.

Contemporary Initiatives

There are several contemporary initiatives which seek to rebuild on the proven methods of the past. Naturally every period in history has its own context, culture, and social background, so the challenges of each will be superficially different but fundamentally the same, as contemporary culture will still have at its root the same rebellion against well-established principles as previous generations.

One such current initiative, named after William Wilberforce and also based at Westminster, England, is "the Wilberforce Alliance" which seeks by 2033 to inspire and equip "a global community of 100,000 men and women to enter public life-driven by the same values that motivated William Wilberforce, by informing decision makers of the cultural, economic, political and spiritual trends of our time, equipping people who have a calling to go into public life to become transformational leaders and inspiring leaders to take on the biggest social and political challenges of our day." The Alliance leaders go on to say that they "have the same inspiration as William Wilberforce, are non-party political, we love democracy, liberty and justice and are global, and are defined by what we are for rather than what we are against." Like the context of this present volume, they seek to transform the mountains of societal influence that dominate our culture.

How Does One Go about This Monumental Task of Transforming Government?

The answer is by starting at ground level and moving up the ladder by small incremental steps gained through experience and trial and error.

Some think that the way to change government is by being elected as prime minister, president, or some other position on the summit of political achievement. That gets us nowhere. In the fall of 2019, I met two candidates who were going to stand for election as president of the United States! I met one in the registrar's office in State House, Concord, New Hampshire, registering his name for the 2020 election. Neither had been in politics before. Neither had a chance.

Politics should be like a profession that is grounded in sound education and training, where aspiring politicians graduate to an apprenticeship, whether as a clerk or otherwise, picking up knowledge and experience incrementally. It cannot be rushed. Professional competence is the reward of those who persevere and keep learning. For 24 years I served as an elected representative. Fortunately, I made my major mistakes in the first five years before I ascended the political ladder! They were no big deal. Only when I was elected to more senior office did I value the lessons I had learned while watching others falling off pedestals. During my teens I studied Richard Nixon very closely. I appreciated his strengths. I learned much from his weaknesses. I have also studied the strengths and weaknesses of Winston Churchill and other leaders. The fact is that all of us have both strengths and weaknesses that we carry with us through life.

The Wilberforce Alliance and others like it are training and mentoring budding politicians through residential and non-residential courses.[71] Another organization, also in London, England, and having a similar name is the Wilberforce Academy, which provides seminars for training not only politicians but also those who are entering non-political public service, such as employees in the public sector.[72] There are similar initiatives in cities around the world. Each is devoted to the formation of competent participants in government. Novices have no part to play in this effort to make a difference in society except to learn by experience and to achieve competence, both of which are paramount.

Political Manifestos Pleasing To Voters

Thought needs to be given the sort of political program that voters favor. As we embark on a program to return to traditional values, that is a much easier than the task facing the illiberal elite, the reason being that tradi-

---

[71] https://www.wilberforcealliance.com/

[72] https://wilberforceacademy.org.uk/.

tional values are innate in human nature, with which we have been endowed by our Creator. Human beings are naturally social. They have always lived in groups. There is one grouping that is paramount above all others—the family, primarily the nucleus of parents and children and secondarily the broader group of kith and kin.

Time and again in elections, the political elite have been flummoxed by what they regard as the myopic perspective of voters. Their primary focus is not on national economic policies and foreign affairs. Their political votes are focused on the essential needs of the family, without which all the national macro-policies are redundant: food and shelter, affordable health care, good education for the children, employment to provide for the family, respect for property rights, respect for individuals and their personal freedoms, safety on the streets, the strong arm of the law to deal with crime and an all-encompassing social stability in the community, city and nation to provide the wellbeing to achieve these things. This encompasses a healthy economy to provide the prosperity and advancement to which people aspire for themselves and their children and as part of their personal freedom, freedom of the exercise of religion, and the right to hold other beliefs and values. To hold these in check governments must be held accountable by periodic elections of parliamentary representatives.

The political manifestos of the illiberal elite, who have highjacked some of our political parties, do not hold these basic family values that are essential to the good of society, so people are wary of them. Parents want to have control over what their children are taught at school. They are unwilling to hand over to extremists the right to teach unhealthy practices in school, and particularly to let the school decide if their son or daughter needs to change gender. These are anathema to most of the population. We need to exert our rights as the majority, while allowing deviation to minority extremists. We need to constantly assert the fact that professional studies have consistently demonstrated that the nuclear family is the most stable and the safest environment in which to raise children. It should also be constantly pointed out that the nuclear family headed by married parents remains a personal ideal even among men and women who do not disapprove of alternative family structures. Published national reports claim that children living in a household with an unrelated adult were about nine times more likely to be abused, whether physically, sexually, or emotionally, than children raised in a family of birth parents and siblings. In turn, these stable families are also able to nurture stable flourishing neighborhoods, communities, towns, and cities, freer from crime, violence, and addictions. These safer neighborhoods are further facilitated by the social support of friends, the broader community, and, in particular, church families.

The Way Ahead

So how do we go about this task in the twenty-first century? We need to include the following:

1. Many Christians in the West (but not elsewhere) are pessimistic that everything is going downhill and that we have lost the battle. We need to open their eyes to the experience of history that shows we can turn things around. When the illiberal propaganda is proved to be vacuous, the majority of the population will be with us, as they already are, albeit secretly.
2. We must challenge young people to go into politics, to attend training seminars, to join a political party, and to start at the bottom.
3. We must get Christians to set up cross-party Christian groups to support people going into politics, to provide them with prayer support and, where necessary, financial support.
4. We need to start social media focus groups on many subjects, and we must lobby decision-makers to follow sound political agendas.

Building Coalitions

The task before us is huge, however, it is not hopeless. As noted above, people know what is right as a result of the innate values imbued in them by their Creator, which should make it easier for us to advocate values that are good for society. We need to enlist their cooperation and work with them to accomplish our desired goals.

The word "co-belligerence" is used to describe people of different faiths or philosophies working alongside others towards a common goal. There are dangers, of course, because there may well be hidden agendas on the part of some to achieve different goals. To work together, we must have a clear purpose, clear outcomes, and clear communication; otherwise we shall get into great difficulty.

Clear purpose. When we work alongside others, we need to have a clear purpose and clear objectives of what we want from a common struggle. We should work these out with those holding different beliefs in advance. We must not fight in just general terms. We must have a good reason for co-belligerence.

Clear outcomes. We and our co-belligerents must know what we want to be the clear outcomes. We must know what our goals are to be. We need to know what we want to achieve. It may be that those fighting alongside us will have different goals. Maybe our goals are not compatible. If that be the case, we need to clarify the disparities and stop our co-belligerence before we start. If our goals can be made compatible, we should do so by negotiation before we start.

Clear communication. If we are going to work alongside others successfully, a lot of effort will have to go into good communication. This usually requires putting something down on paper in clear language. Often lawyers are asked by two parties to write a contract in unambiguous language as to the deal upon which both parties have verbally agreed and have often shaken hands on. There is no disagreement, but they want to be sure that if disagreement arises in the future, they will both know where they stand. If it is appropriate in that situation, how much more important it is for those who have different beliefs, different traditions, a different history and speak different languages to do so while in a mutual conflict situation against a third party.

Even if we adhere to these principles, there will be dangers to consider, such as:

- The danger of losing control. There will not necessarily be much, or any, trust between co-belligerents. The other party may take advantage of us for their own (not common) goals, either unknowingly or deliberately.
- The danger of unacceptable compromise. Our own principles and beliefs will dictate which compromises are acceptable and which are non-negotiable. We may get sucked into unacceptable compromises gradually and insidiously without realizing it.
- The danger of the result being distorted by the co-belligerent. We may find that after all the effort and the apparent trust between the parties, we have been taken advantage of—we have been "used."
- To minimize these dangers:
- We should be alert to what our co-belligerents are doing. We must ensure that we receive regular reports and check up on what is happening.
- We cannot afford to leave anything to trust. In our joint task we can generally leave nothing to trust when working with co-belligerents.

- We must ensure that our co-belligerents know that we are alert and are checking up on everything that is happening. We should encourage them to do the same with us.
- We must keep joint control of the process.
- We must keep good open lines of communication, using clear language in frequent and regular communication.

The Difference One Person Can Make

Individuals throughout history have made a difference. We have noted how William Wilberforce changed his political world. Another great example is Abraham Kuyper (1837–1920), a neo-Calvinist theologian and minister in the Dutch Reformed Church who served as Prime Minister of the Netherlands between 1901 and 1905. He was very well qualified to hold high office, having done his early 'apprenticeship' in politics. In 1879, when he was only 42 years of age, he founded a political party, the Anti-Revolutionary Party. He was also qualified as a journalist, so he was well placed to disseminate his ideas. He went on to establish a newspaper and the Free University of Amsterdam, all good building blocks for creating a just society based on Christian principles. However, he could not achieve all he wanted to do politically on his own, so in 1888 he formed a coalition of his Anti-Revolutionary Party and a Roman Catholic group (not natural allies); this coalition gained power and ended the era of Liberal rule. With vision, courage, wisdom, determination, and perseverance, we can follow in the footsteps of those such as Wilberforce and Kuyper, who made a real difference in former times, and make a real difference in our time.

Chapter 8: Military

Col. Charles E. Reynolds

Col Charles (Charlie) Reynolds is from Bedford, VA. He earned a BA from the University of Richmond and Master of Divinity and Doctor of Ministry degrees from Golden Gate Baptist Theological Seminary. His ministry project, "World Changers" became a National Youth Missions Program. Dr. Reynolds served as a youth minister, a journeyman missionary, a church planter, and a pastor. Col Reynolds joined the California National Guard in 1989 and became an active duty U.S. Army Chaplain in 1993. Following his liaison work with religious leaders in Bosnia, the Army sent him to Princeton Theological Seminary to earn a Master's in World Religions and Culture. Reynolds was selected as the 2004 Officer Instructor of the Year at the JFK Special Forces Training Center, where he taught World Religions, Ethics, and Cross-Cultural Communication. Other military assignments included Eastern Regional Command Chaplain, Afghanistan, Command Chaplain, U.S. Army Africa, Director of the Army Center for World Religions, and Strategic Religious Advisor for U.S. Forces Iraq. After retiring from the military in 2016, Dr. Reynolds was contracted as a religious advisor for the U.S. Army Intelligence and Security Command. COL Reynolds has been married to his wife Marcia Brown for 36 years. They have two children and three grandchildren.

A Strategic Plan for Climbing the Military Mountain

Introduction

It was July 15, 2001. I had just completed my introductory briefing with my new boss, Major General William Gerald "Jerry" Boykin, Commander of the John F. Kennedy Special Warfare Center and School (SWCS), where the U.S. Army trains its Special Forces soldiers. When I finished, the general gave me his first order: "Get on your knees, chaplain!" I immediately dropped to my knees with my hands folded on the chair where I had been sitting. General Boykin came over, placed his hands on my head, and commissioned me as his Command Chaplain. He exhibited the same passion with which he prayed on every military mission he executed, including the attempted rescue of American hostages in Iran, the invasion of Granada and Panama, and the attempted arrest of Mohamed Farrah Aidid in Somalia in what came to be known as Black Hawk Down.

The general said something in his prayer about a commitment he had made in Mogadishu. A week later I heard his testimony. He explained that before every mission, he prayed for his soldiers and they sang *God Bless America* together. There had been injuries, but never had a soldier who participated in this ritual been killed. Boykin prayed with his soldiers before they left to capture Aidid, confident they would all return alive. A few hours later he opened the tailgate of a 5-ton transport and watched as the blood of his dead soldiers came pouring out.

Boykin shared that his first thought was "There is no God," but his stalwart relationship with God would not let him doubt God's existence for long. He recognized that God's existence is not predicated upon the fulfillment of the demands we place upon Him, but rather on His incredible love for us, which is omnipresent in both triumph and defeat. In that moment of crisis, General Boykin discovered the essence of evangelism. Boykin felt an incredible burden for every soldier who would ever serve under his command. He made a commitment to God that all soldiers under his command would have the opportunity to know God and to experience his love before embarking on any mission that might be his or her last.

General Boykin prayed for God to work through me to develop an operational strategy to execute the promise he had made to God. I wrestled with how I could convey God's love to over 3000 Special Forces soldiers who would graduate during my tenure as their chaplain. I determined that it could not be done without forcing soldiers to attend a religious service which, in the Army, I was not allowed to do. I prayed in desperation, as I had never before failed to complete a task assigned to me by a commander: "God, I know this is what my commander has asked me to do, but I can't do it. I don't even know how to begin."

On September 11, 2001, the world changed for every soldier in the U.S. military. In November, when the exploits of our Special Forces in Afghanistan began to emerge in the news, I received a call from the representative of Herald of Truth, a Christian organization located in Abilene, Texas. The group wanted to provide a New Testament for every Special Forces graduate. I hesitated. As a chaplain, it was awkward telling someone I did not want to accept Bibles, but I had cases of Bibles sitting in my office. As I was trying to decide how to respond, he said, "Chaplain, let me send you one of these Bibles. Then you can let me know if you want more." The next week the New Testament arrived. I took one look and thought, Wow! It had a shiny metal cover with a raised cross. The infamous date SEP 11, 2001 was engraved under the cross. I knew that most soldiers would want one of these Bibles.

Rick Warren, the pastor of Saddleback Community Church in California, had just published the New York Times #1 best seller, *The Purpose Driven Life*. I wanted to give a copy to every Special Forces graduate along with a copy of that New Testament. I emailed Rick, who grew up with my wife Marcia, and asked him if he could give me a discount price if I purchased a copy of his book for all of the graduates. I was waiting for Rick to send me a price quote when I received a call from the post office. "Chaplain," the postal worker said, "you need to come down here. Your boxes are filling up our post office." Rick had shipped 72 cases of The *Purpose Driven Life* free of charge. I could not distribute the Bibles at graduation, but the day before graduation, they all came together for a group photo. I set up a table in the same room and placed the Bibles and the copies of *The Purpose Driven Life* on the table. Every soldier, including quite a few foreign nationals, took a copy of both.

In 2004, I registered to attend the Army Survival-Evasion-Resistance-and Escape (SERE) School. SERE is one of the few courses in the Special Forces Qualification Course in which chaplains are allowed to participate. I decided to do some research on the course, at the SWCS library, I discovered a movie that Nick Rowe, the Vietnam POW who had created the SERE course, showed as a part of SERE training. COL Rowe became a Christian during his internment and attributed his survival to his faith in God. In the movie several POWs explain how their faith in God had gotten them through.

The movie was no longer shown in the training, but the training did include several scenarios and situations designed to challenge anyone who believed in God. Our enemies know the importance of faith and have developed techniques intended to create doubt. It was incumbent upon the SERE School to incorporate information about these techniques; however, the tools that strengthen faith, like the movie that I discovered, had been removed.

A couple of weeks after I completed SERE, I approached Major Mike Richardson, the commander of the SERE school. As a part of the training, several former POWS had shared their experience in captivity. All but one had shared the critical role that faith in God had played through this ordeal. I pointed this out and asked, "If the purpose of SERE is to provide all resources that are important for survival, why is faith left out of the training?" There was a pause. "Could I at least provide participants with some scriptures on faith that they could use as a resource?" I asked. "Chaplain," he said, "I will get back to you." A few weeks later Richardson asked to speak with me. "Chaplain," he said, "I did not want to give you an answer until I spoke with the other cadre. We decided not only to let you provide scriptures, but we would also like for you to teach a block of instruction on the importance of faith in the POW environment."

I carefully selected the content for the class. I used two books on the SERE recommended reading list. In *Five Years to Freedom,* Nick Roe explains that he was not a Christian when he was captured. One of his fellow prisoners, Rocky Versace, impressed even his captors with his faith and inner strength as he talked about God and America. Nick came to the realization that Rocky had something that he needed. Nick explained how he learned to depend upon his faith in God to survive.[73]

I shared from another book on the SERE reading list, *In the Company of Heroes* by Michael Durant, who was captured in Somalia. Durant starts Chapter 11 by stating, "On my seventh day as a prisoner of war, I found religion." He goes on to share how he received a packet from the Red Cross. Among the items inside was a U.S. Army Bible that Mike read through the remainder of his captivity.[74]

I also told the story of Patton's prayer, as recalled by the general's chaplain, Msgr. James H. O'Neill. O'Neill's recollection is quite different from the conversation portrayed in the movie. Patton explained to his chaplain,

---

[73] Nick Rowe, *Five Years to Freedom* (New York: Little Brown & Company, 1971).

[74] Michael Durant, *In the Company of Heroes* (New York: G. P. Putnam's Sons, 1980), 265.

"Any great military operation takes careful planning, or thinking. "Then you must have well-trained troops to carry it out: that's working. But between the plan and the operation there is always an unknown. That unknown spells defeat or victory, success or failure.... Some people call that getting the breaks; I call it God."[75]

The famous general was not ordering God to provide good weather. Instead, Patton was expressing his dependence upon God in his desperate circumstance. This is extremely important. If a POW believes that prayer is ordering God what to do, he will likely be bitterly disappointed; the key to survival for many POWs is learning to depend upon God in the midst of devastating circumstances.

The timing of the class was the day after the SERE students completed their three days of POW confinement. This was the last class they would have before receiving their Special Forces Tab that evening. They had two hours of down time following the class. I let them know that I would be hanging around if anyone wanted to talk about faith. After the first class, a soldier came to talk with me expressing his need for faith. As a result of our conversation, the soldier came to know God and committed his life to serving Him.

I was driving back to Fort Bragg from the SERE class at Camp McCall when I heard a still small voice say, "Mission complete." It was not until that moment that I realized that God had answered the general's prayer. He had used me to provide three opportunities for every soldier to know God. Every graduate had a copy of the New Testament and *Purpose Driven Life*. Every soldier had attended my class on *The Importance of Faith in the POW Environment*. Back in my office, I emailed General Boykin and shared how God had answered his prayer. I ended the email with "Mission Complete, Charlie Chaplain." The general replied with a handwritten note that I still treasure: "Charlie Chaplain, Well done! You are a great asset to this command and this community. God Bless You. W.G. Boykin."

I share this story because when Bill Wagner asked me to develop a strategic plan for evangelism for the military, I had similar misgivings to those I felt when I understood the meaning of General Boykin's prayer. The task seems bigger than my capabilities, but I have learned through that experience and many others as a military chaplain that when I allow Him to, God can use my life to fulfil his purposes. The great evangelistic movements in history have been accomplished through ordinary men who have allowed God to use their lives in amazing ways.

---

[75] "Patton's Prayer for Fair Weather and the Turn of World War II," *The American Catholic*, https://www.the-american-catholic.com/2014/12/18/patton-on-prayer/.

The second reason I share this story is that I believe it describes what is at the core of a successful evangelistic strategy. Evangelism must stem from a genuine love for people and a sincere burden for others to experience the fulfillment in life that can only be found in a relationship with God.

What are the obstacles to evangelism in the military?

Obstacle 1: Confusing proselytizing with evangelism

Early in my military career, it was not uncommon for a commander or first sergeant to give soldiers the option of chapel or work detail. I remember one occasion when a soldier chose to perform work detail. His first sergeant, loud enough for the whole group to hear, yelled, "Private Jones, are you telling me you don't think you need to go to chapel?" Pressured by his superior, Private Jones decided to attend chapel. There were also some units where young officers felt that their annual performance report from a religious commander would be influenced by their chapel attendance. These situations constitute attempts to coerce religious experience and are often referred to as proselytizing.

In response to this environment, two groups have emerged. The Military Religious Freedom Foundation (MRFF) is a watchdog group and advocacy organization founded in 2005 by Michael L. "Mikey" Weinstein. The group's stated goal is to "ensure that members of the United States Armed Forces receive the Constitutional guarantee of religious freedom to which they are entitled by virtue of the Establishment Clause of the First Amendment."[76] A second group, The Freedom From Religion Foundation (FFRF), is composed primarily of atheists. These two foundations constantly monitor religious activities in the military, objecting to situations in which they feel military personnel, especially chaplains, are using government funds to promote religion.

The fear of retaliation from these two groups has shifted the pendulum too far in the opposite direction. When I was at the XVIII Airborne Corps, General Daniel B. Allan, a strong Christian, was discouraged by his JAG officer from accepting an invitation to speak at a National Prayer Breakfast. Many commanders are reluctant to say anything about their faith. I served one commander who stopped attending chapel. Commanders talking

---

[76] "Our Mission" Military Religious Freedom Foundation, accessed May 19, 2020, https://www.militaryreligiousfreedom.org/about/our-mission/.

about their faith, which was common when I became a chaplain in 1989, rarely occurs, and when it does, it is carefully worded. The current environment denies commanders the protection of their first amendment rights.

Distinction needs to be drawn between evangelism and proselytizing. Retired Army Chaplain (COL-R) Carleton Birch, the endorser for Converge, formerly called Baptist General Conference, served as the spokesperson for the Army Office of the Chief of Chaplains from 2008-2012. Birch provides excellent insight on this issue:

One of the greatest challenges that we have in defining evangelism to a non-church audience is that many equate evangelism with proselytizing. There are similarities but in a military context they are quite different. Proselytizing is considered 'forcing religion' on someone and is frowned upon or even against some military regulations. Evangelism is sharing the good news of Jesus in a more welcoming and respectful context and is an essential component of many if not most Protestant denominational doctrine and practice. By confusing the two, we take a key component of historical Christianity and make it improper or even illegal in the military. Chaplains and military leaders must be able to articulate the difference and stand up for historical evangelism as an essential component of Protestant worship and practice."[77]

The current environment has caused not only commanders, but also some chaplains to be cautious about any activity that might be construed as the basis for a challenge from MRFF or FFRF. Frank Clawson, Director of Military Relations and Chaplain Services for the Church of Jesus Christ of Latter-Day Saints (CJCLDS) points out, "Chaplains need to be very careful, especially when ministering to atheists, humanists, and non-Christian service members."[78] CJCLDS Chaplains must agree to abide by a "Code of Ethics," which includes a statement that reads, "I will not proselytize those I serve." The greater concern, however, should be that the needs and rights of these groups are addressed. As a chaplain, I always made it a point to let these soldiers know that I respected them regardless of their beliefs.

CJCLDS Chaplains must agree to abide by a "Code of Ethics," which includes a statement that reads, "I will not proselytize those I serve." I sent a short four question survey to over 300 chaplains at Fort Belvoir, VA, and

---

[77] Email from COL-R Carleton Birch, Endorser for Converge, Former Strategic Communications Officer for the Army Chaplain Corps, March 1, 2020.

[78] Email from Chaplain COL-R Vance Theodore, Associate Graduate Coordinator MA Chaplaincy, Bingham Young University, February 28, 2020.

Fort Bragg, NC. I received eight responses. Chaplains have busy schedules, but I believe the greater reason for a lack of response is that many chaplains are hesitant to talk about evangelism. One chaplain wrote, "I think the secular movement in society and the military makes it more difficult to sponsor events that might be construed as evangelizing events."[79]

This reluctance has been further complicated by a change in military policy toward the accommodation of religious practices. In 2014 the military revised Department of Defense Instruction (DoDI) 1300.17 Accommodation of Religious Practices Within the Military Services. The revision replaced the phrase "the U.S. Constitution proscribes Congress from enacting any law prohibiting the free exercise of religion" with the phrase "the DoD places a high value on the rights of members of the Military Services to observe the tenets of their respective religions or to observe no religion at all . . . unless it could have an adverse impact on military readiness, unit cohesion, and good order and discipline."[80] Based on the new guidelines, commanders can prohibit and/or take disciplinary action against any religious activity believed to interfere with good order and discipline. MRFF uses this phrase to coerce commanders into supporting its agenda.

MRFF used this clause against Chaplain Richard Smothers, who sent out an email inviting military leaders to attend an optional seminar called "Lead Like Jesus." In an interview with *Navy Times*, Mickey Weinstein stated, "Nothing could be more disruptive to good order and discipline and unit cohesion than a message like this." He added that those behind the discussions should be "visibly and aggressively investigated and punished."[81] Air Force Brigadier Gen Marty France, an MRFF board member, fired off an email to the base commander, Capt. Ian L. Johnson, urging him

---

[79] Survey emailed by the author.

[80] Section 4. Police tab b, Department of Defense Instruction (DoDI) 1300.17 Accommodation of Religious Practices Within the Military Services, accessed May 19, 2020, https://www.esd.whs.mil/Portals/54/Documents/DD/issuances/dodi/130017p.pdf.

[81] Believers Portal, "Navy Chaplain Accused of Violating U.S. Constitution for Telling Soldiers to 'Lead Like Jesus,'" accessed March 23, 2020, https://believersportal.com/navy-chaplain-accused-of-violating-u-s-constitution-for-telling-soldiers-to-lead-like-jesus/.

to "move quickly on this blatant violation of the Constitution."[82] In Smothers defense, First Liberty Institute, a legal organization dedicated to defending religious liberty, noted that encouraging troops through faith is in the job description of a chaplain. They also pointed out that the seminar was optional and that no pressure was placed on anyone to attend. No serious punishment was given to Smothers for the incident. In separate incidents, Chaplains Wes Modder, Scott Squires, and Joseph Lawhorn were all successfully defended by First Freedom, but they had to go through the ordeal of having disciplinary action overturned.[83] It is understandable that many military chaplains are hesitant to talk about witnessing and evangelism.

Chaplains are wrong, however, if they believe the current environment prevents them from sharing God's love in both word and deed. Chaplains can share their faith. Dr. Steven Keith, director of the Liberty University Center for Chaplaincy, shared in an interview that Liberty University lawyers have searched and found no regulation in the military prohibiting chaplains from sharing their faith.[84]

Liberty University's School of Divinity trains more military chaplains than any other educational institution. I visited Liberty at the invitation of Dr. Keith. I was impressed with their chaplaincy training curriculum. Candidates are trained to deal with situations unique to the military, like deployment, combat injury, and combat-related trauma. Students examine the theological and cultural issues relevant to military populations.[85] Relational evangelism, loving God and loving others, especially soldiers, is the central focus of the training. Keith states, "Chaplains who are a lover of

---

[82] Navy chaplain's 'Lead Like Jesus' message roils command staffs, *Navy Times*, accessed March 23, 2020, https://www.navytimes.com/news/your-navy/2020/01/31/newport-chaplains-lead-like-jesus-message-roils-command-staffs/.

[83] First Liberty Institute, Navy Chaplain Accused of Violating Constitution for Encouraging Personnel to 'Lead Like Jesus,' accessed March 23, 2020, https://firstliberty.org/news/ navy-chaplain-accused/.

[84] Interview with Dr. Steven Keith, director of the Liberty University Center for Chaplaincy, February 19, 2020.

[85] Residential Master of Divinity: Military Chaplaincy, Liberty University Website, accessed February 25, 2020, https://www.liberty.edu/divinity/masters/mdiv/military-chaplaincy/.

soldiers will love doing their job. Taking care of soldiers is what most military commanders are most concerned about in evaluating chaplains."[86]

I commend Liberty for instilling the importance of loving God and loving others. Genuinely showing God's love is the most effective means of evangelism and also the best strategy to combat those who would suppress the right of chaplains to share their faith.

For me personally, some of my greatest moments as a chaplain were those times when God provided an opportunity to share His love with soldiers. I actually had more opportunities to share my faith as a chaplain than I did as a pastor or a missionary. When a chaplain is out with soldiers doing what soldiers do, opportunities naturally present themselves. I did make it a point to be tactful and respectful in how and with whom I did so.

Navy Times featured a copy of the flyer sent out by Chaplain Smothers that caused so much controversy. There is a picture of Jesus with a raised sword upon a white horse leading an army of saints. The picture is reminiscent of the Crusades. In large bold letters is this statement: "Hear why military leaders from all around Naval Station Newport follow Jesus."[87]

While Chaplain Smothers' email was legal, it was not tactful or respectful of the environment in which it was sent. Had I been Chaplain Smothers' supervisor, I would have instructed him to redo the flyer before sending it out. It is my evaluation that in most circumstances where violations were brought against chaplains, the chaplain has not been not tactful and respectful. I believe that Jesus set an excellent example with Zacchaeus and Matthew, non-believers whose lives were changed because Jesus treated them with dignity and respect. I believe it would help chaplains to share God's love more respectfully if chaplains viewed themselves as pastors for all their soldiers, rather than missionaries trying to convert soldiers whom they consider nonbelievers.

Obstacle 2: Failure to uphold the First Amendment.

Any candidate selected as a military chaplain must first be endorsed by a religious body recognized as a legitimate religious denomination or group by the U.S. military. By giving their endorsement, a religious body is saying

---

[86] Interview with Dr. Steve Keith at Rawlings School of Divinity, Liberty University, Lynchburg VA, February 29, 2020.

[87] "Navy chaplain's 'Lead Like Jesus' message roils command staffs," Navy Times Webpage.

that this candidate is a qualified clergyman. Most denominations have separate divisions that are responsible for endorsing chaplains.

Some religious bodies categorize endorsed chaplains as missionaries. Giving chaplains this title implies that their primary responsibility is evangelism. As an example, Southern Baptist chaplains are endorsed by the North American Mission Board and are required to submit a quarterly report stating how many soldiers they have given a gospel presentation to and how many soldiers they have baptized.

Converge, formally known as Baptist General Conference and Cooperative Baptist Fellowship, considers its chaplains to be pastors because the functions they perform are pastoral in nature (preaching, teaching, counseling, weddings, funerals, and staffing).[88] The principal responsibility of a missionary is evangelism. Evangelism is just one of the many responsibilities of being a pastor. The term pastor is a more accurate description of how the military defines the responsibilities of chaplains.

Space does not allow me to examine the regulations defining the duties of chaplains for all five branches of service. Joint Guide 1-05 Religious Affairs in Joint Operations applies to all chaplains from all branches, serving in joint operations. JG 1-05 states, "Chaplains . . . are endorsed by an ecclesiastical organization and commissioned by the US Government to support the free exercise of religion." In the Executive Summary, the Fundamentals of Religious Affairs directs Chaplains to "enable and support free expression of faith and/or religious practice for all assigned personnel." Under Terms and Definitions, religious support is defined as "Chaplain-facilitated free exercise of religion."[89]

There is an important reason why the military emphasizes the responsibility of chaplains to ensure the free exercise of religion. On November 23, 1979, two Harvard Law students, Joel Katcoff and Allen M. Wieder, filed a civil lawsuit in the United States District Court for the Eastern District of New York in Brooklyn. For these two law students, the use of government funds to support the military chaplaincy seemed to be a glaring violation of the First Amendment, which states, "Congress shall make no law respecting an establishment of religion." Tax money is used to pay chaplains, and it would seem difficult to prove that this does not

---

[88] Email from COL-R Carleton Birch, Endorser for Converge, Former Strategic Communications Officer for the Army Chaplain Corps, March 1, 2020.

[89] Joint Guide 1-05 Religious Affairs in Joint Operations, February 1, 2018.

advance religion. The ramifications of the Katcoff and Wieder case threatened the very existence of chaplains in our nation's military and Veterans Administration.

Fortunately, the First Amendment also states that government cannot prohibit the free exercise of religion. The "advancing" and "inhibiting" clauses must be read together as an integration of the establishment and free exercise clauses. If funding appears to advance religion, the refusal to fund would inhibit religion. These provisions serve a maintenance function that provides military personnel the opportunity to continue exercising their religious liberties as they would have had they remained civilians.[90]

The Second Circuit Court of Appeals ruled that the Free Exercise Clause "obligates Congress, upon creating an Army, to make religion available to soldiers who have been moved to areas of the world where religion of their own denominations is not available to them."[91] Since the chaplain ministers to men and women whose work takes them far from home and since chaplains serve personnel of all faiths, the Chaplain Corps is not a religious establishment; rather military chaplains serve to facilitate the free exercise of religion for all soldiers.

The Army Records Management and Declassification Agency website explains how chaplains are expected to balance both clauses of the First Amendment:

Congress recognizes the necessity of the Chaplain Corps in striking a balance between the two clauses of the First Amendment. In the pluralistic setting of the military, the Chaplain Corps provides opportunities for religious support for individuals from all religious backgrounds. Chaplains cooperate with each other, without compromising their faith tradition or ecclesiastical endorsement requirements, to provide comprehensive religious support within the unique military environment.[92]

Problems occur when chaplains' beliefs interfere with their responsibility of ensuring the free exercise of religion for all of their soldiers. This problem was further blurred by the passage of the National Defense Authorization Act in 2013, which ordered that no member of the armed forces

---

[90] Israel Drazin and Cecil B. Currey, *For God and Country* (Hoboken: KTAV Publishing House, 1995), 205.

[91] Ibid., 205.

[92] "The First Amendment," The Army Records Management and Declassification Agency website, accessed May 19, 2020, https://www.rmda.army.mil/civil-liberties/RMDA-CL-programs-first-amendment.html.

may require a chaplain to perform a rite or ceremony that violates the chaplain's beliefs and that chaplains may not be disciplined for refusing to perform such a ceremony.[93] Some chaplains have used this to discriminate against the beliefs of some soldiers and to ignore their responsibility to ensure the free exercise of religion. This opens the potential for future lawsuits. Vance Theodore, Associate Graduate Coordinator for the chaplaincy program at Brigham Young University, shared with me the care he takes to ensure his students understand their responsibility to provide religious support for soldiers of all faith groups.[94]

Unfortunately, no clear constitutional mandate emerged from the District Court's litigation of the Katcoff and Wieder case. The jurisdiction of the ruling applied only to the region under the jurisdiction of the Eastern District of New York. Only the Supreme Court can ultimately determine constitutional legality. A future court could reach a different conclusion.[95] What this decision did confirm is that military chaplains must understand that the only legal justification for their existence is to ensure the free exercise of religion.

If it were demonstrated that military chaplains believe that their primary function is to serve as missionaries, as government employees they would be in violation of the first amendment and the very existence of chaplains paid by the U.S. government could be in jeopardy. Chaplains must ensure the free exercise of religion for all soldiers, to the greatest extent location and circumstances allow.

It is extremely important for institutions that train chaplains and military endorsers to stress this to their students. Regent University has developed a three-step model to encourage their future chaplains to embrace their responsibility to ensure the free exercise of religion. Dr. Mark A. Jumper, director of the chaplaincy training program at Regent University, explains: (1) We begin by providing a Biblical basis. God gave Adam and Eve free choice, so chaplains in providing free choice are following God's example; (2) Candidates are taught that by ensuring religious freedom of

---

[93] "Obama calls NDAA conscience clause for military chaplains 'unnecessary and ill-advised," Daly Caller Website, accessed May 15, 2020, https://dailycaller.com/2013/01/03/obama-calls-ndaa-conscience-clause-for-military-chaplains-unnecessary-and-ill-advised/.

[94] Email from Chaplain COL-R Vance Theodore, Associate Graduate Coordinator MA Chaplaincy, Bingham Young University, February 28, 2020.

[95] Israel Drazin and Cecil B. Currey, *For God and Country* (Hoboken: KTAV Publishing House, 1995), 205.

others, they are also protecting their own religious freedom; and (3) Regent believes that given a level playing field, Evangelical Christianity will prosper well.[96]

Obstacle 3: Assuming military chaplains should be the main effort for the implementation of an evangelistic strategy.

In addition to the limitations on chaplains discussed under Obstacles 1 and 2, the amount of time chaplains have is extremely limited. Chaplains are assigned to military units, most of which have from 300 to 700 soldiers with families. Imagine a church with 700 families and one pastor, Also, not every unit has a chaplain. It is common for a chaplain to provide what we call area coverage for an additional unit and an additional 300 to 700 soldiers. If chaplains are providing area coverage, they should be called upon by that unit only for a crisis or an emergency. The chances of one of those 700 families needing a chaplain in any given week are extremely high.

Also, chaplains cover weddings, memorial services, marriage retreats, etc. as a part of area coverage. During deployments, it is not unusual for one chaplain to be responsible for the families of three to five units at a time when their spiritual needs are even greater, especially when soldiers are wounded and killed. When I was deployed to Afghanistan with the 3rd Brigade Combat Team, 10TH Mountain Division, we had 43 soldiers killed in 16 months. Those chaplains faced immense challenges while covering our five battalions back home.

In addition, being a good staff officer takes at least half of the unit chaplain's time. Every military exercise or operation is the result of an extensive planning process. If chaplains want to provide religious support during a military exercise, which is part of their job description, they must integrate a religious support plan into the overall battle plan. Chaplains can't just show up someplace on a battlefield, hang up a sign, and say, "Let's have church." They must be able to understand the battle plan and determine the best time to provide services for the different components of a unit that is spread out all over the battlefield. Where chaplains are going to be at what time has to be integrated into the operation order. If not, their ministry will not happen. Coordinating a movement plan to get chaplains of all faith groups where they need to be is also a challenge. Once the operation commences, there is an overwhelming chance that everything will change. Chaplains must always be

---

[96] Interview with Dr. Mark A. Jumper, Director of Chaplaincy and Military, Regent Divinity School, March 10, 2020.

prepared for adjustments. Religious support planning for operations may not sound very spiritual, but it is an essential time-consuming task for military chaplains.

This is a chaplain's Monday through Friday job. A chaplain preaching in the chapel service on Sunday will probably not have a chance to work on a sermon until Saturday. Finding any family time is an ongoing challenge, especially when chaplains spend time training in the field, sometimes overnight. Chapel services are great for providing a place for families to worship and find Christian fellowship, but services and chapel activities are rarely focused on reaching the unchurched. A Fort Bragg chaplain stated, "Gospel services at times have 'revival services,' but most are not well attended."[97] Chaplains and soldiers are transitory; therefore, attempting to develop a long-term approach to evangelism is difficult. "The effort really becomes centered on maintaining a few basic programs, i.e. worship services, Protestant Women of the Chapel (PWOC), Youth, and Religious Education," another Fort Bragg chaplain stated in response to my questionnaire.[98]

Lessons Learned from Examining These Obstacles

After examining these obstacles, I believe there are two important takeaways. One is that military chaplains, because of their limitations, cannot be what the military calls "The Main Effort" in evangelism. In the military, the Main Effort is the unit whose success is critical to achieving objectives that lead to victory. As military chaplains perform their assigned responsibility of ensuring the free exercise of religion and perform their role as pastors, opportunities to demonstrate and share God's love arise. Chaplains should embrace those opportunities without any fear of negative repercussions.

Chaplains can be extremely helpful in providing access to military personnel for private Christian military ministries. Chaplains must, however, be intentional in providing that same access to other faith groups. In 2017 the military expanded the number of recognized faith groups from just

---

[97] Survey emailed by the author.

[98] Ibid.

over 100 to 221 as it included the earth-based faiths such as Asatru.[99] A listing of all 221 are found at http://forumonthemilitarychaplaincy.org/wp-content/uploads/2017/04/Faith-and-Belief-Codes-for-Reporting-Personnel-Data-of-Service-Members.pdf.

What private Christian groups are already doing evangelism in the military?

Cadence

When Jesse Miller was a young soldier stationed in the Philippines, he spent many weekends in the home of missionaries whom he called Dad and Mom Brooks. In the Brooks' home, Jesse became grounded in his faith. When the Japanese occupied the Philippines, Jesse endured the infamous Bataan Death March during which he made a promise to God: "Lord, if I ever have a home of my own, you can have it for servicemen." Over the six decades since he made that promise, Cadence has grown from a small Bible study in Jesse's home to an organization with over 200 missionaries who work in over 50 locations worldwide. Cadence serves all branches of the U.S. military in American and overseas locations. Cadence ministers not only to military personnel, but also to their spouses and dependents. In my 28 years serving as a chaplain, I have known of no Christian group more effective in providing ministry for military personnel and their families.

Dave Bobby is a retired Army chaplain who serves as the Eastern Regional Director for Cadence. Bobby explains the Cadence evangelistic strategy:

> Our goal is just ministry to soldiers and their families. No high pressure. We hold Bible studies on some topic at the home. Military families are invited but are not pressured to attend. We provide a loving atmosphere. Most homes have rooms available where single soldiers can spend the weekend. Things happen in the home atmosphere that will never happen anywhere else.

---

[99] Kimberly Winston, "Defense Department expands its list of recognized religions," April 21, 2017, Religious News Service, https://religionnews.com/2017/04/21/defense-department-expands-its-list-of-recognized-religions/.

Kingdom of Ordinary Priests (KOOP)

Kingdom of Ordinary Priests (KOOP) is an evangelistic group that ministers to soldiers. They are currently located at West Point NY, the DC area, Fort Bragg, Fort Campbell, Fort Stewart, Fort Benning, Fort Irwin, and Fort Polk. The group falls under the umbrella of an organization called "No Place Left," which as of January 2020, claimed 118 churches in their network. The network averages 100 baptisms per year.

KOOP leadership coaches soldiers to develop the requisite boldness to share the gospel and mentors Christian converts to persevere against social pressure and ostracism. Their most successful ministry is a network of house churches that has found success training soldiers to reach what they call an *oikos* (Greek for relational network).

New house churches are born out of reaching friends and family members on military installations and beginning to minister to them in homes and public places. Soldiers who have completed military service have organized groups in Huntsville, AL; Columbus, GA; Philadelphia, PA; Albany NY; Cape Coral, FL; Atlanta, GA; and other locations. Overseas, KOOP has worked in India, Pakistan, and South Sudan. Founded in 2012, KOOP is a relatively new organization. Their ministry is not as extensive as Cadence, but they have incorporated some of the same successful practices, and they are growing rapidly.

Jim McKnight, director of KOOP at Fort Benning, is one of the finest Christian officers with whom I served in my 28 years as a chaplain. Jim helped me minister to single soldiers at Fort Drum. When we deployed to Afghanistan, he served as the commander of Alpha company at the Korengal Outpost, the most dangerous location in Afghanistan. Thirteen soldiers in Alpha Company were killed, and Jim miraculously survived a fall from a 50-foot cliff. Jim ministers from his heart, and I am confident that his war experience motivated his love for and desire to reach soldiers.

Officer's Christian Fellowship (OCF)

Officer's Christian Fellowship (OCF) was created 170 years ago by a British Army captain. The mission of OCF is to engage military leaders in home Bible study fellowships and to equip participants for Christ-like service at the intersection of faith, family, and profession. OCF exists almost anywhere U.S. or British Army officers are stationed. In the military environment, it is critical that "The Main Effort" in evangelism has command support. This organization can provide that support.

Club Beyond

Military Community Youth Ministries (MCYM), better known as Club Beyond, focuses on ministry to military high school and middle school kids worldwide. Club Beyond staff and volunteers love young people and are available to journey with them through the hard challenges of adolescence. MCYM was started in 1980 as a cooperative effort between two national youth ministries, Young Life and Youth for Christ. Club Beyond serves many military bases, interacting with nearly 80,000 military teens. More than 90 staff, along with hundreds of volunteer leaders, work in more than 50 military communities around the world. Club Beyond is probably the most evangelistic of all of these organizations. The involvement of youth is critical to the success of any strategic evangelistic effort.

In addition to Club Beyond, Youth for Christ sponsors Campus Life Military (CLM) to help military families deal with normal teenage issues that are intensified by military deployments and the necessity of finding new friends after every move.

Mothers of Preschoolers (MOPS)

Mothers of Preschoolers MOPS started in 1973 when a group of moms of young children banded together to share their lives and parenting journeys. Because of the unique situations that military moms face, MOPS created groups specifically for military wives with the much-needed flexibility military life requires. The group encourages and equips moms of young children to realize their potential as mothers, women, and leaders in relationship with Jesus and in partnership with the local church. MOPS works with local Christian churches of many different denominations and parachurch organizations to maximize ministry opportunities.

MilitaryBeliever.com

MilitaryBeliever.com is a website designed to facilitate military personnel in making connections and finding ministry opportunities where they are currently located. The organization also assists service members and their families in advance of a military move. The website connects military believers and networking efforts with other Christians in one's community and beyond.

Christian Military Fellowship (CMF)

Christian Military Fellowship (CMF), as defined on their website, is an association of believers who are committed to encouraging men and women in the United States Armed Forces and their families to love and serve the Lord Jesus Christ. The video on CMF's homepage is narrated by former Marine Oliver North.

Navigators

This parachurch group ministers primarily on college campuses, but Navigators Military mission has been reaching military families with the gospel since the 1940s. Their outreach includes Bible studies, discipleship, and family support.

The Military Missions Network (MMN)

The Military Missions Network (MMN) has emerged from a common calling shared by evangelical Christians involved in the domain of missional military ministry. MMN creates partnerships between particular churches, chaplains, and ministries linked through a network based on common convictions, mutual benefits, and shared goals. The group builds relationships with a host of chaplains and chaplain endorsers and finds ways to support them and their ministries whenever and wherever they can. Military ministries in local churches are spontaneously springing up near military bases.

Cru Military

Cru Military was established in 1965 as a military ministry at the direct request of Campus Crusade for Christ founder Bill Bright. The focus of Cru is evangelism. Cru operates through small groups, biblical resources, partnerships with chaplains, and church-based ministries, Cru Military helps soldiers develop spiritually throughout their careers. Cru provides resources and lay counselor training for recovery from PTSD and combat trauma, as well as resources and seminars to develop and maintain strong covenantal marriages and godly families.

Christian Groups Sponsored by Military Chapels

Two ministry groups are funded through tithes and offerings collected during military chapel services.

Protestant Women of the Chapel (PWOC)

PWOC is a volunteer organization overseen by the chaplaincy and designed to help chaplains minister to women associated with the military, especially those who participate in a military chapel. PWOC has four primary aims: (1) to lead women to Christ, (2) to teach women God's Word, (3) to develop women's spiritual gifts, and (4) to involve women in Chapel ministries.[100]

The Military Council of Catholic Women (MCCW)

MCCW connects, unites, and inspires U.S. military-affiliated women to grow in their faith. As a non-profit subsidiary of the Archdiocese for the Military Services, USA (AMS), MCCW works with military chapel groups across the globe and at nearly 220 U.S. military installations to mentor women in spirituality, leadership, and service.[101]

Other Groups Classified as Protestant Christians by the Military

These groups are classified by the military as Protestant Christians; however, many Christian denominations consider some of their beliefs and practices to be incompatible with Orthodox Christianity. Both groups have are represented in the military with chaplains, who are classified as Protestant.

Church of Jesus Christ of Latter-Day Saints (CJCLDS)

The CJCLDS does not have an evangelism program specifically for service members, but they do have missionaries who serve in communities near military installations. If invited, these missionaries will share gospel teach-

---

[100] https://thehubpwoc.net/, accessed February 29, 2020.

[101] Military Council of Catholic Women Website, accessed March 1, 2020, http://mccw.org/.

ing with military members. They admonish their members to be an example as believers and to be a light to the world.[102] The CJCLDS, like Cadence, has found their greatest success in building relationships. Frank Clawson states, "I firmly believe that inviting individuals to come unto Christ is all about relationships—one-on-one. They are more open to accepting the two great commandments—love God and love one's neighbor. As they begin to connect with God, they begin to look outward to love their neighbors."[103]

Following 9/11, the CJCLDS leadership saw a need to provide support for military families because of increased deployments and periods of family separation. CJCLDS sent 98 retired military couples to minister to service members who are members of the CJCLDS faith. Clawson explains, "We have found that if we can strengthen soldiers' faith in Jesus Christ and deepen their commitment to live the gospel, the challenges of family separation and reintegration are easier to handle, and the adverse effects of war are greatly reduced. Many of these retirees assist with chaplain ministry programs as needed."[104]

Christian Scientists

I was unable to locate any ministry organizations sponsored by Christian Scientists; however, on the Chestnut Hill Benevolent website, former army chaplain Kim Schuette shares about a ministry of healing of soldiers from smoking habits and alcohol abuse. Chaplain Schuette has written several books on Christian Scientist ministry to the military.[105]

---

[102] Email from Chaplain COL-R Vance Theodore, Associate Graduate Coordinator MA Chaplaincy, Bingham Young University, February 28, 2020.

[103] Ibid.

[104] Ibid.

[105] "Healing and the Christian Science military ministry — Part 2," Chestnut Hill Benevolent Association Website, accessed June 6, 2020, https://www.chbenevolent.org/blog/events/a-former-chaplain-talks-about-healing-and-the-christian-science-military-ministry.

What other religious groups have been successful in military ministry?

Islamic Soldier Ministry Groups

On most military posts, Muslim chaplains offer the five daily prayers and classes in Arabic and Islamic studies. On a post where there is no Muslim chaplain, the military usually contracts an Imam or Muslim Faith Group Leader to lead the daily prayers. I spoke with Command Sergeant Major (CSM) Abdul Mutasa, the current Islamic Faith Group Leader at Fort Bragg. He teaches an Islamic studies class open to all soldiers. The emphasis of the class is the current world situation and military conflicts in Muslim countries. These topics attract non-Muslim soldiers. The content is evangelistic. Off-post mosques serve soldiers and family members. In addition to daily prayers, some mosques have activities designed to attract soldiers. For example, the Islamic Center of Fayetteville has a Saturday breakfast for all men, but the focus is on military soldiers. The Muslims have two national organizations for Muslim soldiers.[106]

Military Muslim Members (MMM)

MMM is an organization providing information, communication, and coordination for Muslims in the U.S. Armed Forces. The leader of the group is Abdul Rasheed Muhammad, who was the first Muslim chaplain to serve in the military, appointed in 1993. Outreach is a part of the group's mission.[107]

Muslim Americans Veterans Association (MAVA)

MAVA was established and certified in 1997. It was organized to be a veterans' service organization for all veterans of the United States Armed Forces, regardless of religion, race, or gender. MAVA is committed to helping all veterans, their families, and their communities. The inspiration for MAVA came from the New World Patriotism movement started by Imam W. Deen Mohammed; it challenged Muslims to "embrace the best America

---

[106] Interview with CSM Abdul Mutasa, Muslim Faith Group Leader, Ft Bragg, accessed March 12, 2020, http://muslimmilitarymembers.org/.

[107] Muslim Military Members Homepage: http://muslimmilitarymembers.org/, March 12, 2020.

has to offer and to stand up as Muslim Americans and lay claim to our 'Shared Freedom Space' as citizens of America." Their goal is to set up branches in states and cities across the U.S. The group commander is Imam Lyndon Bilal.[108]

Judaism

Jewish Chaplains Council (JCC)

JCC sponsors education and cultural centers, groups for spouses, children, and teens, counseling, education scholarships, and many other services.[109] The organization was also charged in 1917 with recruiting and training rabbis for military service and continues to function as the endorser for Jewish chaplains. The rise of social media has led to a variety of other vehicles for connecting Jewish service members with each other and to outside groups.

Buddhism

The percentage of Buddhists in the military is very small. Only 5,287 of 1.4 million military personnel are Buddhist. Buddhism is a very diverse religion of multiple groups with divergent beliefs and practices. I spoke with LTC Ann Tran, the faith group leader at Fort Bragg. Her most popular ministry is an *Introduction to Buddhism* class. Ann did point out that it was difficult to find a chaplain to sponsor her group. She was not aware of any national organization for Buddhist soldiers, and I was unable to locate one.

There is a Facebook page titled "US Military Buddhist". The site states, "We are a small minority in the U.S. Military. Let's connect with each other and help each other realize that we aren't alone. Let us breathe, smile, connect, and live in the present moment. Please spread the word."[110] There is also a more formal website called "Buddhist Military Sangha" that is an

---

[108] Muslim American Veterans Association Homepage, accessed March 12, 2020, https://mavanational.org/.

[109] Jewish Chaplains Council Homepage, accessed March 14, 2020, https://jcca.org/what-we-do/jwb/.

[110] US Military Buddhist Facebook Page, accessed March 1, 2020, https://www.facebook.com/pg/usmilitarybuddhists/about/?ref=page_internal.

online resource for Buddhists associated with the United States Armed Forces.[111]

What well-defined activities could be used as models upon which to build?

Small Groups

The model that has clearly been the most successful in reaching military personnel and their families is small groups. Eleven of the seventeen organizations mentioned utilize small groups to minister to military personnel. These groups, sometimes called share groups, allow participants to share common experiences and challenges. Those who are more mature in their faith can provide testimonies of the importance of their relationship with God in facing these challenges. The most successful organizations are those that emphasize ministry in the home. Cadence, which makes home groups the centerpiece of its ministry, is by far the most successful group in reaching military personnel. Military families, especially those serving overseas, are often separated from their extended families by long distances. The Cadence Hospitality Houses fill this emotional gap. The Cadence staff and the families who gather in these homes become family. Dave Bobby explains, "Guests who visit are loved into the family of God."

Kingdom of Ordinary Priests, whose primary focus is one-to-one personal evangelism, has still found their greatest success in home churches. The Church of Jesus Christ of Latter-Day Saints (CJCLDS) is known for door-to-door ministry, but this approach has become less and less successful. The CJCLDS family ministry, which emerged with the extended wars triggered by 9-11, utilizes home groups run by missionaries similar to the Cadence Hospitality Houses.

Religion Classes

Another ministry that appears to be successful is the religion classes taught by Muslims and Buddhists. CSM Mutasa, who leads the Muslim class, stated, "Soldiers want to learn about religion."

When I was the XVIII Airborne Core World Religion Chaplain at Fort Bragg, I taught a class called *Exploring Religion*. I only invited chaplains, as

---

[111] Buddhist Military Sangha Homepage, accessed March 1, 2020, https://buddhist-militarysangha.blogspot.com/2008/08/requirements-to-become-buddhist.html.

the intent of the class was to improve their understanding of world religions. However, several soldiers who were not chaplains attended the class because they wanted to learn about different religions. A class on Christianity or world religions could be an avenue to reaching military members.

What guidelines can help us in the development of a mega strategy for evangelism?

To develop a strategic strategy for evangelizing the military, I will use the analogy of a jigsaw puzzle. On the outside of the puzzle box is a picture of what the puzzle should look like. I cannot provide a picture of the completed puzzle, but I can provide a picture of some of the components that I believe would be seen on the outside of the puzzle box.

Picture 1: The strategy must have God's fingerprint.

In Avery Willis's discipleship program, Master Life, he places emphasis on the reality that God is always working and on the importance of our being a part of what God is doing. This is God's fingerprint. What was most evident in the story I shared about God answering General Boykin's prayer was God's hand at work. Another example occurred at Fort Drum in 1998. When I arrived, I immediately noticed the ministry gap that existed from not having a Cadence Hospitality House. I called Cadence headquarters to see if they might be interested in starting a ministry at Fort Drum. I was informed that just before my call, the Cadence leadership had been praying about where they should start their next ministry. Fort Drum was one of the possibilities. Less than six months later, missionaries Tim and Bobby Bettger arrived and opened the Fort Drum Hospitality House.

Tilden Edwards from The Shalom Institute states, "Great minds can develop successful strategies. But successful strategies without God's presence can be perfidious." While working at the American Embassy in Baghdad, I attended a weekly gathering of atheists. I discovered that for most of the participants, their decision to become an atheist was not the result of intellectual pursuit, but rather from an encounter with a person of faith that was devoid of God's love. Too often I have seen evangelism strategies where the primary focus is on converting people rather than on loving people and sharing God's Love. On the outside of this puzzle box I see the fingerprint of a God who loves soldiers.

Picture 2: The strategy reflects the ecumenical environment of the military.

Any successful religious strategy in the military must be ecumenical. One of the things I enjoy most about the military is the comradery with other chaplains. This comradery is much more like the demographic I envision heaven to be than attending a denominational annual convention. The General Protestant Services are composed of Christians from multiple Protestant denominations. I believe this movement will incorporate Roman Catholics as well. We must look beyond the suspicions that separate us and unite around the essentials of our faith. I believe God enjoys working outside of the boxes in which we attempt to confine Him. Father Larry Hendel, Father Phil Denig, and Cardinal Bertrand Law are three Catholic priests who had a profound impact on my spiritual growth. I will share one of these stories.

My military career began in the California National Guard where I served from 1989 until 1993. Each year we had a two-week annual training exercise at Camp Roberts, CA. Every Sunday I accompanied my Brigade Chaplain, Major Larry Hendel, a Roman Catholic priest. We traveled all over Camp Roberts together to provide religious services. Sometimes there were no Catholic soldiers and my brigade chaplain would attend my service. If there were no Protestant soldiers, I would attend his mass. We did this for five years until I was selected for active duty in 1993. Our annual training was in August that year, and I was scheduled to begin my active duty career in October. We knew this would be the last time we would travel together. There was some sadness as we had become close friends. At one location there were no Protestant soldiers, so I attended his mass. When the last soldier had been served, Larry walked back and offered me the Eucharist. He knew what he was doing was wrong according to the teachings of his church, and I knew what I was doing was wrong according to the teachings of my church. We were expressing symbolically what could never be put into words. In that moment, we both drew a little closer to heaven.

Picture 3: The strategy respects the pluralistic environment of the military.

In the military environment, soldiers of other faith groups are our comrades, not our enemies. This understanding is essential. We need to move past the confrontational mindset toward other religions that has caused so much misunderstanding and strife. When I was the Eagle Base chaplain

A Strategic Plan for Climbing the Military Mountain | 181

in Bosnia, a Rabbi chaplain came once a month to lead Jewish services. One day he came into my office. "Hello, Charlie," he greeted me with his boisterous voice. "How are JC and the boys doing today?" "Fine, I answered. "How are Moses and the kids?" "Oh, they are a little rebellious as usual, but otherwise everything is fine," he said with a smile. Because the Rabbi knew that I respected his faith and I knew that he respected mine, we could hold this conversation. This, I believe, is the kind of relationship we should have with military personnel from other faith groups. Any evangelistic strategy for the Military Mountain must be respectful of others and their religious beliefs.

Picture 4: The strategy is built on a home group family environment.

Based on what is effective now, I believe a revival in the military will emerge from a missionary led small group family ministry, meeting in homes that provide a family atmosphere for military personal separated from their families. Since workers and missionaries for these ministries are not paid by the government, they are not subject to the same restrictions as chaplains. Chaplains can play a critical role by making it easy or difficult for these groups to operate in the military setting. Chaplains should be careful, however, to provide that same access for other faith groups. In my picture on the outside of the puzzle box, churches or Christian individuals who want to influence the Military Mountain are supporting these home groups. In my picture churches near military bases are supporting the local Hospitality Houses financially, donating supplies, and providing volunteer workers. As the number of personnel attending grows, Christians all over the area are opening their homes for small group meetings and ministry to service members and their families. Groups continue to multiply and grow. There are three potential mediums to connect the larger group: (1) someone taking leadership to organize the division of groups and training of leaders, (2) a weekly worship service designed for those involved in small groups, and (3) a website.

Picture 5: The strategy utilizes the Internet.

The importance of the Internet cannot be ignored. The current military leaders, with the exception of a few general officers, are Generation X. The emerging leaders are Generation Y, and the incoming privates are Generation Z. A common characteristic of all three is their extensive use of Internet. Millennials, who are the emerging military leaders, prefer back-

and-forth conversation rather than a monologue.[112] When I glanced at the top 50 religious blog sites, one stood out: *Building a Church Without Walls*. On the outside of my puzzle box there is a military cyber church without walls. The website has many resources, like a referral site for soldiers who are moving, but there is also a blog site, operated by a retired chaplain who can help soldiers, airmen, and marines with some of the difficult questions and struggles they have about their faith. This chapel without walls would play an important role in a revival of faith in our nation's military.

My Challenge To You

The often-quoted statement, "There are no atheists in foxholes," is not a fact. I have met a few. However, I can attest that when one is in harm's way, there is an intensified awareness of God's presence. My most profound cases of awareness of God's presence all occurred as I was walking in the shadow of death. I believe military personal do have a greater curiosity about religion than the average person on the street. Should the Holy Spirit facilitate a great awaking in the United States, the military would be a logical place for it to begin. The military is a microcosm of the U.S. No institution is more represented by all segments of society than our military. Every unit is like a slice of an omelet whose ingredients come from all over the continent. A revival in the military could rapidly spread throughout the nation. There appears to be a curiosity, if not a thirst, for religion among military personnel.

If you are in the U.S. military or retired military, a military family member, or one who feels called to serve the military, I would challenge you not to simply view this moment as the completion of another chapter in a book. Before you put the book down, I ask you to pause a moment. Take a few deep breaths and center your mind on God's presence. Pray this prayer: "Holy Father, if you want your spirit to move in the US military, I am available for you to use me to be a part of what you want to accomplish in whatever way you choose." Then I ask you to pray this prayer every day for the next forty days. As you are praying, listen for God's burden.

---

[112] "Boomers, Gen X, Gen Y, and Gen Z Explained," Kasasa Webpage, accessed March 13, 2020, https://www.kasasa.com/articles/generations/gen-x-gen-y-gen-z.

Chapter 9: Sports

Hans-Günter Schmidts

Hans-Günter Schmidts (60) has been employed by SRS e.V. since 1984 and has been the head director since 2003. The Christian non-profit sports organization supports and challenges athletes of all ages and abilities as well as those whom they influence in their settings by providing a variety of offers to help them in life and sports situations. SRS is active in 30 sports and works closely with local churches and congregations. Together with the sports and seminar hotel Glockenspitze, SRS offers an excellent contact point for teams, top athletes, associations, companies, and communities, and is also the host of the permanent exhibition "Hall of Fame of German Sports." SRS supports and accompanies sports missionary projects in approximately 40 countries.

Internationally, Schmidts served on the board International Sports Coalition from 2007-2019, which, among other things, organizes pastoral care at Olympic Games and World Championships. He has served as chairman of the Evangelical Alliance Altenkirchen since 2012.

He is an elder in his congregation, the Evangelical Free Congregation in Altenkirchen.

Hans-Günter Schmidts is married to Judith. Together they have four adult children, three children-in-law, and six grandchildren.

Sports Today: A World Phenomenon

Introduction

Sport—Next to culture and music, it is one of the great languages of the world. Sport plays a major role in the lives of people in all parts of the world, both passively as fans, watching with enthusiasm on television or in the stadium, or actively, from health sports to top-class sports. The question is, what role does sport play in how we as Christians are involved in our society? What does the building of the Kingdom of God look like in the area of sport? Do we already have global strategies, and if so, which ones? How must the church of Jesus adjust to the world's largest community of interest?

The Power of Sport

> *"Sport has the power to change the world."*

If the head of a Christian sports organization makes this comment, it sounds subjective, exaggerated, presumptuous, even arrogant. If an Olympic champion with multiple medals or a world class soccer player says it, that person sounds one-sided and perhaps selfish. However, when the President of South Africa, Nobel Peace Prize winner Nelson Mandela, says it, the effect and the weight of this sentence are quite different. Mandela made this statement in the year 2000 in Monaco at the first presentation of the Laureus world sports award, one of the highest awards in sports. He did not mean it only as a polite sentence for the present athletes, politicians, and VIP guests. He proclaimed a message stemming from the profound experiences of his own life.

In 2016 I had the opportunity to visit Nelson Mandela's cell on Robin Island, near Cape Town. Four square meters, a blanket as a bed, a tin bucket as a toilet, a table, a chair. He spent eighteen years in this prison. How did he survive there, physically, mentally, and emotionally? The guide who led us through the prison was a fellow inmate of Mandela's. I listened intently to what he had to say about that brutal time, and I was amazed when he said, "One of the things that kept us alive was this place here. Here we were allowed to play soccer for an hour every afternoon." He was looking at a concrete slab, exposed to the hot sun, with no shade. Even enthusiastic soccer players would not want to play there, yet for Mandela and his fellow prisoners, it was the highlight of the day. Then he was liberated and rose to the presidency, where he learned and experienced, from a completely different perspective, how divided, torn, and hateful South Africa was, this country that had now elected him as president. He also quickly discovered the power for change, paradigm shift, and reconciliation through sport. The well-known movie *Invictus* tells the story of Mandela shortly after his election as president, when he put all his energy into overcoming the apartheid that lived on in people's minds. Convinced that enthusiasm for sport could unite people, he wanted South Africa's soccer team to win the Rugby World Cup in his own country. They did. In a sensational way. The then chaplain of the South African rugby team, Pastor Cassie Carstens, wrote a statement for this book:

> Sport has made a major contribution towards reconciliation in South Africa in 1995 through the World Cup of Rugby, when Nelson Mandela recognized and used the influence of sport to bring peace to a nation that was on the brink of bloodshed. We have seen this again in 2019 when the Springboks won the World Cup again with a black captain and a mixed team. This is why Mandela said: "Sport has the power to change the world. It has the power to inspire. It has the power to unite people in a way that little else does. It speaks to youth in a language they understand. Sport can create hope where once there was only despair. It is more powerful than government in breaking down racial barriers.

"Sport has the power to change the world." Does this statement have meaning for today and worldwide or was it applicable only in a special, unique, historically justifiable time and region? If so, what does it mean for us Christians and for the church of Jesus worldwide?

Let me begin with three current contemporary witnesses who have very special experiences of the potential of sport for social change through the Gospel of Jesus Christ. Even though all three of them have gathered experience in many countries of the world through many missionary assignments and travels, they primarily represent the culture and social reality of their respective countries and continents. For security reasons I have made them anonymous:

Africa: This pastor has travelled to 120 nations and stays in contact with people of sports' ministries in 215 countries.

> We have seen how sport has provided substitute fathers for a fatherless generation in many countries of Africa over the last 16 years since we have started a Fathering program through sport. In one of the big townships in Africa, which is a very poor township with many people living in shacks, we have seen how sport has been the medium to raise the dignity level of the

marginalized youth by bringing them identity and purpose. Jesus assigned all Christians to be leaders when He said: You are the salt and the light of this world. Paul and John add later that we are kings and priests and will reign forever with the Father and the Lamb. This is why I would love to see Christians to step up in responsibility. Since sport has such a massive width of influence, Christians should fill most of the responsibility positions in sport. They should be the managers, coaches and captains of teams. Since sport is a microcosm of life where all the emotions of life is experienced in a condensed form, Christians, who understand what life is, better than anyone else, should show the way! We have enough training material now to train coaches and players on life!

India: This pastor is serving in South India, but his influence reaches his whole country as well as established sports ministries in all regions of India with thousands of sport missionaries.

We all know that the Gospel is the answer to the problems of the world and so to see so many from other faiths coming to know the Lord and become transformational leaders in their homes, schools, Colleges, communities and at their work through Sports and Mission has been very satisfying. It is time now for the Global Church wakes up to reality of the enormous potential of Sports and Mission and use all its resources to use this strategy for the extension of God's Kingdom.

Eurasia: This pastor was expelled from his home country because of his allegiance to Christ. He was flown to the United States at the expense of the UN. From there he was able to establish, mentor, and multiply sports-oriented mission teams all over the former Soviet Union.

In my experience traveling to more than 50 countries around the world, I have seen the power of sports to connect people of different cultural and religious backgrounds. Whether it is international sports like soccer and basketball or more local and traditional sports like kurash, turon, and boyqurgan in Central Asia, sports has a significance to become modern-day parables of Jesus to create a familiar experience for people of our days to present unfamiliar principles of the Kingdom of God. During Euro2012, the partnership of 54 denominations and 67 mission agencies united to serve Ukraine during the European Soccer Tournament. Besides community transformation activities in 212 cities for 30 days, they were able to change the national law prohibiting alcohol consumption at the stadium. It is a significant cultural change for Eastern European country like Ukraine, which struggles with alcohol addiction. We believe that that the body of Chris is called to make disciples in all segments of society in cities; therefore, every representation of the sports in a community is a segment to focus to see discipleship in.

I could provide many more such experiences and cases of lasting social change; however, as an introduction to the questions of missionary strategies "in sports," "with sport" and "through sport," I would like to report four of my own very different experiences and my insights into the potential of sport.

June 1, 2002, Shizuoka/Japan: 'Soccer World Cup in Japan and South Korea.' Germany played its last group match against Cameroon and had to win to get into the final sixteen. I had the privilege of being in the stadium. The outcome of the game was not a foregone conclusion. In the fortieth minute, Carsten Ramelow was given the red card, and the German team had been decimated; now the play was getting even more difficult. In the fiftieth minute, Marco Bode scored, making it 1-0. Behind me in the stands were some other German soccer fans. They fell into each other's arms and cheered. Suddenly I recognized one of them. He was a well-known and popular TV moderator. His normal desire to distance himself from "autograph hunters" had disappeared as the common cheering and the joy about the German goal prevailed. Social distances no longer existed. In a report on the behavior of soccer fans, one of the leading German television stations reported, "25,000 people in the south bleachers cheered their team on—whether university professor, retiree, or prostitute."

July 2004, Worms, Germany: FSV Mainz 05, which had just been promoted to the first Bundesliga, played against the Norwegian champions Rosenborg Trondheim. At the request of our friend Rune B., the manager of Trondheim SRS organized the match. After dinner, each player received an Athlete Bible. Our colleague B. handed one player a second Bible to give to the coach of the second team, who was not present. Later I asked B. if he knew this coach personally or why he wanted to give him a Bible. He replied, "No, but God put him on my heart." The next morning the coach received this Bible. None of us knew that he had received the same Bible from a fan months before and had angrily and blasphemously thrown it in the trash. Now he received the same one again. This time, however, he was in a professional and family crisis, and he did not throw it away. He started to read it, alone in his hotel room. God met him in a special way, and he started a life with Christ and began to be involved in sports mission activities. Professionally, he developed into a very successful women's soccer coach, cup winner, Champions League winner, and national coach—and was privileged to share Christ and lead several players and friends to the Lord.

Spring 2010 Chennai, India: I visited my friend X. Some years previously, he had started to play soccer with children who lived at the garbage dump. What began as a mere game developed into training sessions. X. got his coaching license and formed a team. Today, when I watch a game, I notice that it is all about promotion to the national league. The game is won; the promotion is certain. Most of the players who started out in the garbage dump have come to believe in Jesus Christ on their way between the dump and the championship. Instead of having a big party after the game, the players take an overnight bus ride to the next bigger neighboring city to use the weekend for missionary outreach, to witness for the gospel and give testimony about the changes they themselves have experienced.

These stories are three of many experiences and miracles of God that give some insight into the transformative power of sports.

The History of Sport

I would like to touch on this one. With the creation of man, God gave the mandate to shape this earth. The first humans fulfilled this mandate. The first town builders, the first professions, the first musicians began developing: culture was being shaped (Gen. 4:17-22). From the historical literature of ancient times, we know they had sports: chariot races, boxing, wrestling, running, archery, lancing, and other modern events. From these playful and combative beginnings, intentional sporting competitions were developed: the Pythian Games, the Isthmic Games, the Nemean Games, the Actual Games, the Capitol Games, and finally the Olympic Games, which since their beginning in 1896 have developed into the largest sporting event in the world today.

The Importance of Sport Today

The Greatness of Sport

One could mention a variety of statistical values to show the size and importance of sport. I will limit myself to a few numbers.

In terms of the global importance of sport, 207 of about 239 nations (the number of recognized nations varies) were represented by their athletes at the last Olympic Summer Games in Rio de Janeiro.

In terms of the worldwide interest in sports, a total of over 8 billion viewers watched all the 2014 World Cup games in Brazil on television, with 410 million tuned in to the final alone. In Germany, 35 million people, 40% of the population, watched, setting a new record for a TV program.

In relation to the media in Germany, if one looks at the TOP 10 TV programs in Germany, in terms of viewing figures, only five of the TOP 10 sports programs are broadcast in the odd years while ten of the TOP ten are shown in the even years, as the Olympics, the World Cup, and the European Football Championship take place in the even years.

In terms of economic power, in Germany, the current total for active sports is 80 billion EUR in expenditure. This amount does not include expenses for interest in sport such as tickets, travel expenses, magazines, books, or Pay TV licenses to watch sport.

The Motives for Sport

The motives for people to participate in sports are very complex and different. They depend on whether we are talking about interest in sports, occasional health sports, hobby sports, or competitive or high-performance sports. We will come back to these distinctions later in the strategies. Of course, the motives for children in the bush of Burundi are different from those for senior citizens in a small German town, families in a Chinese provincial metropolis, or young people in the deepest winter of Alaska. Mentality, origin, age, and culture play a major role.

If you look at the current study by the Zukunftsinstitut Frankfurt (Future Institute Frankfurt), you gain a different insight into the motives for sport and, above all, the expectations of sport. This study, "Sportivity," examined sport as a model of postmodern society and found that sport addresses seven needs of modern societies:

- Entertainment
- Self-presentation
- Compensation
- Health maintenance
- Self-expansion
- identity building
- Thrill

The Impact of Sport

Here, too, one cannot generalize and must differentiate greatly due to the differences in this world. In Western society and culture, the effect is particularly evident in the report of the German Federal Government:

> Hardly anything brings people together as much as sport and play, overcoming the barriers of different languages, skin color and religion almost effortlessly.

> As the central content of our everyday culture, sport encompasses all social classes, genders and age groups and thus acts as a connecting link for people from different social groups. For many it is the most popular form of leisure activity, conveys joie de vivre and thus contributes to a better quality of life (10th Sport Report of the Federal Government, p. 10).

Other proven effects of sport continue to manifest themselves:

- the improvement of the learning ability of children and young people
- the social integration of people on the margins of society, refugees, prisoners and drug addicts
- Physical, mental and emotional health.
- In other parts of the world this is defined differently, but sport has its impact, locally, nationally and globally.

Mission of the Municipality

To go into the strategies for social change, we need to recall briefly the mission of Jesus to His church. It is complex and happens on several levels. I would like to reduce it to three dimensions.

The Discipleship Call: "Make disciples and teach them..."

The so-called Great Commission is clear and unambiguous. Jesus gives the baton to his disciples and to us: "As the Father has sent me, I also send you." Thus, the strategy is inherent in the commission exactly as Jesus Christ understood his mission, which means specific attitudes and behaviors.

Close to the People

Jesus came into this world; he did not save mankind by preaching from heaven: "We saw his glory," "We have seen him, we have heard him, we have touched him." Jesus himself says in John 7, "He who believes in me, from his body will flow rivers of living water." We must ask, "Are we close enough to the people so that they can get wet?"

Serving, not Dominating

In Matthew 20:25ff Jesus says that He came to serve and not to rule and he washed the disciples' feet—not their heads. What an example and model he provides for us and our topic. It is important to work out how we can serve people in sports to change culture.

Saving, not Judging

In John 12:47 Jesus gives us another challenge. In his first mission as Messiah, Jesus came to save, not to judge. No doubt, he will also be the judge. We often confuse these two: we judge and then ask Jesus to save. He gives us the mandate to save and forbids us to judge.

Dependence on the Father

Perhaps Jesus's most important strategy was the intimacy and connectedness to the Father. He would not and could not do anything without the Father (John 5:19.30). From this dependence he experiences the great freedom and sovereignty to act in different ways. Whether a person is a criminal, prostitute, king, religious leader, or employee, he meets everyone confidently, willing to serve, help, give direction, and liberate.

The Mandate of the Diakonie

"Break the bread with the hungry . . ." This phrase sums up the mission of social work. Unfortunately, in the history of the church, mission and social help have too often been pitted against each other, but the one does not work without the other, nor is one a means to an end for the other. If you only want to help so that someone is converted, then you should leave it alone. When another person becomes an object of conversion, instead of being the subject of our love and service for him, we are not only no longer in the mission of Jesus, but we are also subject to an enormous pressure to perform, which makes us ill.

The Mandate for Social Change—the Cultural Mandate

How else can we understand the word of salt and light if not that we also have to develop a power of change. When we pray "Your kingdom come," we are relating not only to eternity, but also to today's reality; we want to build the kingdom of God already here and not enjoy it only in the future. This multi-faceted commission of Jesus to His church must now be interpreted and broken down, even into the world of sports. The world of sports cries out for help and needs mission, social help, and change.

If one looks at the grievances in the world and asks oneself which topics are independent of continent or skin color, some major problems become apparent that are similar worldwide:

- Lack of morals and values
- Decay of marriage, family, and education
- Corruption
- Looking for alcohol, drugs, etc.

If one compares "shall and is" in the worldwide church of Jesus to the mission described above, there is still much to do.

The Importance of Sport for the Christian Community

The Perception of Sport

The other day I attended a seminar in a church to look at the issues of sport and church. This church is located in small rural village with 900 inhabitants. At the beginning of the seminar, I asked what kind of sport they were familiar with in this village. The first responses were answers like "There is no sport here" or others similar to it. I then asked the 30 or so participants to think about this question, write it down, and respond on paper. When we collected the notes, they had identified 27 sports being practiced in this village. When asked about sports facilities and location, their response was similar, but in the end, they named 13 places in this village where sports were practiced. The seminar got a new direction and dimension because we realized that the topic of sport has a relevance.

After speaking at church services of various denominations, my experience is often similar to this quotation of the pastor: "You do a good job, but in our village we have not much access to sports." I replied, "Oh, that surprises me. What does your Monday newspaper look like?" "I don't understand. What do you mean?" "Well, does your Monday paper look different from the other days?" "Well, yes, Mondays are always much thicker because of many pages of local sports with all the results and charts."

These responses clearly show that our perception is often related to our interests—we don't pay attention to what doesn't interest us. Why do church leaders show so little interest in sports, particularly in Europe?

The Problems from the Church in the Field of Sport

This chapter is not the place for theological discussion, but we have to acknowledge that there are still quite a few regions in the world where great tension exists between the Christian congregation and sports; therefore, Christians do not see sport as their responsibility. Let me mention two issues.

The Sunday Question

There is the competition on Sunday morning between worship and sports. No question, Christians need fellowship, Christians need places and a framework for ministering to one another by encouraging, admonishing, and exhorting others in their spiritual walk toward maturity in Christ. Acts 2 states the core elements of Christian community: prayer, teaching, the Lord's Supper, and fellowship. In our Christian culture, Sunday morning is the traditional time for worship and fellowship. There are good reasons for that. The New Testament teaches, however, that there are no times and places more holy than others. In contrast to the Old Testament, we do not need a temple, nor a Sabbath, nor a mediating priest to be in fellowship with God. We can come directly to the Father as his child at any time and in any place in the world. This great truth does not yet solve the pragmatic questions in this field of tension, but it frees us from a dogmatic and uptight approach. When we are concerned about people, their need for help and salvation when the focus is on ministering for Jesus, solutions to pragmatic problems can always be found.

Not Being Unequally Yoked with Unbelievers

A misunderstanding of the phrase "in the world but not of the world" is more present than one might think. Paul exhorts and encourages us to think differently, to have a different attitude, a different worldview, and new values, which are also possible with Christ in us. Jesus himself and the writers of the New Testament letters do not speak of social distancing from non-Christians, quite the contrary. The first Christians, of whom historians say that they changed the world, had the courage to go to the remote hospitals of plague patients and help them, even if it cost their own lives. "Social distance" is important for fighting the Corona pandemic, but it is not the strategy for changing the world.

Existing Strategies

Target Group Oriented Strategies

Sports Ministry Map

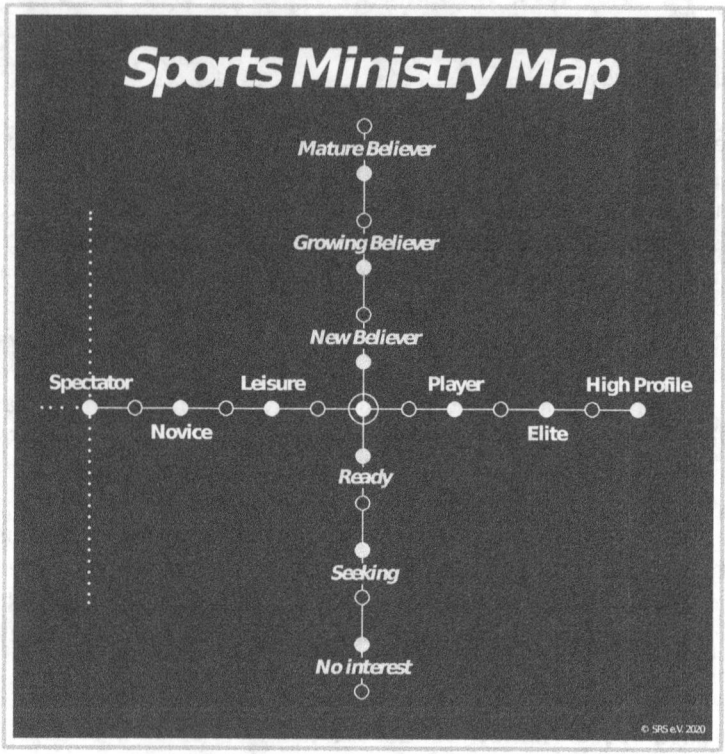

The sports ministry map is a simple diagram with two axes placed on top of each other. The horizontal axis shows us a person's mentality and intensity on the topic of sports. Billions of people are enthusiastic about sports and follow sports in stadiums and in the media. In the case of sports broadcasts, the viewing figures rise to the highest level. Many people engage in sports because they are good for them and there are health benefits. Still others do sport because they enjoy biking, volleyball, swimming, or soccer. There comes a point, however, where people think and act differently due to their createdness: they want to train, they want to get better, they want to measure themselves, they want competition. Here we are in competitive sports, then in high-performance sports, and finally among the world's elite.

The vertical axis stands for our relationship with God. From the bottom upwards, we have descriptions of a completely convinced atheist, followed by the spiritually interested person, the really searching person, and then comes the point of a clear decision for Jesus Christ and the process of growth to maturity in Christ as described in the New Testament.

If we place the horizontal and vertical axes on top of each other, we get four quadrants, each of which describes a very different target group in sports. Of course, the squares have different sizes. The horizontal axis is not central, but very far to the right in terms of the quantity of athletes involved, and the vertical axis of faith is unfortunately very high up and not central, let alone at the bottom. The graph helps to understand that we cannot generalize in the field of sports. Individual and targeted models, methods, tools, and speeches are needed to reach and change everyone individually in his or her situation.

Sports Enthusiasts and Fans

For this target group, the primary approach lies in the media. Whether it is from books, video clips, autograph cards, magazines, or blogs, fans like to see, hear, and read about their stars and the athletes they admire. The interest often goes beyond the pure sport. They want to know the interests of the athlete, what he does in his free time, how he thinks and what he believes.

Since the turn of the millennium, "public viewing events" have been particularly popular when major team sports events such as a soccer World Cup are taking place. All over the world, churches and Christian communities have opened their doors for such low-threshold offerings. Sports associations, such as FIFA, have offered non-profit broadcasters the transmission free of charge, unlike commercial providers. The live broadcasts are supplemented by entertaining program elements from the local community and culinary offerings. In Germany alone, around 3,000 churches and communities took advantage of this opportunity during the 2006 World Cup. Many of them have made use of this form of event regularly since then. These offers are supplemented by printed testimonies from Christian publishing houses and missionary societies.

Children and Youth

If you want to influence the future or even want to determine its outcome, you need children and young people. This insight is not new. As with all target group-oriented models and strategies, it is about the respective target group, in this case the children themselves, and not about the strategy as an end in itself. Nevertheless, the strategic point of view is not wrong; on the contrary, it is important. It must only suppress the subjective motivation, shaped by unconditional love. "KidsGames" are an outstanding format of all children's missionary models. The American Eddie W. an American friend wrote in July 2020,

> 20 years ago, God did something that was unprecedented and counter intuitive which opened the doors for sports as a means of ministry. Churches and agencies in the Western world accepted sports as a means of ministry and missions. But for the other 80% of the world, then 5 billion people, the church seldom accepted sports for ministry. In fact, the church was antagonistic. God took the unprecedented idea of children, sport, and experiential Bible lessons and KidsGames was born in the Middle East. When millions of children accepted Christ and hundreds of thousands of churches in that 80% part of the world were part of KidsGames, their eyes were opened to serving athletes, coaches and sport in the church and to many forms of sports ministry.

Kidsgames is a multi-day, cooperative, sports-oriented, Bible-based, and worldwide initiative for children aged 6-14 years.

It is of interest to note that the first "kidsgames" took place in Cairo, Egypt, a Muslim Country. These games were inspired by the Olympic Games and were successful, thus giving Christianity a great boost. The games were held in the largest stadium in Cairo, and many of the events were held in local venues around the city. Both the opening ceremonies and the closing ceremonies were a big success.

The successful concept multiplied all over the world in a short time. In Madagascar, for example, only three years later 200,000 children were able to take part in the kidsgames. The program contents are translated into about 50 languages.

High Profile Athletes

A few years ago a colleague and I spontaneously visited the captain of a Bundesliga soccer team, the highest league in Germany. We had to make a detour due to an accident on the highway, so we came through the place where this player lived. We knew from the media that he had suffered a serious injury, but we had had no contact with him until then. It was not difficult to find his home. When we rang the doorbell, his wife opened the door and kindly asked us inside. We talked for a while, tried to encourage him, and gave him a Bible. I will never forget his response when I said goodbye:

"You know, I've been injured for 12 weeks, but you're the first to ask about me. No one from the club, none from the media, none from the fans."

The German talent of the century Sebastian Deisler ended his career completely and unexpectedly at the age of 27. He played for the German champions Bayern München, was on the national team, and was the idol for millions of people. In an interview, he said,

> Soccer is very much about status, power, ego, and title. The business took possession of me too quickly. I've never had time to grow, never time to grow up. I was wearing a mask, inside I rebelled against it. But I felt so ridiculous. I was sitting in my apartment, I was known all over Germany. I had reached the top and there was a Mercedes in front of the door. Nothing of that made me happy. I asked myself: was that it? I was very unhappy.

Probably the most valuable aspect when dealing with elite athletes is the question of identity. Who am I? What makes me valuable? The number of fans cheering me? The sum of the last transfer proceeds? The number of titles or medals?

Former top gymnast and paraplegic Samuel K wrote in his book the following statement and brought it to the point:

> That's how I imagine God to be: He loves me because I am—that's all I have to do or accomplish. The vast majority of people seem to live by that principle:
>
> > Doing-Having-Being.
>
> In other words, they are doing something: working, building, creating, achieving, earning and so on.
>
> > Then they have something: money, a degree, a doctorate, influence, success, well-behaved children, a house and so on. Only then are they something: they are someone, because they have done something and achieved something. They measure their value by their achievements. A principle with which one can live well for 102 years and also become happy. But what if the house burns down, someone else gets the job or the ravages of time gnaw at the beautiful appearance?
>
> > I have made the experience that I am happier if I turn that around:
>
> > > Being-Having-doing.

We are valuable simply because we are. This gives us something, a value, and from this we can do something. If we stop doing something, we'll still be somebody in the end. Maybe that is why it is called "human being" and not "human doing."

In the series of target group-oriented strategies, we could continue with the officials, the referees, the Paralympic athletes, the physiotherapists and all groups of people in sports, but I want to introduce other approaches to strategies.

Event-oriented Strategies

Many missionary strategies can be designed in the context of sports events. The network report "Major sports events host partnerships" describes how hundreds of congregations, organizations, and Christian works have come together in the past 20 years and reached millions of fans and athletes with the gospel in major events like world championships, Olympic Games, or World Cups.

Strategies for Events

In addition to the great missionary and societal changing potential, sport also has a diaconal effect. Whether in the slums of Africa, the outskirts of the war-torn Syrian city of Aleppo, the refugee camps in Greece, or many other places around the world, sport is the only remaining joy, community, and relationship-changing chance on a hopeless day. I was particularly impressed by Julian B. As a swimmer, he was a multiple Olympian for Sri Lanka. After the devastating tsunami in 2004, the children in Sri Lanka were traumatized. They no longer dared to go into the water and therefore did not learn to swim. Julian then set up a national swimming school under the name "Swim Lanka" and was able to give the children new hope and perspective.

Influencer Strategies

Sports offer a special opportunity for individuals to become prominent influencers and to shape an entire generation. I would like to introduce three influencers.

Trainer

How to deal with children and adolescents also applies to any other group in sports; therefore, the first interest of the trainer is, of course, his own person and his salvation. At this point, however, I would like to examine the strategic possibility of a trainer. The role of a trainer is perhaps the greatest sustainable way to change a society. To support this thesis, let me introduce two facts. First, a great need exists for trainers, especially in the children's and youth area. There are 91,000 sports clubs in Germany and almost every one lacks coaches. Second, trainers are very special. For children of certain ages, the trainer is more influential than teachers, pastors, and sometimes even more than parents. The trainer is the hero. He helps the child to become better in areas where he or she would like to be successful. The belief that the coach shapes is sociologically undisputed. The question remains: is it positive or negative? Is the adolescent encouraged by or at risk from the trainer?

If someone comes to the pastor with the question of whether he or she should become a trainer in the sports club because it is particularly important to him or her, many pastors will answer, "I think it's good that God has given you a heart for children, but we urgently need someone for **our** kids program. The sports club will find someone."

If we were to make a paradigm shift here and started as churches to support young coaches, to bless them and send them specifically out to do this ministry, in the process of sending thousands of Christian coaches into the world of sports, we would change our society sustainably. Children would have role models and would themselves become value carriers of our society. The believing former European boxing champion Alexander Dimitrenko once said, "Without my trainer I would have become an extreme criminal."

Officials

The most powerful sports association in the world is FIFA. It has been experiencing a major crisis in recent years. Corruption, abuse of power, manipulation, and fraud are dominant headlines. A good friend of mine, the devout former President of the English Football Association, Vice President of UEFA, and member of the Executive Committee of FIFA, told me with dismay that he was rejected by a Christian fellowship because he was never there. What wasn't seen is that he was the only one in the Christian community in England who had a direct influence on FIFA's president and officials. Instead of offering him fellowship and prayer, they just wanted to offer him guest member status. What a mistake in brotherly dealings and what a mistake in strategic thinking.

Top Athletes

We have considered top athletes as a target group. Now I would like to underline the opportunities that believing athletes have in making a difference and changing a society in the long term.

The ice hockey professional Paul Kobylarz switched from the New Jersey Devils to the Swedish professional league. After completing his career, he graduated from Bible school, became pastor of a church, and volunteered to set up a national sports missionary work. Despite being in his mid-30s, he still played in the local hockey club in the third division when time allowed it. One Sunday in Advent, he was once again asked to help out in the first team for an important championship game. The current community situation particularly challenged Paul on this day, so he could be there only for the last third. When he began to play, his team was 0: 4 behind, but Paul scored five goals in the last third. His team won and the Swedish media had a sensational story: "Pastor comes in and scores five goals." This report was also read by the King of Sweden, and since that day, Paul, together with the king, has been able to distribute Bibles to the athletes at the official World or European Championships on Swedish soil.

There are other professional teams around the world that are deliberately led as Christian associations, whose players are committed Christians and, far beyond the sport, involve themselves in their communities as well as Missions. These groups sometimes have to make critical decisions. Often times, faithful top athletes are put under pressure to be successful so that the gospel has even more open doors. Doing so is dangerous and not in line with the gospel. Can God use an athlete's gold medal to be honored by this athlete's testimony and people to believe? Definitely. Does God need the gold medal in order to be honored and thereby people bring to faith? No, God is not dependent on a gold medal.

Strategies through Change Processes

The strategies described so far have, depending on a particular culture, different possibilities and effects. The value system of the postmodern societies of the West is completely different from the value system of the emerging powers like China or India or of the economically developing regions of Africa.

Value Campaign

Everyone has them. Everyone needs them. Whether we like it or not, whether we are aware of it or not, they are simply there: values. Values shape what we do and our actions shape our values. They determine life and thus extend to the last corner of society, to our dealings with wealth and poverty, with time, work, stress, and leisure, with sexuality and relationships, with friends, family, and neighbors, with power, control. and trust. They classify what we perceive as right and wrong, as good and bad, as valuable or without value; all of these are based on our personal concept of values.

Values are not tangible. They cannot be checked or evaluated because they are individual ideas in the minds of people. It is only through the actions of a person do values become visible and can be experienced. As already described, socially recognized and central values can be conveyed in a unique way in sport. Politics, education, science, and economy all clearly recognize the important role of sports. They use the socially indisputable relevance of sports in a variety of ways; sport connects people regardless of age, religion, skin color, or social status and allows them to attain new goals.

The decay of values and the degeneration due to a lack of values are particularly striking in the Western world. In Germany, the Christian sports organization SRS launched a value campaign in sports in 2017 in order to promote and motivate an opposing development. The SRS values campaign in the fields of youth sport, integration, and trainer forum would like to portray and multiply key values based on those exemplified by Jesus Christ. This campaign has resulted in more than 20 projects and models being adopted at various locations.

The Global Strategy—Locally through the Community and Teams

All of the strategies described above already exist, have been tried and tested, and are constantly multiplying. They are known under the name ReadySetGo, summarized at the website ReadySetGo.ec. Thousands of sports missionaries, pastors, and youth missionaries support this initiative with their collective experiences and models. The aim of the "global movement" network is to reproduce it and carry it on. All materials are license-free and presented primarily in this form so that many may simply use it. "Copy, right?" is the philosophy. Everyone should use it.

But who are all? All the previous thoughts, strategies, and needs flow into the most important strategy. Jesus himself founded and specified it—the local church. Compared to the immensity of the world of sports and the mission of Jesus, Christian sports organizations and sports missionary works could still employ thousands of sports missionaries and it would be a mere "drop in the bucket." Only if the local church of Jesus and his teams discover and implement the responsibility for sport, the possibility through sport, and the potential in sport can the world of sport be changed, and with it, society. Sport makes it clear: the world is crying for a change from corruption, violence, manipulation, and doping. We Christians know the one who is the only one who guarantees real change. Now it's up to us to pass this baton on.

Conclusion

It is necessary to inform, motivate, and qualify the body of Christ worldwide about these strategies. Four different approaches are needed.

The Local Church

Sport always takes place locally, on the spot. The church of Jesus is the best structure worldwide to act locally; therefore, the local Christian church must recognize the possibilities in and through sport, realize the potential and implement the most diverse models. Just as there are staff members for child and youth work, women's work, work with senior citizens, integration and family work, there is a need for women and men to work in the area of sport. There is a need for sports advisors and sports missionaries.

The Associations of Municipalities

In addition, municipal associations must promote the topic and tap into resources. The themes and strategies must be integrated into the annual meetings, conferences, and pastors' meetings.

The Bible Colleges

The next generation of pastors and leaders in church and ministries must be trained in a targeted manner. Knowing Hebrew and Greek is important, but it is just as important to know and be able to communicate in the current languages of this world. The language of sport is universal and independent of age, gender, skin color, education, and social status. It is not a question of whether students at Bible schools, seminaries, and theological institutions are interested in sport, but whether they are people oriented.

Media

Just as important is that the Christian media, books, magazines, digital and social media, and radio and television stations communicate the themes, models, and personal stories and inspire others.

The success of these efforts requires teamwork. Let us start today.

Chapter 10: Technology

Dr. Walker Tzeng

Walker Tzeng is the Executive Director of the World Evangelical Theological Institute Association (WETIA), a non-profit service and research organization supporting a network of approximately 400 evangelical theological colleges and seminaries with education technology resources. This includes an E-Learning and Student Database platform called EdBrite, which he created in 2014 for theological seminaries in the majority world. He has also been involved with the World Evangelical Alliance (WEA) for nearly 15 years, currently serving as Executive Director of its IT Commission.

After graduating from the University of California Los Angeles (UCLA) with a Bachelor of Science degree, Dr. Tzeng earned his Master of Divinity and Doctor of Ministry at Olivet University. He has been involved in education technology and higher education for nearly 20 years, since getting started as Chief Operating Officer of Olivet University. He has or is currently serving in leadership or board roles for the Association for Biblical Higher Education (ABHE), the National Association of Evangelicals (NAE), the Global Great Commission Network (GGCN), and City Vision University.

He and his wife Julia are based in San Francisco, CA, where they are raising three boys. In San Francisco, he is Senior Pastor of Gratia Community Church and University Chaplain of Olivet University.

A Biblical-Theological Approach to Transforming Technology

Introduction

How technology has changed the world is obvious to anyone who became an adult by the turn of the century. Life before the turn of the century meant talking to friends on a landline phone, reading the paper to find out the news, going to work or class, and visiting the library to conduct research on a topic. Now, we have a plethora of mobile phones, social media applications, video conferencing, online news, online classes, and a sea of information, all available at our fingertips.

How did it all change so quickly? Simply speaking, the advent of the Internet triggered exponential growth in the pace of technology development, the technology industry, and the use of technology across the globe. This exponential growth is not unique to this era; technology cycles have always occurred throughout history, as Moore's Law has shown.[113] The difference is that where technology cycles previously took millennia, then centuries, then decades, now they take only a few years and or even just months and can be seen by anyone of us in our day to day lives.

These changes make one wonder about some things. If mankind had not fallen in the Garden of Eden, would God have allowed us to reach this stage in technological development much faster, without the millennia of suffering and death? When His Kingdom comes on earth, will we develop technologies even faster, beyond imagination, without the hindrance of sin? These are the types of questions about which Christians involved in technology think.

For the better part of the past two decades, I have been working with Christians around the world in using technology for their ministries. Through this time, I have come to view technology in a positive way, as a good gift of God and a tool to better accomplish the task of the Kingdom; however, I have to accept that not everyone takes my view. Technology was used in history in many bad ways, and that misuse continues today. Nonetheless, my view has always been that our good, loving God in His providence is guiding history in a righteous, true way and that good or bad technology will ultimately be judged under His authority. We can, therefore,

---

[113] Gordon E. Moore, "Cramming More Components onto integrated circuits," *Electronics*, Volume 38, Number 8 (April 19, 1965).

positively accept much of the technology we see as tools to further God's Kingdom. Overcoming the "mountain" of technology is critical for the development of a mega-strategy of evangelism in this era or in any era.

In this chapter, I will be exploring three areas of technology: using technology in evangelism, distinguishing truth amidst a sea of disinformation, and finally, developing a Kingdom worldview for Christians in technology. For each area, I will look at the theological, biblical, and historical background for why each area is important, consider what is being done in each area, and put forward a mega-strategy for that area.

Technology in Evangelism: Background

Many definitions can be found for the word *technology*, but I want to consider a definition applicable to our discussion. For the purposes of evangelism, I would like to propose a definition for *technology* as any tool that allows humans to extend our reach within the boundaries of our current state of finitude, namely time and space. Others have alluded to this definition of the word *technology* as they have observed the impact of technology through the centuries. When Samuel Morse invented the telegraph, one of the first its observers wrote, "Time and space has been completely annihilated."[114] C.S. Lewis noted, "For magic and applied science alike the problem is how to subdue reality to the wishes of men."[115]

The fact is, humans are finite, while God is infinite. As the Lord said through the Prophet Isaiah, "'For my thoughts are not your thoughts, neither are your ways my ways,' declares the Lord. 'As the heavens are higher than the earth, so are my ways higher than your ways and my thoughts than your thoughts.'" (Isaiah 55:8-9). As this verse shows, the Bible teaches us that our Creator completely transcends us, which means He transcends the limits of our reality. Augustine of Hippo surmised that time itself is an objective reality that God created and believed that only the creation is bounded by time.[116] Our reality may be limited by the finitude of time and space, but a variety of technologies have allowed humans to extend our reach within the boundaries of these limits.

---

[114] Rebecca J. Rosen, "Time and Space Has Been Completely Annihilated," The Atlantic, February 14, 2012, accessed July 1, 2020.

[115] C. S. Lewis, *The Abolition of Man* (New York: Collins, 1978), 46.

[116] Augustine of Hippo, *Confessions*, Book IX, translated by J. G. Pilkington, originally published in *The Early Church Fathers and Other Works* (Edinburgh: Wm. B. Eerdmans, 1867).

It was the technology of writing that first allowed our Biblical ancestors to take God's word from oral traditions to written scriptures and to translate them into Greek for the whole world to receive. This is God's word, originally spoken at a certain time and place in history and gathered together with other recordings over thousands of years for any other person in any time or place to read. When the Apostle Paul was confined in jail, God's word overcame the limits of time and space of Paul's solitary prison to reach all of us who read those letters today.

A look at Paul's mission strategy makes it clear that he went to the largest cities in order to spread the name of Jesus more widely and rapidly. Why were the largest cities important? They were centers of commerce because technology and civilization had advanced to reach a global scale with the empire of Rome. Again, technology helped overcome previous time and space limits.

It was a synergetic moment in history when Luther's 95 Theses could be widely published as a result of the invention of Gutenberg's printing press, the first mass communication technology. This invention allowed the Reformation leaders and their followers to gather around the simple idea of returning to the Scripture and accepting justification by faith through grace alone. Without the technology of the printing press overcoming previously existing time and space limitations, it would have been much more difficult for the Reformers to overcome the power of the institution of the Catholic Church.

Seafaring technology allowed the Gospel to cross oceans into the New World. Further advancements in travel by land, ocean, and air continue to spread the Gospel to unreached people groups.

Recording technology is perhaps the clearest example of technology allowing the Word of God to be preached across time and space. A person can now go online and listen to full sermons that Billy Graham preached decades ago. No longer are those sermons limited to the thousands present in those large stadiums; anyone in any time or place can hear his preaching. These advances just go to show how the grace of the Holy Spirit has no boundaries in time and space.

History has shown that the work of God's Kingdom has advanced as Christians have utilized whatever technology is available for evangelism. The technologies that transcend time and space have advanced the Gospel beyond former limits. Indeed, we must look at all technologies and discern how a particular technological tool can be used to save souls.

Technology in Evangelism: Global Strategies Today

Christians have been at the forefront of innovation for centuries. Alfred North Whitehead and J. Robert Oppenheimer, both renowned philosophers and scientists of our era (but not Christians themselves), have said that modern science was born out of the Christian worldview.[117] Although the Catholic Church as an institution has well-known conflicts with innovation, many renowned technology and science innovators came from a biblical worldview. Some of these include Blaise Pascal (1623-1662), Sir Isaac Newton (1642-1727), and Samuel Morse (1791-1872), which shows us that it is possible for technological and scientific innovation to develop out of those with a Christian worldview. At the present time, however, the realm of technology and science is almost completely secularized. Still, there are Christians today with an innovative mindset who are utilizing a wide variety of technologies in evangelism across the globe. Many of these organizations go under the radar since they are not gathering large in-person crowds like mega churches do. Instead, they reach individuals at any time and any place with the good news of Jesus Christ, including hard to reach places around the globe.

Global Media Outreach

The mission of Global Media Outreach (GMO) is to "share Jesus online in every country of the world and help believers grow their faith using cutting-edge technology."[118] It accomplishes this goal by placing ads across the Internet and social media, reaching people who are seeking answers about God. GMO then presents the Gospel across its vast array of websites and other media. Seekers are given the opportunity to pray to accept Jesus into their life as their Lord and Savior, which includes a click of the "yes" or "no" button. Either option will lead them to connect with an online missionary who will further their discipleship with a variety of biblical resources and guide them to a local church.

To date, GMO has presented the Gospel to over 120 million unique IP addresses, and over 16 million individuals have clicked "yes," indicating a decision to follow Christ. Languages in which GMO reaches out include Arabic, Chinese, English, Farsi, French, Hindi, Portuguese, Russian, Indonesian, Spanish, Turkish, and Urdu. Many of the people whom GMO reaches

---

[117] Francis A. Schaeffer, *How Should We Then Live* (Old Tappan: Revell, 1976), 132.

[118] Global Media Outreach, accessed July 1, 2020, https://globalmediaoutreach.com/.

are in the hardest to reach part of the world, places where clicking "yes" on an Internet browser may be the only way to indicate a decision for Christ.

Internet Churches

Congregations gathering on the Internet do so at varying degrees. At the fully immersive end of the spectrum, Virtual Reality Church gathers on the Altspace VR social platform where congregants attend from home using their own virtual reality technology headsets. Congregants are represented by avatars and can virtually attend services at their mega church campus and have fellowship in their virtual social gathering places.[119]

Internet Churches also gather in virtual worlds like Second Life and gaming environments like Roblox. These churches are accessible through any computer. Again, congregants are represented by avatars. The Robloxian Church, which exists literally within the game of Roblox, preaches the Word of God mostly to teenagers and young adults who play the game.[120]

Churches with an Internet Presence

Many larger churches have a strong Internet presence with their own church platforms. These include Church of the Highlands, North Point Community Church, and Saddleback Church. Life.Church has the largest congregation, with over 70,000 members, and it even offers its online platform for free for any church to use.[121] Since these churches have a strong, well-established infrastructure, they provide the potential for in person discipleship that internet evangelism and churches cannot provide.

Web and Social Media Efforts

A variety of efforts are being made to bring the Gospel using websites and social media. Many of these organizations use the same methods that the growing numbers of influencers use to grow their follower base. In fact, creating popular content is now being strategically studied. No longer are viral videos created spontaneously; instead, they are created intentionally. Ministries like The Bible Project are using many of these

---

[119] Virtual Reality Church, accessed July 1, 2020, https://www.vrchurch.org/.

[120] The Robloxian Church, accessed July 1, 2020, **Fehler! Linkreferenz ungültig.**.

[121] Life.Church, accessed July 1, 2020, https://www.life.church/.

methods, while GotQuestions.org uses search engine optimization strategies to answers questions people have about the Bible through their website.

Technology in Evangelism: Mega-Strategy for the Future

As long as technology keeps developing at the exponential pace it is now, the use of technology in evangelism will continue to expand. With every new technology that is developed, new churches and ministries will use that technology for evangelism. Some of these new methods may eventually eclipse traditional methods used now because these technologies will help us evangelize in hard to reach places where we could not share the Gospel before. They will also help us evangelize hard to reach people who ordinarily would not respond to the Gospel but may be more receptive over a new technology medium.

This inevitable expansion in the use of technology for evangelism will require new theology, specifically in the area of soteriology. We know this will happen because soteriological questions are already starting to arise from current use of technology in evangelism. For example, take the case of a person who visits GMO's pages and is asked to make a decision on accepting Jesus Christ. If he or she clicks "Yes," should we consider that person a Christian? Of course, the answer to that question is something known only to God; however, as Christian leaders, we also need a sense of our congregation and to whom we are preaching. Another example is the case of an individual who wants to be baptized in a church over virtual reality. Through a virtual headset, the individual is virtually asked baptismal questions by the minister, who is also wearing the virtual headset. Then the individual's virtual avatar is immersed in virtual "water." Is this considered a true baptism? Later in the service, the entire congregation, via their virtual avatar, eats the virtual "bread" and drinks the virtual "wine." Is this a holy communion given before God?

Now, project this setting into the future when we go beyond simple virtual reality technology and get into the realm of holographic projections with tactile technology. This development means that people from around the world can gather simultaneously in a virtual room; it looks and feels like they are actually interacting while gathered in person. The people are not physically gathered, but it looks and feels physical, so how do we deal with baptisms and holy communions?

Any mega-strategy for world evangelization must factor in the inevitable developments of technology and the theology needed in this new environment. Christian leaders should anticipate these developments, organize relevant theology, and be more accommodating to new methods and traditions that will happen in new technology mediums.

Also, as new technologies come out, Christian leaders should collaborate together on how the new technology can be used in a mega-strategy on evangelization. When we work separately, then we divide resources and duplicate work. Technology is well established as an industry where collaboration can happen easily. Take, for example, the many open source platforms that are widely used and developed together. Moodle, which was developed collaboratively, is an open source online education platform used by over one billion students.[122] Christian leaders must collaborate together and ask themselves how they can work together for the same vision of the Kingdom that we all have. We live in a world where 3.5 billion people own a smart phone, so how can we work together to get the Gospel on everyone's smart phone?[123] What collaborative strategies do we need for app development, marketing, community interaction, and more in order to accomplish this?

Any viable path to collaboration will need to use technology to mediate this collaboration; therefore, we need technology platforms to facilitate the collaboration among Christian leaders. A mega-strategy will not happen behind closed doors with a handful of leaders. It will happen in the open, on technology platforms that bring together churches, denominations, ministries, and companies.

It also will not be just one technology platform that brings everyone together. The key cultural mountains identified in this book have different needs for collaboration, so different types of platforms will need to be developed. Think about the difference between Facebook and LinkedIn or Twitter and Instagram.

Something that all these platforms have in common is that they will need to span time zones and language barriers. Technology tools will need to be primarily asynchronous, able to facilitate ideas and cooperation even when leaders are not awake at the same time. Artificial intelligence can be used to bring out the most important personalized content and help with

---

[122] Moodle, accessed July 1, 2020, https://moodle.org/.

[123] Statista, "Number of smartphone users worldwide from 2016 to 2021 (in billions)," accessed July 1, 2020, https://www.statista.com/statistics/330695/ number-of-smartphone-users-worldwide/.

translation issues. An example of one such platform that is being built for collaboration in missions is called "Connect." It is built by an organization of which I am a part, the Global Great Commission Network.[124] The platform has asynchronous tools to share discussion topics, news, events, prayer topics, and much more. The platform brings together mission agencies and ministries that are focused on discipleship and the work of the Great Commission, as the name implies.

Distinguishing Truth: Background

One of the primary advances that the Internet created was the advent of the information age. A flood of information on any subject or news item is available to almost anyone, anytime, anywhere. While this tool has advanced the acquisition of knowledge for all people, it has also created a major problem in terms of distinguishing truth.

The problem is particularly bad for news articles that now, quite appropriately, have the moniker of being "fake news." Every major news organization clearly has the political bias of the authors in their writing. It is now very difficult to find news articles that stick to succinct, clear, and obviously factual information because simple new articles do not draw any attention and the economics of news agencies require a political bias. Beyond that, most people are now getting their news through social media, which will always be qualified with personal commentary from the person sharing the news.

The current situation is that regular people can now acquire as much knowledge as they desire, but they then have the task of figuring out what information they can trust. How can regular people distinguish truth? How does anyone distinguish truth? This problem has faced mankind since the Fall of Adam.

Most people in the world would say that they can determine truth by adding up all the facts. This theory is why we have such a plethora of "fact-checking" websites that claim to reveal the truth. News organizations also write fact-checking articles that claim truth amidst their sea of fake news. In actuality, however, these fact-checking articles are very often biased and can also be called fake news themselves. The conclusion is that there is no method in the world that can give us definitive truth.

Christians can appreciate this method of adding up all the facts to find truth. Indeed, this is the premise for natural theology. Romans 1:20 says,

---

[124] Global Great Commission Network, accessed July 1, 2020, https://www.ggcn.org/.

"For since the creation of the world God's invisible qualities—his eternal power and divine nature—have been clearly seen, being understood from what has been made, so that people are without excuse." This verse means we can look out into the world and extract truth by looking at all the facts we see in the world because God created this world; however, natural theology is limited because humans are limited. As much fact-checking as we can do, we are still finite. Our finitude does not allow us to reach the infinite absolute truth of God. The same problem that fact-checking websites have is the same limitation Christians have in using natural theology, which is why revealed theology is needed. The Bible reveals God's absolute truth to us in an immediate way, so having a Biblical worldview is important. While we may not be able to interpret every news item and social political issue when it first appears, a Biblical worldview gives us the framework we need to begin to navigate it.

As Christians, we claim that truth, "logos," was fully incarnate in Jesus Christ, which means that more than a knowledge base of truth, our basis for truth is the person of Jesus. Our primary view of truth comes through the channel of faith and our personal relationship with Jesus, and then secondarily, it comes through knowledge. Faith and a personal relationship with Jesus allow us to interpret truth in the world in ways that the method of extraction and fact-checking cannot do since those methods rely solely on a knowledge base of truth.

Christianity has a long history of dealing with issues of truth based on the absoluteness of God. In the flood of information that has come through the advancement of technology and Internet, Christians remain best equipped. The revelation of the person of Jesus Christ and a Biblical worldview give us all we need to take hold of the mantle of truth in this world.

Distinguishing Truth: What is Being Done Today

The problem of truth amidst the flood of information and content is well recognized by the large technology companies. In particular, Facebook and Google have faced strong criticism from various ideological streams on their handling of information, especially fake news and misleading content.

The fact is that it is impossible to hire enough people to sufficiently filter the flood of information, news, and content on the Internet. Even if there were enough people, there would inevitably be bias and differences in how people would filter the information, which is why the large technology companies are building artificial intelligence technologies to automatically filter the information posted on their websites. However, artificial intelligence comes with its own set of problems. As people browse content on the Internet, what they will often notice is that related content appears right next to what they are looking at. This is artificial intelligence technology working to give more content and information about what they are interested in. The problem of truth comes in when artificial intelligence technology leads a person down a "rabbit hole" of content whereby he or she loses perspective on the bigger picture. For example, let's say a person starts looking at conspiracy theories on YouTube and finds a video that interests him or her. Looking at recommended videos of other people speaking about similar topics could get that person stuck into a rabbit hole of conspiracy theories, making him or her lose perspective.

In essence, artificial intelligence is creating self-perpetuating distorted worldviews in people. As they look at some content, the technology self-perpetuates them into a false sense of how things really are. The danger of artificial intelligence isn't robots taking over the world as in movies, but it is in people being swallowed up by false information, lies, and distortions.

While major technology companies are investing in artificial intelligence technologies related to truth in content, there are currently no major Christian efforts in developing this type of technology. Instead, Christians have focused on the overall impact of artificial intelligence as it relates to ethics, rather than how it relates to distinguishing truth. For example, the Evangelical Statement of Principles on Artificial Intelligence, endorsed by 65 evangelical voices, was made in 2019.[125] It is an excellent statement covering a wide range of ethical concerns, but it lacks any engagement in the area of truth.

One area where Christians are engaging in truth on the Internet is with online news. For example, The *Christian Post* and *Christian Today* are major online newspapers covering world news items from a Christian perspective. These news organizations use search engine optimization tools to make sure those searching on the Internet will find them when browsing a particular topic.

---

[125] The Ethics and Religious Liberty Commission of the Southern Baptist Convention, "Artificial Intelligence: An Evangelical Statement of Principle," April 11, 2019, accessed July 1, 2020, https://erlc.com/resource-library/statements/artificial-intelligence-an-evangelical-statement-of-principles/.

Distinguishing Truth: Mega-Strategy for the Future

For any mega-strategy of evangelism, revealing truth and being part of the flow of information in the world is crucial. Christians should consider this area a critical component for Kingdom work to penetrate into the world. If we overlook it, we run the risk of losing control over information and the world's perception on truth. Of course, truth will always be revealed, but Christians should be a part of revealing that truth.

First, as previously mentioned, no major Christian efforts are being made to develop artificial intelligence technologies related to filtering information on the Internet. Since it is people's first point of contact with information, it is very important area. It is also a massive undertaking to develop this type of technology, which is why most of this work is being done by the large technology companies. Nonetheless, there are steps that Christians should take now, including recognizing Christians who are in in the technology industry and are working in information artificial intelligence. Giving them a platform from which they can spur discussion can increase Christian exposure to this area and influence development of these technologies.

Second, Christians must endeavor to publish more good, holy, and true knowledge. The Bible keeps it simple; there is the knowledge of good and evil, which means there is good, holy, and true knowledge and then there is evil, depraved, and deceitful knowledge. Most information and news on the Internet is full of half-truths, using the same strategy as the Devil, which draws people into evil knowledge.

The battle for information is becoming a battle over which kind of information can overwhelm the other. Christians can be part of this battle of information by simply creating good, holy, and true content that comes from the Bible and a proper Biblical worldview. We can do this on the individual level on our social media postings with blogs, videos, prayers, and devotions. It can also be done on the institutional level with ministries focused on getting searchable content and news on the Internet. Therefore, developing communications technology is also very important. It is simple really. Technology is the best tool for communication. The world leverages technology to flood the world with secular information. Christians must do the same, leveraging technology to flood the world with the holy knowledge of the Lord.

Third, education remains important on all levels from primary schools to higher education. It is important to educate truth and to strengthen our next generation's ability to distinguish truth by teaching with a biblical worldview in education. In addition, efforts should be made for increased

A Biblical-Theological Approach to Transforming Technology

usage of technology in education. Allowing the next generation to become accustomed to learning on the Internet will help them in the future as they strive to create good, holy, true knowledge for the Internet.

Of course, there are many institutions that are using technology in education, and I want to highlight one institution that has been using online education for decades. South Africa Theological Seminary has over 3000 students in 80 countries.[126] The institution has faculty members all around the world, coordinated by a staff in Johannesburg. The institution is accredited by the South Africa ministry of education. They are an example of an evangelical institution using technology to educate the next generation to distinguish the truth.

Kingdom Worldview: Background

Perhaps the biggest challenge might be bringing Christians who are in the technology field over into working for the Kingdom. Inherent postmodern worldviews exist within the industry, making it difficult to embrace a Kingdom worldview. These inherent worldviews are by no means held by every Christian who works in technology, but they are still commonplace because of the nature of the industry. I will explain three postmodern attitudes, standing side by side in the technology industry, with which many deal, either knowingly or unknowingly.

The first is an attitude of scientism and the need to have empirically verifiable information. This is an attitude of needing provable data to understand reality. This attitude tends to be critical of anything invisible, intangible, or unproven. In the same way, technologists tend to proceed systematically, based on what is empirically provable first, before moving forward. For example, the "lean startup" method tries to get proof of a concept for a new technology by seeing if a lean, cheap beta-version of the technology works well before investing more time and money.[127] Likewise, Christians in technology want this empirically verifiable information before moving forward on anything, including Kingdom work.

The second is an attitude of existentialism, common across this postmodernist age, but especially manifested within the system of the technology industry. An existential attitude starts from the individual, finding his

---

[126] South Africa Theological Seminary, accessed July 1, 2020, https://www.sats.edu.za/.

[127] The Lean Startup, "The Lean Startup Methodology," accessed July 1, 2020, http://theleanstartup.com/principles.

or her own purpose, meaning, and structure in life. The technology sector responds well to the existential needs of an individual, by providing systematic career paths, while still giving plenty of autonomy. Based on certain certifications, qualifications, examinations, and experience, people move along fairly structured paths across the industry, irrespective of the company. In fact, technologists tend to move around companies quite a bit in their careers. This is also about a systematic way of looking at life—study at a good college, get a nice internship, graduate, find a nice company, get promoted, get an increase in salary, become financially stable, get married, buy a house, have children, retire, and travel. This is a common life path that individuals in technology hope to accomplish for themselves.

An outgrowth of the first two attitudes is, finally, a nominalist attitude. This attitude treats everything and everyone on a one to one basis, rather than seeing universal ideas and meaning. Engineers tend to focus on what is in front of them and what they can see, rather than on what is unseen. Innovative ideas and thoughts that break through to the community with interconnectedness are not common among engineers. Rather, it is the rare technology entrepreneur who breaks through the nominalist attitude and innovates the industry—these are exceptions from the typical engineer. Examples of those who break through include the big names in technology whom we would expect, including Steve Jobs, Bill Gates, and Elon Musk.

In a world without answers for post-modern worldviews, the technology industry has a comparatively good response. It is one thing to win over a person to Jesus Christ, but it is quite another thing to win over a Christian in the technology industry into giving his or her life for the Kingdom.

Kingdom Worldview: What is Being Done Today

Now that I have described the kind of worldviews with which Christians in technology must deal, the next step is to consider how they are being addressed. How can a Biblical-Kingdom worldview overcome these three attitudes? Unfortunately, there is not one resource or ministry dealing with these three attitudes together, side by side. Instead, various ministries are trying to address them individually, bringing the Bible or Kingdom purpose to believers and non-believers alike who have these worldviews.

Biologos

Biologos.org is a website started by Francis Collins, Director of the National Institutes of Health and a renowned biologist who led the human genome project.[128] Its mission is to let the church and the world see the harmony between the Bible and science. Generally speaking, the authors of the website are evangelicals who uphold the authority and inspiration of the Bible and at the same time affirm the evolutionary creation of God. For those growing up in the modern education system and the scientific worldview, theological writings like those seen in Biologos.org are critical for them to fully accept the truth of the Bible.

Global Great Commission Network (GGCN)

The late Dr. Ralph D. Winter wrote extensively about the need for a global-level association of mission agencies, which led to the organizing of a 2010 meeting in Tokyo, on the 100th anniversary of Edinburgh 1910.[129] Following the Tokyo 2010 meeting, the Global Great Commission Network was started to serve mission agencies, churches, and ministries that are striving to see all people discipled in our generation. I previously mentioned one of the key networking tools developed by GGCN called Connect. Connect is a secure technology platform for mission leaders around the world to connect, communicate, and collaborate together globally. Platforms like Connect are critical for Christians in using technology to go beyond their individual silos and to interact with organizations on a global level.

IT Degrees with a Biblical Worldview

Several institutions in biblical higher education offer technology degrees. The Association for Biblical Higher Education (ABHE) represents over 200 institutions of biblical higher education in North America. Their requirements for accreditation include an emphasis on a biblical worldview for all degree programs, including undergraduate degrees with at least 30 hours of core Bible/Theological studies.

Columbia International University, Prairie College, and Olivet University are a few examples of ABHE-accredited schools that offer technology degrees with a biblical basis. These programs are drastically different from getting a technology degree at a typical secular institution. Students matriculate through the programs by taking Bible-core classes and getting spiritual formation through Chapel and Christian service requirements,

---

[128] Biologos, accessed July 1, 2020, https://biologos.org/.

[129] Global Great Commission Network, "Dr. Ralph D. Winter and GGCN," accessed July 1, 2020, https://www.ggcn.org/dr-winter-ggcn/.

while also taking technology courses that will help them professionally in using technology to help build the Kingdom.

Apologetics Ministry Ravi Zacharias

Ravi Zacharias started his apologetics ministry in 1984, and it has grown to nearly 100 speakers around the world.[130] Throughout his ministry, Zacharias emphasized a coherent worldview that only the Bible gives satisfactory answers to four big questions: origin of mankind, meaning of life, morality, and destiny. The focus on worldview has had an impact on millions of Christians and non-believers who have grown up in a modern secular worldview and need answers from the Bible.

Kingdom Worldview: Mega-Strategy for the Future

Bringing Christians in technology into a Kingdom worldview is critical for a mega-strategy of evangelism. Many Christians are working in the technology field, but very few Christians are using their technological skills for the Kingdom. Perhaps the first step in discipleship is giving a convincing argument for the Kingdom to Christians who are well settled in their technology careers.

In the case of the scientism attitude, technologists have a desire for empirically verifiable information for the vision of the Kingdom. What data can the Church provide to show that we are making a tangible impact in building the Kingdom? How will we know when we reach the goal of building the Kingdom? Short of that, what are some key milestones and data points to show we are making progress? These are the kinds of questions that technologists with a scientific worldview will ask when they are making a decision to commit to a vision.

It is for this reason that I believe Dr. Ralph D. Winter was the most influential missiologist of the past century. From his engineering background, he revolutionized statistics and analytics in missions. Where before, mission agencies worked country by country, Winter popularized the term "unreached people groups." Instead of reaching each country, we need to find out which people groups are unreached and send missionaries to them. In essence, Winter reframed a tangible goal for the Kingdom and

---

[130] Ravi Zacharias International Ministries, accessed July 1, 2020, https://www.rzim.org/.

gave us a new way to make clear milestones to show we are making progress in the Kingdom. One of the ministries he started, The Joshua Project, still continues to track these statistics to this day.[131] If we are to win Christians to the idea of using technology to work for the Kingdom, continued expansion of this type of research and data analysis for the Kingdom is necessary to address this scientism attitude.

The existential attitude is a difficult one to tackle because of the systematic nature of the technology industry that gives clear outcomes for those who pursue this career path. For most Christians in technology, faith becomes a footnote. Their job gives them a seemingly clear purpose to create a nice tool, and creating that tool is a clear, tangible result that gives them meaning in what they are doing. When asked to compare that to their walk of faith, they ask, "What can the Kingdom do for me? What tangible purpose can I see for my life?"

Fortunately, technologists are a logical bunch, and the answer to these questions can be taken to their logical conclusion. Technology moves so quickly that any technology created now tends to become obsolete in a few years. Of course, technology developed now is meaningful because it contributes to future development; however, because how it will impact the future is unclear, it is common among engineers to feel empty when their technology becomes obsolete.

Several questions arise at this point: Does anything I do have any lasting value? What is the impact in future generations? What impact does it have for history? The evidence is clear about what the Bible teaches us. Earthly treasures rust and are destroyed, but heavenly treasures are eternal. What we are doing now during our short time on earth has lasting eternal impact only if it is for the Kingdom of God. Even the best technological tools will become obsolete in some years, but anything for the Kingdom of God will last eternally.

Our preaching, writing, and counseling with Christians in technology should all have this Kingdom framework in mind. What we are doing now has meaning only because it is dependent on the eternity of God. Technologists know better than anyone how finite we all are. As theologian Friedrich Schleiermacher said, we have an absolute dependence on God.[132] In other words, we depend on going towards an eternal purpose, and that purpose is the Kingdom. The Apostle Paul says in Romans 8:24 that "in this

---

[131] The Joshua Project, accessed July 1, 2020, https://joshuaproject.net/.

[132] Friedrich Schleiermacher, *The Christian Faith* (Edinburgh: T & T Clark, 1999), 33.

hope we were saved," meaning we depend on the hope of historical salvation. We are already saved by Jesus Christ, yet we depend on the eternal dream Jesus gave us for the Kingdom of God as we live. This is the clear position the Bible teaches us, but much of it is lost to people. So much preaching, writing, and counseling cedes to existentialism. Salvation in Jesus Christ has become escapism from the world, rather than impacting the world for the Kingdom. Any mega-strategy for evangelization must have clear Kingdom preaching in it.

Finally, the nominalist attitude needs to be overcome so Christians in technology can actually make a difference for the Kingdom in this world. As mentioned, nominalism limits the engineering worldview to only what is in front rather than what is beyond it all. So even if an engineer has some creativity bubbling up inside, it is limited by the nominalist worldview. Many technology entrepreneurs have been able to overcome the nominalist worldview and innovate technology as we see it, but what happens even to them is that their creativity runs up against the next level of nominalism. In many cases, even the most innovative technology entrepreneurs are just innovating within the social structures of the world. That is why we have so many social media companies.

Of course, from a secular perspective it is possible to keep finding more levels to break through, but Christians in technology have more to offer We have the Kingdom worldview from the Divine one, which means we have the infinite worldview that is not limited by the secular structures of the world. Christians in technology must realize this deep meaning of the position they are in and be able to lead. We must not stand behind and allow the secular world to lead us, but we must lead innovation from the front. I believe God gives us this potential because He gave us Jesus Christ and the cross and the dream of the Kingdom before us.

It is just as Luke wrote about Apostle Paul in the Book of Acts, saying, "Boldly and without hindrance, he preached the kingdom of God and taught about the Lord Jesus Christ (Acts 28:31)." That exhortation comes to all of us in technology to dream about the Kingdom and live boldly in Jesus Christ.

Chapter 11: Religion

Thomas K. Johnson

Thomas K. Johnson is a foremost evangelical voice on human rights and religious freedom, as well as a crucial participant in growing intrafaith and interfaith cooperation to address global issues. He is senior advisor to the World Evangelical Alliance (WEA) Theological Commission and Office of Intrafaith and Interfaith Relations. In 2016 he was named the WEA Special Envoy to the Vatican. In 2020 he became the WEA Special Envoy to Engage Humanitarian Islam.

As a philosopher, Johnson is known for writing on human rights and the universal (natural) moral law; as a theologian he is known for writing about God as Trinity, as well as the role of Christianity in society. Johnson has authored six books and more than 250 articles, essays, and book chapters in several languages. He has edited 25 books on religion in society, along with editing and translating numerous reports on human rights, religious freedom, and intrafaith relations. His best-known work is *Human Rights: A Christian Primer*, a standard evangelical resource since its publication in 2008. The 2016 edition was jointly released by the WEA and a Vatican-based institute.

After an informal Bible college in Germany and university and seminary degrees in the US, Thomas received a Fulbright/DAAD grant to research religious and philosophical responses to the Holocaust at the Universität Tübingen (Germany), leading to a Ph.D. in ethics and philosophical theology at the University of Iowa (USA). He pastored churches in the U.S.

and the former Soviet Union and taught philosophy or theology at eleven universities in nine countries, including the anticommunist European Humanities University in Minsk, Belarus (now exiled in Lithuania), Charles University in Prague, and Martin Bucer Seminary. He is board president of the Comenius Institute (Prague) and an ordained minister of the Presbyterian Church in America.

The Word of God and the Mountains of Culture

Introduction

Jesus' prayer for the Body of Christ: "They are not *of* the world any more than I am of the world. My prayer is not that you take them out of the world but that you protect them from the evil one. They are not of the world, even as I am not of it. Sanctify them by the truth; your word is truth. As you sent me into the world, I have sent them *into* the world" (John 17:14-18; emphasis added).

The 2006 mass murder of children in a school in Pennsylvania brought our attention to a Christian group that is very intentional about relating their faith to secular culture: the Old Order Amish.[133] This growing group of some 200,000 is mostly descendant from Swiss and Alsatian Anabaptists of the sixteenth century. From the beginning of their movement, they have said that true believers must be serious about holiness and that holiness means being separate from the world, even withdrawal from the world. This withdrawal relates to the State but also to technology and labor-saving devices. Some say selfish pride is the fundamental motivation for modern technology; therefore, serious believers must avoid self-serving technology. Instead, we should practice true humility, which means hard physical work with hand tools. Biblical verses they often quote include 2 Corinthians 6:17, "Come out from among them and be separate" and Romans 12:2, "Be not conformed to this world." According to the Old Order Amish, Christian holiness requires the formation of humble communities of true believers. This model of relating

---

[133] The reference is to the murder of four girls in the West Nickel Mines Amish School in Lancaster County, Pennsylvania, on October 2, 2006.

God's Word to cultures can be called *"Holy Withdrawal."*[134] Technology and government are the mountains of culture given prominence.

If we are serious about following Jesus, we should have moments when we think this way. I sometimes wonder why we Christians do not set up separate communities of faith, diligence, learning, and virtue. Why not withdraw from much of the world, even if I take my computer and mobile phone along? The reason why not is simply what Jesus said, "My prayer is **not** that you take them out of the world" (verse 15). Jesus has called us to be holy, not conformed to this world, but he wants us to be **in** the world. Jesus, it seems, recognized that the problem with worldliness is not something in the world *per se* but rather something deep inside us—our unbelief, pride, and ingratitude toward God. The sin inside us will follow us if we withdraw from the world into holy communities. If this assumption is true, the Amish may have misinterpreted the biblical text about "coming out and being separate."

An entirely different move in relation to culture was that of the so-called "German Christians" during the Nazi period. These serious Christians were enthusiastic supporters of Adolph Hitler; many thought they should support Hitler as a Christian duty. Their reasoning went something like this: God's law comes to us partly through the creation orders. Those creation orders include the people (*das Volk*) and the State; therefore, the laws of our people and of our State reflect the laws of God. In a time of economic and political chaos, God had, they thought, given a new leader who could restore the people and the State. Therefore, Christians should support Hitler enthusiastically.

I remember vividly the first time I read a book by a German Christian author. The book was in the old Germanic alphabet, which was always difficult for me. I read a few paragraphs and asked myself, "Did he really say what I think he said?" I went back and read it again. When I realized I had understood him correctly, I was appalled. I wondered, "How could believers support something so obviously evil"? Yet they thought they were following the Bible honestly.

Before we congratulate ourselves for not doing something so evil, we need to pause. The German Christians of the 1930s read the Bible through lenses coming from their culture, Nazi-colored glasses, which led to a mis-

---

[134] Some of the terminology used here comes from H. Richard Niebuhr, *Christ and Culture* (New York: Harper & Row, 1951). Building on Niebuhr's descriptions of historical models of Christian ethics, this essay attempts to move to prescriptions of models for evangelical missiology.

interpretation of the Christian faith that unduly supported their political/cultural bias. We can call it *accommodation* to secular culture—in this case Nazi culture; if you prefer, you might call it *compromise* with culture. In Jesus's terms, these believers were "of the world." Their story became famous because it reflected one of the worst tragedies of the twentieth century, but we can easily do something similar, even if our cultural agenda might seem more respectable.

My cultural/political sympathies might be described as "compassionate conservatism," but I must be careful not to say that God is a compassionate conservative; nor may I say that compassionate conservatism is God's will or read the Bible through these cultural lenses. Rather, compassionate conservatism is my part of the world, but I still am to be *in* the world but not *of* the world. I am called to bring the criticizing and reforming Word of God into that part of secular culture we call compassionate conservatism.

What does Jesus want in our relation to "the world"? In John 17 Jesus prays that God would help us to be "in the world" but not "of the world." Thereby he calls us to be "in" but not "of" the world, which means we should live in real living contact with the world, without having our identity, thoughts, priorities, feelings, and values controlled by the world. Instead, our identity, thoughts, priorities, feelings, and values should be continually sanctified by the truth—the living Word of God. As sanctified people, Jesus sends us into the world in a manner similar to how the Father sent Jesus into the world. We can probably summarize the central thrust of this biblical text by saying *Jesus wants us to be in the world but not of the world for a very specific purpose: He has sent us into the world as hearers and bearers of the Word.*

It may be helpful to define the term *culture*. Many of my university students spend time studying abroad, and they all come back talking about culture shock. When I then ask them what culture means, they usually say culture is "how we do things here," wherever "here" is. I then ask, "Is that all culture is?" In the following discussion, it usually becomes clear that culture is much more. Culture is also how we think about things, how we feel about things, and how we talk about things. Culture is what we have made out of nature, or in theological terms, culture is the entire human sub-creation developed from the creation as it came from the Father's hand. Culture includes customs, theories, ideas, practices, habits, role models, slogans, proverbs, and much more. It is all that we pass on from one generation to the next. Education is partly about passing a culture from one generation to another; all of us who received an education were

The Word of God and the Mountains of Culture

educated into a culture or cultures. It is now common to talk about participating in culture through its several dimensions or "mountains."

How do cultures relate to faith? Is there a connection? Many observers of culture, especially anthropologists and sociologists, point out that particular cultures are frequently shaped by a particular religion. Philosopher Paul Tillich summarizes these observations into a slogan, "Culture is the form of religion, and religion is the substance of culture."[135] What must be added to Tillich's observation is that much religion is idolatry. Whatever culture it is that we inhabit, it is partly formed and directed by idolatry and unbelief. The Old Order Amish are not all wrong when they say that modern technological culture is the organized expression of individualistic pride. Oh, that the Nazi Christians had seen that Nazi culture was the expression of a war-religion!

The apostle Peter reminded the first-century believers of an important principle in this regard (1 Pet. 1:18, 19). He said, "You know that it was not with perishable things such as silver or gold that you were redeemed from the empty way of life handed down to you from your forefathers, but with the precious blood of Christ." His term "way of life," *anastrophe* in Greek, is close to our modern word "culture." We were all redeemed out of a godless way of life into a new way of life. That means that being a Christian is the ultimate cross-cultural experience. We were redeemed out of a godless culture into a renewed culture by the precious blood of Christ, and that happened when we first began to hear the redeeming Word of the gospel. But as Jesus emphasized, we are not only redeemed out of a godless culture; we are also called to be "in the world," that is, sent back into the world as people who are both hearers and bearers of God's Word. This command makes the relation of the Word of God to culture and its several mountains very urgent.

The relation of the Word of God to cultures is complex.[136] I hope someone reading this chapter will ask, "What about . . ."?, thereby helping me

---

[135] Paul Tillich, *Theology of Culture* (Oxford University Press, 1959), 42. There seems to be conscious exaggeration in this slogan, since some commonalities among all cultures flow from our common humanity, created in the image of God. These commonalities allow communication across cultures and worldviews, though religious and cultural differences make communication more difficult.

[136] This complexity arises from the way in which we are addressed by God's revelations in creation and in scripture, the way in which the biblical message contains both law and gospel, as well as the multiple proper uses of God's moral law. For

learn something more! I am sure, however, the Word has at least four complementary relations to culture, each of which can be summarized with a "c": critic, correlation, creation, and contribution. Our life and witness will become unbalanced if we implement only one or two of these relations. In each of these four relations of the Word to culture, we are simultaneously hearers and bearers of that Word. We are always members of particular cultures who need to hear the divine Word while we are also, in word and action, bearers of that Word into the various cultures in which we live.

The Word of God Is the Ultimate Critic of

We should all know what a social critic is: the person who attempts to stand over against his society to articulate what is wrong. The words of good social critics often land on the editorial pages of newspapers and websites. A good social critic has a valuable role in society; however, the ultimate social and cultural critic is the Word of God, which has always been fearless and profound in its confrontation of sin. We must hear the Word's confrontation of our sin while also communicating that confrontation with sin into our world and culture.[138] Sin does not end at the level of actions; like culture, sin extends to actions, thoughts, feelings, and speech.

The Word of God Condemns Sinful Actions

The prophet Amos is a good example. He wrote, "This is what the Lord says: 'For three sins of Gaza and for four, I will not turn back my wrath. Because she took captive whole communities and sold them to Edom'" (Amos 1:6). The sin mentioned is slave trading; the people of Gaza kidnapped whole communities and sold them to the slaves in Edom. Similar things happen today. Many of the prostitutes in Prague (where I lived for 20 years) are slaves, kidnapped from their homelands. We must hear the Word of God as it confronts sins that may even be acceptable within our cultures. God's

---

more on this see Thomas K. Johnson, "Law and Gospel," *Evangelical Review of Theology* (2019): 43:1, 53-70. Online: https://www.academia.edu/38262994/Law_and_Gospel_How_the_Reformation_Applied_the_Bible.

[137] This relation of God's Word to cultures should be compared with what the Protestant Reformers frequently called the "theological use" of the law.

[138] It should go without saying that believers should affirm and give thanks for all that is good, just, true, and beautiful in each of our cultures. We must be grateful for creation and God's sustaining grace.

Word has always condemned those matters mentioned in the Ten Commandments: e.g., idolatry, murder, stealing, lying, dishonoring parents, adultery, and Sabbath breaking. We must hear and communicate God's displeasure at such practices.

Our Values Can Be Sinful

Sin extends to the level of values. Some of our core values are wrong. A generation ago Francis Schaeffer observed that in the West, "the majority of people adopted two impoverished values: *personal peace* and *affluence*."[139] I think he was right, though we might want to add that personal peace probably includes what we might want to call safety or security. These values quickly become our idols, our God-substitutes, which shape our personal and cultural life. Listen to the priorities one hears in the political campaigns. Prosperity, comfort, and personal peace are what the various parties tend to promise, the differences often being how we might pursue those values.

The Word of God challenges these basic values. The prophet Micah says, "He has shown you, O man, what is good. And what does the Lord require of you? To act justly and to love mercy and to walk humbly with your God" (Micah 6:8). Justice, mercy, and humility before God should be our basic values. Surely the Old Order Amish are right in their belief that God-fearing values will make us very different from today's secular, hedonistic culture, but we are not only to hear the Word of God about basic values; we are also to carry that Word into the secular world. Our entire lives, lived in the world, should be a dramatic statement that there is an alternative to the world's impoverished values.

Multiple social critics have claimed that a central characteristic of the West is outward prosperity joined with inward emptiness. We can call it

---

[139] *The Complete Works of Francis Schaeffer*, Vol. 5, *The Christian View of the West* (Crossway Books, 1982), 211. Schaeffer's definition is worth noting: "Personal peace means just to be let alone, not to be troubled by the troubles of other people, whether across the world or across the city — to live one's life with minimal possibilities of being personally disturbed. Personal peace means wanting to have my personal life pattern undisturbed in my lifetime, regardless of what the result will be in the lifetimes of my children and grandchildren. Affluence means an overwhelming and ever-increasing level of prosperity — a life made up of things, things, and more things — a success judged by an ever-higher level of material abundance." Schaeffer, *The Complete Works of Francis Schaeffer*, 5:211.

"The Western Paradox."[140] The pursuit of personal peace and affluence has left the lives and hearts of millions of people largely empty. In stark contrast, as believers, our whole way of living and talking should be a statement that prosperity or affluence is not the highest good though we may not like poverty. The internal emptiness of the West must be criticized, but it can be filled with faith, hope, love, and gratitude, which can be joined with justice, mercy, and walking humbly before God.

Sinful ideas Stand under Critique

Culture is the realm of ideas, and many of the most important ideas we hear in education and the media are abhorrent to the Word of God. Some of the ideas that are most important are those about what a human being is. Though European communism is largely gone, Marxist ideas are still very influential, and one of the most influential Marxist ideas is that human beings are fundamentally economical creatures. Marx thought that economic relations determine a person's and a community's entire way of thinking and living. Today, this idea is often given a capitalist spin, but it is still a similar view of a person. This view of a person seems prominent among political scientists and sociologists in the U.S. and in the EU; however, Jesus directly rejected this idea when he said, "Man does not live by bread alone." If we have partly accepted this view of a person, Jesus would call us to repent of a sinful idea, and we, as bearers of the Word into the world, should use every opportunity we have to say we are more than what we eat or what we own.

In theoretical ethics today, one of the questions that most concerns me is why human life is valuable. Among European and American philosophers, the majority point of view seems to be that human life is valuable because of the unique abilities and functions that human beings have. Functions such as reason, speech, and creativity provide the basis for human value; of course, a being without those functions does not have any value. There is an organic tie between the theories of the philosophers and

---

[140] An early social critic to speak in these terms was Abraham Kuyper. Describing modern secular culture under the code name "Babylon," he writes, "The most glittering life on the outside joined with the death of the heart, that is Babylon." *De Gemeene Gratie* (Kampen: J. H. Kok, 1902), Vol. 1, 456, my translation from the Dutch. A similar assessment of western life is found in the excellent book by David G. Myers, *The American Paradox: Spiritual Hunger in an Age of Plenty* (N.p.: Yale University Press, 2000). Most of what Myers writes, as summarized in his subtitle, can also be said of European life.

the practices of racism, abortion, active euthanasia, ageism, and tolerance of infanticide. Ideas have consequences.

Against that sinful idea, the Word of God says that humans are valuable because each person is created in the image of God. This God-given value cannot be lost, even if a person loses many normal human abilities. As bearers of the Word into the world, we should take every opportunity to say human life is valuable with a God-given value, even if a person has lost some normal functions. Doing so will mean criticizing other ideas about why human life is valuable, and some people will listen to what we have to say.

The Word of God stands over against culture as the ultimate critic, calling us and the world to repent of sinful actions, values, and ideas. As bearers of that Word into the world, we should take every suitable opportunity to communicate, by word and deed, that ultimate criticism of sinful actions, values, and ideas.

The Word Correlates with the Ultimate Needs of Cultures[141]

The Word of God has a negative relation to cultures as the ultimate critic; fortunately, our message, which we hear and communicate, also has a positive relation to culture—*the Word correlates with the questions, needs, and problems of culture.* This means that the Word provides responsive solutions to the entire range of human needs. Let me explain.

The Word Provides Honest Answers To Honest Questions

This concept was an important slogan of Francis Schaeffer.[142] Many people have honest, important questions. What is the meaning of life? Can we know that God really exists? Can we know if absolute truth exists? Can we

---

[141] Though this terminology reflects Paul Tillich's "method of correlation," it does not imply agreement with the rest of Tillich's theology. Some other Protestant theologians of the twentieth century, such as George Forell and Wayne Johnson, talked about the gospel correlating with the deepest needs of humanity because those needs arise in the encounter of all people with the general revelation of God's law in its theological use.

[142] In Schaeffer's terms, "Every honest question must be given an honest answer. It is unbiblical for anyone to say, 'Just believe.'" *Complete Works*, Vol. 1, 189. He also said, "Rightly understood, Christianity as a system has the answers to all the basic needs of modern man." *Complete Works*, Vol. 1, 93.

really know right and wrong? Can we know if Jesus really was raised from the dead? Can we know if the Bible is reliable? Can I know that my sins are forgiven? Can I know if I am justified and adopted by God? Can I know how God wants me to live? We could list additional important, honest questions that people raise, and these questions are, in principle, answered by the Word of God.[143]

This does not mean that there is a single verse of scripture that we can use to simply answer complex questions, such as, "How can we know for sure that God exists?" What I mean is that the Word provides principles for understanding human life and the world that enable thoughtful and reflective believers to give substantial answers. Because we have the Word of God in our midst, there are, in the body of Christ, people who can give honest answers to the vast array of questions that arise in the world today. In this sense, the Word correlates with culture by means of giving answers to the questions that arise in the minds of men and women.

We should also notice why people ask serious questions: because God is a question-asking God. Since the Garden of Eden, when God came to Adam and Eve with the question "Where are you?" God has been asking questions.[144] People do not always realize that God is pursuing them with such deep questions, but those questions are part of how God drives people to himself, so that they find answers in the Word. This explains the correlation between the questions in our minds and the answers in the Word.

The Word Addresses Our Deepest Anxieties

Since Adam and Eve, people have been an anxious bunch. We worry all the time, not only because we are paranoid, but also because things really go wrong. *Anxiety is the unclarified sense of the fallen condition of our world.* What will happen to us? How will life turn out? What will be our calling and destiny? We are anxious about suffering and death. We face guilt and shame. We are plagued by emptiness and meaninglessness. Such anxieties become not only the matters of sleepless nights and countless hours with therapists; they are also the themes of important movies, novels, and songs. Culture in all its dimensions expresses anxieties of the full range. The human

---

[143] For a good comparative study of how such universal questions occur to all people, see J. H. Bavinck, *The Church Between Temple and Mosque: A Study of the Relationship Between the Christian Faith and Other Religions* (Grand Rapids: Eerdmans, 1981).

[144] For more on this topic, see Thomas K. Johnson, *God's General Revelation* (Bonn: VKW, 2014), 79-95. Online: https://www.academia.edu/36885979/Gods_General_Revelation.

heart cries out in its deep spiritual need, calling for answers in the various mountains of culture.[145]

We can be grateful that the Word correlates with the human heart by speaking to our deepest needs. This communication is not intended only for believers; it can also become the cutting edge of bringing the Word into the world. All around us are people whose hearts are bleeding with spiritual need. We have the solution to the cries of their hearts—cries that can be heard whenever we listen. To repeat: the promises of God's Word correspond with the deepest hurts of fallen men and women that we hear in all the mountains of culture. Listen for guilt, shame, fear of fate and death, or a sense of meaninglessness, and you will have opportunity to talk about the promises of God.

The Word Addresses Our Comprehensive Alienation

Since Adam and Eve, people have suffered under a state of comprehensive alienation, separation from God, separation from each other, separation from ourselves, even separation from creation. This disconnection is experienced by all and is articulated by many, becoming a widespread theme in some dimensions of culture. Many good novels and movies depict our alienation and the attempts to overcome it, and the theme is also prominent in politics and economics.

As a young man, Karl Marx offered a sensitive and moving analysis of human alienation while his own alienation from God came to expression in his atheism. The tragic effects of Marxism and Communism flow partly from setting the wrong message in correlation with human alienation. It is important to see that the biblical Word is the right message to respond to our comprehensive alienation, and it does so by means of bringing reconciliation. The Word offers reconciliation with God; in addition, the Word leads to reconciliation with each other, to reconciliation within ourselves, and maybe in some ways, to reconciliation with nature. In this life, reconciliation is never total or complete. Reconciliation must always be worked out day to day because new conflicts always arise, and those new conflicts always bring the stench of death back into our lives.

Reconciliation is constantly made possible by the Word of God. In this way, the Word responds to the deepest human needs. It is important that

---

[145] This paragraph is dependent on Paul Tillich's analysis of anxiety in *The Courage to Be* (Yale University Press, 1952).

the church become a community in which reconciliation is constantly occurring so that restored relationships within the Body of Christ stand in contrast and correlation with the alienated condition of our world.

We must hear the Word of God both as it is the critic of our sin and as its promises correlate with our spiritual needs. It is crucial that as we carry the Word into the world, we bring that Word in a balanced relation to culture. The Word is the ultimate critic of culture, but it is also the ultimate healer of the painful cries of our world. The Word speaks healing to anxious hearts and brings answers to tortured minds. We must be careful to hear and to communicate both the criticism and the answers, critique and correlation, in a balanced manner.

The Word of God Creates a New Christian Counter-culture.[146]

John Stott's excellent study of the Sermon on the Mount is entitled *The Christian Counter-Culture,* and there is good reason for talking this way.[147] Jesus came to recreate us to be new people with new relationships, new ways of thinking, new ways of talking, and new ways of doing things. This plan was already evident in the work of redemption in the Old Testament. The people of Israel were supposed to be a redeemed nation, not just redeemed individuals. As a redeemed nation, they had a complete cultural expression of their redeemed status. They had a tabernacle with an elaborate system of sacrifice and worship. They had music and visual art. They had a political structure and a system of laws. All this was created by the Word of God in ancient Israel to be the cultural expression of God's work of redemption.

After the death and resurrection of Christ, the Body of Christ became the new people of God sent into both Jewish culture and Roman culture. At first, the early believers were only a poor, frightened, socially marginalized, and persecuted minority. Very soon, however, the basic Christian confession became "Jesus is Lord!" This confession stood in contrast with the claim of the Roman emperors that "Caesar is Lord." Of course, Caesar claimed to be Lord of everything, so the claim that "Jesus is Lord" meant that Jesus is also Lord of everything—a truly revolutionary idea.

---

[146] This relation of the Word to cultures should be compared with what was called the "third use of the law" in Reformation theology.

[147] John R. W. Stott, *Christian Counter-Culture: The Message of the Sermon on the Mount* (Downers Grove: InterVarsity Press, 1978).

It was only about a century ago that Abraham Kuyper wrote the famous words, "There is not a thumb-breath of the whole realm of human life of which Christ, the sovereign Lord of all does not cry out, 'It is mine'!"[148] This slogan is relatively new, but this idea was already powerfully active in the early church. It meant that all of life was coming under the Lordship of Christ. This is the starting point for the full cultural expression of our faith. In the time of the Old Testament, the people of God were set apart from the surrounding cultures by national and language barriers, in a defensive posture in relation to the surrounding cultures, but the new people of God, the Body of Christ, was sent into both Greco-Roman and Jewish culture, with all their dimensions and mountains, as a countercultural presence. Like the people of Israel, their condition as the redeemed people of God slowly started to come to complete cultural expression.

There was, I believe, an ordered progression of the cultural growth of the Christian counterculture in the early centuries. It was something of an inside moving toward the outside type of progression in the embodiment of the faith.

The Word Creates New People with New Hearts and New Relationships

We see this in the New Testament. People were saved. Families were reconciled. Small communities of believers were gathered around the gospel. Love became the mark of the Christian and of the Christian community. Much of the teaching of the New Testament epistles addresses the kind of people we are to be as a result of the gospel, including the right kind of relationships in marriage, family, work, and church, and the resulting types of communities we are to be.

The Word Creates New Ways of Thinking and Talking

In the centuries following Pentecost, there was an exciting period of growth, not only in numbers, though the numbers of believers exploded for a period of a few centuries. *There was also real growth in new ways of thinking and talking.* Simple believers learned how to think and to talk about complicated doctrines such as the Trinity, the Incarnation, and the two natures of Christ. They were soon discussing society and ethics. This new level of thoughtfulness and cognition was, I believe, an expression of the new hearts that had been given by the gospel.

---

[148] Abraham Kuyper, *Souvereiniteit in eigen kring* (Amsterdam: Kampen, 1930), 32.

The newness of what the early Christians had to say pushed them to explain to both Jews and Gentiles why they believed these things to be true. Some of this is seen in the New Testament, and it flourished in the following centuries, becoming the roots of Christian theology, apologetics, and ethics. The intellectual complexity of the faith, joined with the intellectual complexity of the interaction with the surrounding world, created a community that was studying and learning. Such a community of learning was previously conceivable only to a tiny elite.

The Word Creates New Cultural Institutions

Already in the Roman era, believers started all sorts of new things. Orphanages and programs to assist people in need came early. schools, cathedrals, and some forms of art followed. Then there appeared universities, great music such as Bach or Handel, while there was also great literature and philosophy. One can almost tell the history of the Body of Christ by looking at the continuing series of new cultural institutions produced by believers in response to the Word of God. In more contemporary terms, new mountains of culture were created by believers because they believed and obeyed God's Word.

This is an exciting story; it would take many hours to tell, enough for a university course of study.[149] All I can do now is to say that the story exists, and the story is worth hearing. Across the centuries, the Word of God has indeed moved believers to create many new cultural institutions and ways of life. Believers today should be courageous in following our believing ancestors in being willing to try to create new organizations, activities, and movements for the glory of God. History is not finished. Believers should again become courageous in starting new cultural activities for the glory of God.

The Word Contributes To Cultures[150]

This contribution is important for us who live in the post-Christian West. What does this mean? Even though much of the secular West denies or neglects the Christian heritage that shaped it, there are many elements in

---

[149] A good resource for this history is Kenneth Scott Latourette, *A History of Christianity*, 2 volumes (New York: Harper & Row, 1953 & 1975).

[150] This relation of the Word to cultures should be compared with the "civil use of the law" in Reformation teaching.

European civilization that were produced or developed under the influence of the biblical message. These are activities, institutions, or ways of thinking that hardly seem to be consistent with an unbelieving worldview, and which seem, historically, to be the result of the impact of the biblical message on Europe and later the Americas. As believers, we can see this as one of the ways in which God has been at work to make our world a much more humane place to live. This is a long story to tell; I can give only a few illustrations.

The Word Contributes Practices To Cultures

Notice that in the West today, when an ambulance comes down the street with lights flashing and the siren screaming, everyone knows to get out of the way. We all know that someone is injured or seriously ill and needs help quickly, but at many times and places in human history, this would not have been true. It was *not* always obvious to all people that someone who is injured or seriously ill should be helped. At many times in human history, people thought the injured or ill should be left to their fate. I would suggest that many people know to get out of the way of the ambulance because of the contribution of the biblical message to western civilization.[151] It is because of the influence of the biblical worldview that many know we should help people in need; and this principle, learned from the Bible, is the background for the European interest in humanitarian aid for people in need, while Europeans also work hard for political reconciliation. There is a whole set of important practices that make western life more humane and compassionate that arose partly because of the contribution of the Word to the world.

The Word Contributes Key Ideas To Cultures

Even in the post-Christian West there are many key *ideas* that arose partly due to the contribution of the biblical Word. I can mention only a few examples. The idea of human rights is a good example. In western history, some of the first people to talk much about human rights were the Christian philosophers in Christian cathedral schools and universities. These were people like Thomas Aquinas and Albertus Magnus in the thirteenth century. They thought humans have rights because they were created in

---

[151] For this illustration I am indebted to Wim Rietkerk, of L'abri, having heard it from him in a lecture or personal conversation.

the image of God.[152] Today most Europeans want to discuss and protect human rights, though they may not have a good explanation of why people have rights or where those rights originate. In some cases, the protection of human rights seems inconsistent with modern secular worldviews although this does not seem to prevent people from often becoming energetic protectors of at least some of those rights. I think we believers should rejoice that the Word has contributed a central idea to western culture—that of human rights.

Another key idea contributed by the Word to secular European society has to do with the possibility of natural science. History shows us that the early modern scientists, especially in the late sixteenth and early seventeenth centuries, were mostly serious Christians and that they developed modern science because of their Christian beliefs. They thought that the world is God's good creation, which we can and should try to understand. Christian beliefs contributed to the start of modern science.[153] Today science, along with the technology and health care that depend on science, is one of the most important institutions of western culture. Of course, many scientists are not yet believers, and many do not know the extent to which the biblical message contributed to the initial development of science. We can rejoice and give thanks to God for the way the biblical Word has contributed ideas that helped start an institution and movement that is so important and valuable today.

The Word Contributes Institutions To Secular Culture

One of the true radicals in western history was Jan Amos Comenius, also known as Komensky. One of his most radical ideas was that girls should be allowed and encouraged to get an education. Comenius is known as the "Father of modern education" because of his educational writings and practices. He was also an evangelical pastor and theologian. Sending girls to school was directly a result of his evangelical faith.

Today every western nation encourages or even demands that girls get an education, often without even knowing that the education of girls

---

[152] Some this story is told in Thomas K. Johnson, *Human Rights: A Christian Primer*, 2nd ed. (Bonn: WEA, 2016). Online: https://www.academia.edu/36884876/Human_Rights_A_Christian_Primer.

[153] This story is effectively told by Nancy R. Pearcey and Charles B. Thaxton in *The Soul of Science: Christian Faith and Natural Philosophy* (Wheaton: Crossway Books, 1994).

started as a distinctly Christian institution. I would suggest that the education of girls is a whole institution contributed to western culture by the biblical Word, and for that we should be profoundly grateful. There are other institutions in western culture that seem to be largely the result of culture-forming by believers. We could mention orphanages and humanitarian aid organizations as good examples.

History is not finished. Maybe some of us will be used by God, used by the biblical Word, to bring entirely new contributions into secular culture. Maybe someone reading this essay can be used to start something just as radical and new as education for girls, humanitarian aid, or modern science. The Word continues to be active as a key force that contributes new mountains to cultures.

Conclusion

A great European preacher of a century ago, J. Christian Blumhardt, had a fascinating saying, "A man must be converted twice, from the natural life to the spiritual life, and after that from the spiritual life to the natural life."[154] We must be converted from the world so that our identity, values, beliefs, and priorities are not those of this world. We must be converted back to the world, knowing that God has called and sent us to serve the Word in the world.

The Old Order Amish are, I worry, once-converted people. They have been converted away from the world, and that is necessary for each of us, but Jesus also wants to convert us back to world, to live in the world, to be sent as his representatives into the world. That means bringing the Word to culture with its many mountains. What I have presented is little more than a progress report on what I am learning about how that Word relates to culture. I really hope some of you are thinking, "Does not the Word relate to culture like this. . . .?"

I am sure that the Word is the ultimate *critic* of culture, laying bare before God the sinful acts, values, and ideas of the unbelieving world. That Word, especially the gospel and the promises of the Word, *correlates* with the deepest needs expressed in culture, the need for honest answers, the need for comfort in our anxiety, and the need for reconciliation in our alienation. The Word also *creates* entirely new cultural entities, ways of thinking, living, and ordering our world, that bring glory to God. The Word

---

[154] Quoted by Herman Bavinck, *Wijsbegeerte der Openbaring* (Kampen: J. H. Kok, 1908), 207.

has a long history of *contributing* key ideas, practices, and institutions even to those cultures that do not acknowledge the Word, and for that we should be profoundly grateful.

Our challenge today is to live as twice-converted people, called out of the world to a life of faith and then sent by God back into his world as hearers and bearers of the Word. As we take the Word into cultures and the several mountains of culture, it is important that we do so in a balanced and complete manner. It would be a mistake to apply God's Word in only one way. But we see in Christian history that believers do develop the level of complexity to consider themes such as the Trinity and the two natures of Christ. It is well within our capacity to consider how God's Word relates to culture and its mountains in multiple ways at the same time. Then we may see a more full-orbed result of missions.

Chapter 12: Immigration

Alan Cross

Alan Cross is a graduate of Golden Gate Baptist Theological Seminary in Mill Valley, California, with a Master of Divinity degree and with a focus on Intercultural Studies. He has also engaged in post graduate studies at the University of North Carolina, majoring in Public Administration. He holds a secondary education degree in Social Studies from Mississippi State University. After pastoring for 18 years in Montgomery, Alabama, Alan began working with churches across the Southeastern United States, helping them engage their immigrant and refugee neighbors with love, good deeds, and the gospel. Alan also led the nonprofit Community Development Initiatives that facilitated Christian mission, advocacy, education, and relief work in places such as North India, Haiti, and across the U.S. He served as a Missional Strategist for the Montgomery Baptist Association from 2016-2019 where he focused on racial reconciliation work and migrant ministry. Alan is the author of *When Heaven and Earth Collide* and *Racism, Southern Evangelicals, and the Better Way of Jesus*. He has written for the *New York Times*, Religion News Service, *Providence Magazine*, *Christianity Today*, *The Bulwark*, *Time*, and other publications.

Alan now pastors Petaluma Valley Baptist Church in Petaluma, California, where he lives with his wife and children.

Receiving Faith: The Hospitality of God Amid the Crisis of Global Migration

For the Lord your God is God of gods and Lord of lords, the great God, mighty and awesome, who shows no partiality and accepts no bribes. He defends the cause of the fatherless and the widow, and loves the foreigner residing among you, giving them food and clothing. And you are to love those who are foreigners, for you yourselves were foreigners in Egypt. —

— Deuteronomy 10:17-19

*no one leaves home unless
home is the mouth of a shark
you only run for the border
when you see the whole city running as well*

— "Home" by Warsan Shire

Introduction

According to the International Organization for Migration of United Nation's World Migration Report for 2020,[155] approximately 272 million people fit into the category of migrants globally as of 2019. Factors contributing to global migration include war, economic upheaval, climate change causing food shortages, religious persecution, political unrest, violence, and failed state and local governments who cannot provide for or protect their people.

We now have 79.5 million forcibly displaced people worldwide, including 26 million refugees with 45.7 million people internally displaced within their countries and 4.2 million asylum seekers, according to the United Nations Refugee Agency.[156] Mass migrations of people fleeing violence, persecution, and economic deprivation are changing both the countries to which they are going and the countries they are leaving behind. As this phenomenon increases, it is being accompanied by a growing backlash

---

[155] International Organization for Migration World Migration Report, 2020 (2019), https://www.un.org/sites/un2.un.org/files/wmr_2020.pdf.

[156] United Nations High Commissioner for Refugees, (2020, June), Figures at a Glance, accessed August 15, 2020, https://www.unhcr.org/en-us/figures-at-a-glance.html.

among nations receiving migrants, refugees, and asylum seekers as nationalists fear that they are losing their own countries to newcomers. Conflict between people groups is accelerating as immigration, migration, the plight of refugees and asylum seekers, and what happens to the vulnerable and persecuted promises to become one of the major challenges of the 21st Century.

What role will the global church play in dealing with these conflicts and their challenges? Will we cling to our national identities and look to our nation-states to protect us from "foreigners" and those some say are "invaders" of our own cultures? Will we see our nationalistic identities as primary and enfold our church expressions back into our own countries? The possibility of these reactions exists only for the church in countries with freedom of religion. Currently, OpenDoorsUSA lists at least 50 countries[157] where Christians face high or extreme levels of persecution, so finding refuge in nationalist identities is not even possible for them. Or, forsaking our hope in the kingdoms of this world, will we see the bigger picture of what God is doing globally with 272 million migrants on the move?

Perhaps we might then embrace the full meaning of Acts 17:24-28:

> From one man he [God] made all the nations, that they should inhabit the whole earth; and he marked out their appointed times in history and the boundaries of their lands. God did this so that they would seek him and perhaps reach out for him and find him, though he is not far from any one of us. 'For in him we live and move and have our being.' As some of your own poets have said, 'We are his offspring.'

If we believe that God is in control of the movements of people around the world so that they will seek Him and reach out to Him and find Him, then instead of seeing mass migration as a threat, we might instead see it as a massive opportunity to reach the nations with the gospel not only by *sending* missionaries to the nations (*ethne*, or people groups), but by also *receiving* the nations when they come to us. To receive the poor, cast out, homeless wanderer spoken of in Isaiah 58:7, we will have to take on the ethic and nature of Jesus as exhibited through his journey to the Cross and his death and resurrection where he lowered himself, gave up the divine prerogative, loved sacrificially, and took on the nature of a slave to secure our salvation. Taking on this character of Jesus requires us to receive faith

---

[157] World Watch List, 2020, January 15, accessed August 15, 2020, https://www.opendoorsusa.org/christian-persecution/world-watch-list/.

from God that exhibits itself in the hospitality of God, with sacrificial love for the stranger.

I met Hector[158] at an incredibly difficult time for our entire community, but especially for his family and people. It was a day full of grief and rage over a senseless murder that shook the Mexican immigrant community in Montgomery, Alabama. Hector came up to me to ask me about what was going to happen next and to talk to me about his own family. People were gathered all around the house—family, friends, neighbors. Police cars drove by slowly to check on the neighborhood and to provide a secure presence. Teachers from Maribel's middle school came by to offer condolences to the family and to check on her younger siblings. We had gone by the day before to visit Maribel's grieving mother and found the family almost inconsolable. I'd never met Maribel or her family before this tragedy happened, but I was doing all I could to hold back the tears that kept welling up inside of me.

Hector was Maribel's older cousin. He spoke English well, and he explained to me the dynamics of the family and the poor neighborhood in North Montgomery where Maribel lived with her large family. Hector and his family lived several doors down and, as an extended family, they were all close. As we talked, he told me his family's story—and his story. He was brought to America from Mexico illegally when he was just two years old. He was now 27. He grew up in America; it was the only country he knew. Hector was a beneficiary of DACA (Deferred Action for Childhood Arrivals), a program for undocumented immigrants who were brought to America when they were children years ago. Hector married here and had children, all of whom were U.S. citizens. We talked about his life, his family, and his cousin Maribel and the tragedy that had overtaken this poor community of Mixtec immigrants in Montgomery, Alabama.

I had gotten the call about Maribel's murder a couple of days before. Our city's police chief called me looking for ministers who knew the Hispanic community and who could come in and help out. He told me that a 13-year-old girl had been shot and killed the night before at her home. He didn't have many details to share, but he asked if I could help minister to the community. I was out of state at the time, but I headed home and went to the neighborhood the next day. I met up with Lisa, the community ministries director with our Montgomery Baptist Association. She already been there the day before, making a visit as soon as she heard.

---

[158] Name changed to protect Hector's actual identity.

When we arrived at the house where Maribel's mother was this first day (I met Hector a couple of days later), we saw a couple of dozen people standing outside. We said hello and went in the house where family was gathered. Maribel's mother was grieving deeply. I won't share all that happened inside the home, but it was a house of tragedy and great sadness. After listening to them and praying for them, we went outside where I saw the large group of Mixteco men gathered around the house.

I walked up to them, introduced myself, and told them I was a Baptist minister in Montgomery. The men were uncles, cousins, and friends of the Barrera family. They were there for support and to just be present. Most didn't speak English. They had their heads down and were shaken. Maribel, their cousin, niece, family member, had been senselessly killed. I learned more about what had happened. It was spring break, and everyone was out of school. She was up late and was sitting in a room when the house was sprayed with bullets; one of them struck Maribel, killing her instantly. Her poor immigrant family and community were devastated.

Maribel was a U.S. citizen, born in the United States. Her family had lived in the area for many years. Many of those gathered that day on the lawn telling me what happened were not citizens. Some were in the U.S. illegally. Many had arrived years before. Some had arrived more recently. They were family and extended family. Right then, they were all grieving, afraid, and utterly powerless. What happened next wasn't planned, but it changed me and gave me a new perspective on immigrants, the immigrant community, and how we engage in Christian ministry to those who are new to our country, our cities, and our towns. In the midst of great grief and tragedy, I engaged in *welcoming faith* with those who were suffering.

After we had talked for a while, I asked them if we could pray together. The men said yes and began to circle up. Around the circle were men, young and old. Some were grizzled with deep lines etched in their faces, their hands calloused. They came from their jobs as manual laborers and had ball caps on. Others were elders who were retired. Some of them were younger and had their whole lives in front of them. Whatever their age and situation, they were all family, and they were connected, and they were grieving. The thought occurred to me that they weren't "them" or "they." They were "we" and "us." We were together simply as neighbors.

I told those men gathered there that they were not Mexicans. They were not foreigners. They were not immigrants. They were Montgomerians. They were a part of that community, and Maribel had been one of us; her death had affected us all. I told them that they were not powerless or separate from us who had perhaps lived there longer than they had. That town was their town and we were their people. I told them that the churches and schools and police and businesses and people of Montgomery would rally around them and embrace Maribel's family. I said that their pain was our pain and their struggle was our struggle and that we would look to Jesus together. We all bowed our heads and cried out to God for mercy and for justice for this family in the midst of this senseless murder. When I made this declaration, I had no idea what was going to happen, but I felt it deep in my bones to be true.

The next day, I met Hector on the front porch of the family's house and heard his story. He was grieving for his family and trying to take care of his wife and children in the midst of all their grief. A news station reporter came out, and I acted as a spokesman for the family there at the beginning. I said for the news the same things that I had told those men the day before—something along the lines that the violence had affected all of us in Montgomery and that we were one community and we were going to suffer and get through the pain together as one people. Over the next couple of weeks, my words proved to be prophetic and the churches and city of Montgomery responded in amazing ways.

The city newspaper, The *Montgomery Advertiser*, perhaps tells the story better than I could:

> Sometimes you don't have to speak the same language to understand the pain. Gloria Barrera speaks Spanish, but on a recent morning outside her daughter's school, she didn't have to say a single word in any language to know her hurt. Capitol Heights Middle School planted a Japanese maple tree in her daughter Maribel Barrera's honor after she was shot and killed in the middle of the night inside her home during a drive-by shooting. Police believe Maribel was completely innocent, and her home in the Chisholm neighborhood was an unintended target . . .
>
> Maribel was 13 years old. She was soft-spoken with a beautiful smile, family and school administrators said. Charming, intelligent and approachable, they said. She loved music and the color hot pink.
>
> She didn't deserve to die.
>
> . . . Churches and Maribel's school have rallied around the Barreras and cocooned them in love, compassion and tenderness. The show of humanity gives us great comfort, knowing that when a family has been broken, this community is there for them.
>
> The Barreras are immigrants, but there was no wall trying to keep them out of comfort in their time of need. What their church and what Maribel's school did for them was love. It was the kind of grace we should all live in. It

was the kind of empathy we should have for everyone we come in touch with.[159]

The newspaper described the reaction of churches and the community to this tragedy very well. A massive funeral at a local Catholic church with city leaders attending was followed by a large meal provided by the churches of the Montgomery Baptist Association and local businesses. Friends, relatives, close family members, and the community itself came out to celebrate Maribel's life and to grieve her loss with her family. The tragically shortened life of a little girl whom most in the city didn't know ended up affecting us all.

I continued to talk with Maribel's cousin, Hector, after this. We would talk on the phone and meet from time to time. As a DACA recipient, he had lots of questions about what was happening with immigrants. More than anything, though, I learned his story and what his life was like as an immigrant to America. He didn't choose to come here, but he was here, nonetheless. His whole life was one of living between worlds. Not fully American because of legalities beyond his control. Not living in Mexico. His children were U.S. citizens. He had nowhere to go, so he kept his head down and tried to provide for his family where he was. He would write me and tell me he was afraid of what would happen to him and his family. What if DACA was rescinded? What if he could not work any longer? What if he were deported? What would happen to his family? Where would he go? We prayed together, and I kept trying to bring a solution to this situation for Hector. For Maribel's family. For those men I prayed with on the street after her murder when I told them we were all in this together.

The Mixtec are an indigenous people group from the southern Mexican states of Oaxaca and Guerrero. A subgroup, the Metlatonoc Mixtec[160] of Southeastern Guerrero state in Mexico came to Central Alabama by the thousands in the 1990s and early 2000s, and by the late 2010s they had put down roots. They migrated to the United States looking for work after the North American Free Trade Agreement (NAFTA) severely altered the market for corn by introducing cheaper U.S. corn into their own economy. They had been growing corn as their main agricultural product to survive

---

[159] http://www.montgomeryadvertiser.com/story/opinion/editorials/2017/04/06/our-view-after-girls-fatal-shooting-there-no-wall-communitys-compassion/100098830/, accessed October 21, 2017.

[160] PeopleGroups.org., Southeastern Guerrero Mixtec of United States, accessed August 15, 2020, https://www.peoplegroups.org/explore/groupdetails.aspx?peid.=49275.

in the hill country of southern Mexico for generations. The men who migrated north to America for work to support their families after the collapse found it in America, in the poultry plants and agricultural industry of the Deep South. Some of them became my friends.

At that time, this particular subgroup of Mixtec were considered to be the largest Unreached Unengaged People Group (UUPG) in the Western Hemisphere by the International Mission Board (IMB) of the Southern Baptist Convention, and the largest group of them lived in neighborhoods and communities close to both my church and where I lived. The Montgomery Baptist Association identified the Mixtec as our primary mission to unreached peoples, and we engaged them both locally in Montgomery and in Central Alabama as well as connecting with their home region in Southern Mexico. As time went on, relationships were built, the gospel was shared, and a Mixtec church was formed in Montgomery. The IMB has now changed the designation for this people group to "engaged, but unreached." We were able to see the Bible translated into their language along with the Jesus Film. The gospel is now being shared among the Mixtec of Central Alabama and in Southern Mexico as well. Global Migration is a platform for Global Mission.

Overcoming Fear of Migration Through Gospel Eyes

Xenophobia is a Greek word that means "fear of the other" or *xenos*. When we look upon sojourners as a danger and as people to fear and to pull away from, we no longer see them as fellow image-bearers of God, but rather as those who are both less than us and those who would take from us. When our identity is found most significantly in our heritage, our blood, our race/ethnicity, the land (or soil), and our shared cultural history, we see sojourners from other lands, nations, ethnic groups, and races as threats. We fear that they will change the world we know and love. We fear that they will take our jobs and that our lives will somehow be depleted by their presence. We fear that "the other" who has come among us will change our "way of life." None of that fear is from God, and it demonstrates a perspective that fails to understand how God is working to shake the world to bring the gospel to those who have not yet heard and to strengthen the church around the world through the realignment of God's people. Instead of seeing global migration according to what we might lose, perhaps, as followers of Jesus, we should think about what we might gain.

How Migration Is Changing the World

Does global migration change countries? Yes, but not how you would think. In a paper entitled "Migration and Cultural Change," released in June 2020, Hillel Rapoport, Sulin Sardoschau, and Arthur Slive argue that migration has more of an effect on the home country from which migrants travel than it does on the host country to which migrants go. They note, "While migrants do act as vectors of cultural diffusion and bring about cultural convergence, this is mostly to disseminate cultural values and norms from the host to the home country (i.e., cultural remittances)."[161]

In other words, when migrants come to a country, their home country is changed more than their host country through these "cultural remittances." Rapoport, Sardoschau, and Slive explain,

Migrants can also affect cultural change in the home country by transferring host-country cultural values, preferences, beliefs and social norms to their home communities. Migrants are selected to be closer to the destination culture than their average compatriots and, moreover, may assimilate, be transformed by their exposure to new cultural, social and institutional norms. They can then transfer these norms back home through communication within family, social and community networks.[162]

All of us concerned with global mission and the spread of the gospel should recognize how receiving migrants with sacrificial love and biblical hospitality affects not only the migrants, but also communicates back to their home countries the love of God and the salvation found in Jesus. In a world that is globally connected through technology and travel, global mission is not just about sending missionaries to the ends of the earth. It is also about receiving sojourners from unreached people groups with sacrificial love, hospitality, and the gospel. Just as we are preparing missionaries to go, we should also be preparing churches to receive the sojourner, refugee, and wanderer who comes to us.

In 2016, missiologist Ed Stetzer wrote the article "The Immigration Crisis and the Great Commission." In it, he refers to the work of Philip Connor and his book, *Immigrant Faith*, which showed that "when people migrate they tend to become less religious rather than staying the same. Over time,

---

[161] Hillel Rapoport, Sulin Sardoschau, and Arthur Slive, "Migration and Cultural Change" [Scholarly project], from Weatherhead Center for International Affairs, Harvard University, accessed August 15, 2020, https://seminars.wcfia.harvard.edu/files/.pegroup/files/silve_et_al_7.28.pdf.

[162] Ibid.

however, they will become just as religious as the dominant culture around them. Connor calls this a 'disruption in religiosity,' followed by an 'adaptation in religiosity.'"[163]

Stetzer goes on to say,

> This means that migration as a disruptive event allows us, the Church, to speak into people's lives at a key time. We can be the hands and feet of Jesus, offering love in His name, showing and sharing the love of Jesus to immigrants. But, later on, this can be more difficult. Over time, immigrants become generally more religious in their homeland's religion if they are living in the southern U.S. (where the culture is more religiously active). If they live in the northern or western U.S. (where the culture is relatively less religious), they generally become even less religious. Either way, religious patterns start to seep in over time, and the opportunity to share the gospel and minister to felt needs starts to lessen. If both of these things are true—migration is a missiological opportunity and immigrants tend to shift in their religiosity when they migrate—we must seize the opportunity before us to care and share.[164]

Stetzer, building on Connor's work, reflects on the research developed by Rapoport, Sardoschau, and Slive as well as the work and testimony of thousands of Christian workers receiving and ministering to migrants around the world with the hospitality of God. Because of transition, hardship, a shaking and disconnection with old norms and relationships, and the need for new connections in their host country, immigrants and refugees are initially open to being welcomed and received by those who would engage them in hospitality. Those caring, welcoming relationships become the foundation for the gospel to be lived, shared, received, and then transmitted back to their home countries. This receiving of sojourners, sharing of love and life, and spreading of the gospel back through relational networks has a transformative effect on everyone involved in these relational networks.

My own work traveling through the Southeast from 2015 to 2019 demonstrated this theory. I saw churches in rural areas and big cities open their doors to migrants and refugees in Christian love and hospitality. The result was that the gospel spread to newcomers who had recently traveled

---

[163] Ed Stetzer, January 19, 2016, The Immigration Crisis and the Great Commission, accessed August 16, 2020, https://factsandtrends.net/2016/01/13/the-immigration-crisis-and-the-great-commission/.

[164] Ibid.

from other parts of the world, and they were filled with hope and dynamism for the future. Their energy and openness spread back to the churches who received them, and an exchange took place where both receiver and guest were built up, encouraged, and assimilated. Fear gave way to faith and churches and communities were renewed, immigrants came to Christ or helped strengthen churches if they were already Christians, and the gospel spread back to their homelands.

I wrote about this dynamic in Alabama for the *New York Times* in April 2019, in an article entitled "Alabama Is More Pro-Immigrant You Think." As I traveled across the state, I engaged pastors and church members who were following God's commands to welcome the sojourner and to share the love of Jesus with all people. One such place was a little town called Union Springs and Eastside Baptist Church.

> Eastside Baptist Church, located in Union Springs, an old cotton town around 45 miles southeast of Montgomery, began reaching out to the town's immigrant community eight years ago, providing tutoring, mentoring and other assistance. Gene Bridgman, the pastor, told me that it all started when a woman in the congregation brought by 10 children whose families came from southern Mexico, part of a large influx of agricultural workers. She was already doing what she could to help them—and soon the rest of the church was, too.
>
> What gives me hope is that this openness isn't just on the individual or congregational level; it is spreading across communities, as their faith overtakes their fear. Earl Hinson, a former mayor of Union Springs and a member at Eastside, said that while the arrival of so many immigrants had taken some adjustment, the town's residents have come to accept them. "Once people get to know them, their hearts change," he said. "The perception that people have against them mostly comes from the news."[165]

I once asked Mr. Hinson what would happen if the immigrants all left Union Springs. He told me that the town would dry up. The chicken plant would leave, and the plant nurseries would go elsewhere, taking the tax base that was left in the county with them. Then the utility companies wouldn't be able to provide water and electricity because the businesses would be gone. He said that it would be a disaster for the town and for the county. In many ways, the influx of the immigrant workers from Mexico

---

[165] Alan Cross, Alabama Is More Pro-Immigrant Than You Think, May 1, 2019, accessed August 16, 2020, https://www.nytimes.com/2019/04/30/opinion/alabama-evangelicals-immigrants.html.

years ago had saved the town. The church was growing in vibrancy as it welcomed and ministered to forty Mixtec children each week.

Receiving and welcoming immigrants, however, is more than a church revitalization strategy. It is more than a way to reach the nations. It is that, but there is even more going on here. When we welcome the sojourner with biblical hospitality and sacrificial love, we connect with the heart of God and we are able to know him better. Opening our homes, churches, and communities to refugees and migrants and receiving them as we would receive Jesus helps us to connect with God's heart for the stranger and the sojourner and helps us better understand the gospel. Receiving the wandering stranger is a way that we worship God.

The Hospitality of God

> *"I was a stranger and you welcomed me."*
>
> — Matthew 25:35.

Jesus told his disciples in Matthew 25:31-46 that for the Great Judgement, the nations would be judged and divided up like sheep and goats based on how they treated the hungry, the thirsty, the stranger, the naked, the sick, and those in prison. When he said these words, he did more than tell them to do good to those in need because good works would gain them approval. He said that how they treated the "least of these" was how they treated him. He made their good works toward the poor part of their devotional lives. Our love for God is directly proportional to how we love those around us in need, especially those who are of the people of God. We are not saved by doing good works, but if we know Jesus and love him, then we will love those who Jesus loves.

First John 4:20 says, "Whoever claims to love God yet hates a brother or sister is a liar. For whoever does not love their brother and sister, whom they have seen, cannot love God, whom they have not seen." This point is what Jesus is getting at. If we claim to know God yet we turn away from people in need around us, then how can we claim to belong to Jesus who gave his life for the very enemies of God (Rom. 5:6-8)?

The concept of biblical hospitality is a key theme throughout Scripture. We are commanded to be hospitable. First Peter 4:9 tells us to show hospitality without grumbling, and Hebrews 13:2 tells us to not neglect to show hospitality to strangers. That is actually what the word hospitality, or *philoxenia*, means: love for the stranger. When Jesus tells us that those who belong to him and will spend eternity with him are those who welcome strangers, he is saying that receiving strangers (foreigners, sojourners, migrants) is the same as receiving him. If we have faith in Jesus, if we have received Jesus by faith, then we will also receive those whom he loves and died for. We will open our lives and hearts to strangers to welcome them the same way that Jesus welcomes us.

The word that Jesus uses for *welcome* here is *synegagete*. It comes from the root word *sunago* and means to "gather together, collect, assemble, receive with hospitality, entertain." It is a harvest word, and the connotation is that we are to gather together strangers or sojourners and receive them unto ourselves with love, just like we would receive Jesus. When we have that kind of open heart to strangers and migrants who are fleeing violence, war, poverty, and persecution, we will welcome them in such a way that the love of Jesus will flow from us to them and the gospel will be proclaimed to them through the way that we love and receive them.

Furthermore, we get the concept of the *synagogue* from sunago, which was the Jewish gathering for the reading of Scripture, prayer, and worship. The New Testament church, or the "called out ones," is very much based on the concept of the synagogue. It isn't too much of a stretch to say that when Jesus told us to "welcome the stranger," he was really saying that we are to open up our lives with the kind of faith that received Jesus himself and then receive into our lives the migrant, refugee, and wanderer in a way that would "church" them. Welcoming the Stranger is far more than a good work or command. It appears to be a major way that Jesus wanted the gospel to interact with the movement of peoples around the world, and only those who know and receive him will really do this. The "goats" who reject the stranger also reject Jesus and show that they do not really know him.

Now, at this point, an objection will arise along the lines of legality, rule of law, and our limited ability to receive and welcome all people. Are we really saying that our faith in Jesus is being held up for scrutiny by how well we welcome the stranger in need? Yes, I think so. While we are not able to set a nation's immigration policy and while we agree that a nation has every right and ability to police its borders and enforce the rule of law and that we should obey the law unless it calls us to disobey God, the disposition of the Christian who follows Jesus should always be that of sacrificial love for the stranger (philoxenia or hospitality) in the same way that we love and welcome Jesus. Instead of pulling back in fear of the other (xenophobia), we are to open our hearts and lives in hospitality and love for the stranger (philoxenia). Followers of Jesus who are full of faith in God are to be different from those who do not see the world according to the Kingdom of God and who seek to protect their own way of life because of fear.

A Warning: Zechariah 7 and the Whirlwind

How we treat the widow, the orphan, the sojourner, and the poor is so important that God announced again and again to his people that they would be judged based on their hearts toward the least of these. One of those warnings comes in Zechariah 7 when the Jewish people had returned from exile in Babylon and they inquired of God about whether or not they should continue fasting at set times now that they were back in the land. God asked who they were fasting for. For him, for themselves? God then put before them what he really wanted from them in verses 8-10: "And the word of the Lord came to Zechariah, saying, 'Thus says the Lord of hosts, Render true judgments, show kindness and mercy to one another, do not oppress the widow, the fatherless, the sojourner, or the poor, and let none of you devise evil against another in your heart.'"

Do justice. Love mercy. Be humble. Treat the widow, the orphan, the sojourner, and the poor well. How we treat the least of these is directly proportional to how we see God and worship him. If we want to influence nations for God, we must reflect the heart of God toward the marginalized and dispossessed. That is how God wants the nations to see Him: through the lens of sacrificial love, which would then prepare the nations for the message of the Cross of Christ.

The Jews, however, refused to listen. The rest of the chapter reads tragically: "But they refused to pay attention and turned a stubborn shoulder and stopped their ears that they might not hear. They made their hearts diamond-hard lest they should hear the law and the words that the Lord of hosts had sent by his Spirit through the former prophets. Therefore great anger came from the Lord of hosts."

There is a progression here that goes from not listening to instruction to turning away from God to removing themselves from God's Word altogether to their hearts becoming diamond hard. How God's people see and treat the poor, the vulnerable, and the sojourner is directly proportional to their relationship with God himself. When they treat them badly, it is a sign that they have already been turned over to judgment and are living apart from God.

Often, we mistakenly only see God's judgment as a meteor from heaven, an earthquake, or some kind of massive calamity, but what if God's judgment is being turned over to hard and rebellious hearts that do not adequately care for others around us and that grasp for power to protect our own way of life? What if the judgment and loss we fear is already at work within us when we refuse to love and care for the weakest among us, those whom God has brought our way to receive? What if the sojourner, the immigrant, and the refugee in our midst is a test to reveal to us our hearts and whether or not we are with God? If we turn away from them, perhaps that just reveals that we have also turned away from God Himself.

God responded to them by saying, "'As I called, and they would not hear, so they called, and I would not hear,'" says the Lord of hosts, 'and I scattered them with a whirlwind among all the nations that they had not known. Thus the land they left was desolate, so that no one went to and from, and the pleasant land was made desolate.'" Those who fail to treat the widow, the orphan, the sojourner, and the poor well and reject God's Word on this will not be heard by God. The whirlwind will come and scatter them among the nations, and they will be poor wanderers without a home to dwell in, cut off from relationship. Their pleasant land will be made desolate. This is quite a warning.

How we treat people matters. How we treat the sojourner who comes before us matters deeply to our own spiritual walk and to our relationship with God and with one another. When we reject those in need around us, the result is a hardened heart that is then broken off from the relationships that we once had.

Jesus calls us to a better way: the way of the Cross. In Isaiah 58:7, we are told to provide the poor wanderer with shelter. The concept behind the "poor wanderer" is "one who is cast out." He is a refugee, so to speak. When we loosen the bonds of injustice and oppression, share our food with the hungry, cover the naked, and bring the wanderer into our house, the result is an outpouring of the Spirit of God upon us. Isaiah 58:8-9 says, "Then shall your light break forth like the dawn, and your healing shall spring up speedily; your righteousness shall go before you; the glory of the Lord shall be your rear guard. Then you shall call, and the Lord will answer; you shall cry, and he will say, 'Here I am.'"

The result of addressing injustice, doing right, opposing violence and oppression, and caring for the poor and the cast out wanderer is that God will cause our light to break out like the dawn and our healing will come upon us. Our influence upon the nations will grow proportionally to how we care for those God loves. We will then be strengthened by the Lord, and we will get to see our age-old foundations renewed and our cities rebuilt. Isaiah 58:12 makes this promise, "And your ancient ruins shall be rebuilt; you shall raise up the foundations of many generations;

you shall be called the repairer of the breach, the restorer of streets to dwell in."

Conclusion

With the largest refugee crisis in world history upon us and almost 300 million migrants on the move, the opportunity before the church to reach the nations by welcoming and having the faith to receive the sojourner is before us like never before. When we open up our hearts and lives with concern and compassion, we will find an openness to the gospel emerges. We will gain the right to minister healing and welcome to those who have left everything they know behind, and the love of Jesus will penetrate hearts through those relationships.

As we engage in this welcoming and receiving ministry, we find that we are actually welcoming Jesus into our midst, and he strengthens and comforts us. The ancient ruins and foundations are rebuilt, and our streets will be restored. God's light will shine upon us, our healing will appear, and we will be a light to the nations.

The way to express the influence of Christ upon us is through the Cross and through sacrificial love. When we grasp after power and try to protect ourselves against others, we actually lose power and our hearts become hard. The whirlwind comes and our land is left desolate, but when we love God and love the people whom Jesus loves and we gather them to ourselves with the hospitality that God shows us, we will see a chain reaction that will reach around the world.

CHAPTER 13: CHRISTIAN EDUCATION

Jenny Clark

Jenny Clark is the director of a London-based language and further education institution called Global London College. She previously served in a wide range of Christian ministries, companies, and churches in various countries. Having grown up in Los Angeles, she dedicated her life to Jesus as a university student and spent much of her 20s as an overseas missionary, involved in campus outreach and missions. She has worked for a Christian media company, Christian Today, and has gone on to find her passion in education. She holds a Bachelors of Theology (B.Th), as well as a Masters of Divinity (M.Div), and at present she has successfully completed her dissertation and oral defense for her Doctor of Ministry (D.Min) at Olivet University. Jenny has been married to her husband, Andrew, for 15 years, and they have two children, Peter and Grace.

The Alarming Decline of Christian Theological Education in the UK

Introduction

In recent decades, there has been overwhelming evidence that theology and religious studies disciplines are shrinking in the higher education sector in the United Kingdom. A constant stream of private Bible colleges has downsized, sold off their major assets, shut down core theological courses, or even closed their institutions altogether. Public universities have not been exempted, with many theological departments merging with secular humanities departments and others halting their theology offerings and shuttering their doors for good. The major concern has been that the erosion of the Christian higher education sector in the UK does not appear to be a mere temporary bump in the road, but rather a relentless decline that has now gone on for decades. The changes that we are seeing at present threaten the very existence of Christian education in the UK as it has stood for generations. Furthermore, the evidence and signs of this decline are not isolated to the UK alone; similar signs may be seen in many Western countries, which could indicate a comparable path of decline in those nations in the coming years and decades if something is not done to address the core problems. The landscape of theological education in much of the Western world could be changing forever.

A report by the British Academy in 2019 exposed the depth of the problems facing the Christian education sector in the UK. Following an extensive examination into the state of theology and religious studies in UK universities, the prominent research institution declared that "theology and religious studies risk disappearing from our universities" altogether unless something is urgently done to confront the "significant challenges" facing the sector.

The British Academy report, "Theology and Religious Studies provision in UK Higher Education," highlights an alarming and steep decline in student enrollment in theology and religious studies courses in UK universities. In just the six-year period leading up to 2018, there were about 6,500 fewer students on degree courses in this sector. One can only imagine the acceleration of the decline in this sector—course offerings being devastated and theology departments shuttering altogether—should this decline continue over the coming decade as universities face funding challenges.

Will Christianity still have a place in the higher education sector in the UK a few decades into the future? If so, where will that future be and what will it look like? These are vital questions to answer if we are to prepare theological institutions to enter this new modern era, not just to survive, but rather to flourish with a clear understanding of its identity and mission, as well as its relevance to society and the Church as a whole.

The Landscape

The landscape of universities, higher education, and Christian colleges is ever changing. In modern day form, the institutions can range from those that have been widely secular from their establishment to those that were founded by Christians but are no longer recognizably Christian. There are also others that are supported in various ways by Christian churches, and still others that have maintained their character as devout institutions with a clear Christian identity, where they require exacting standards of belief and behavior of their staff and students.

In the United Kingdom, there are public universities that are heavily reliant on state funding for their operations. There are also, however, private institutions, often called Bible colleges or schools of theology, that have largely developed without state funds, and so encounter varied and wide-ranging challenges because of it.

Across the full range of institutions, multi-faceted problems face all establishments of higher education, such as issues concerning governance, curriculum, teaching methods, and standards; however, Christian institutions today face many additional problems to varying degrees, often related to their existence within a multi-faith or secular modern-day society.

The Secularization of The Christian 'Ancient Universities'

When one thinks of universities in the United Kingdom, the two so-called ancient universities in England spring to mind: Oxford and Cambridge. Both had Roman Catholic foundations, but later became exclusivist Anglican universities; however, they have evolved so much in modern times that they can no longer rightly be considered Christian universities and must be reckoned more-so as secular universities. Oxford and Cambridge can to a certain extent be used as examples of universities established with Christian roots but have, over time, become indistinguishable from other universities founded on a purely secular platform.

Oxford and Cambridge were established in the 13th and 15th centuries, and both were founded with the support of Roman Catholic orders.[166] In many ways, in their operations following their founding, both could be considered as Catholic universities, even though only Cambridge was in fact given formal papal approval, with Pope John XXII in 1318 proclaiming a *studium generale*—the old customary name for a medieval university in medieval Europe.

The evolution of these universities took a sharp turn under the Elizabethan statutes of 1570 and the Laudian statutes of 1636.[167] These statutes required that both universities subscribe to the Acts of Supremacy and Uniformity,[168] which meant the institutions would now exclude all Catholics and Non-Conformists. It should be noted at that point in time, both Oxford and Cambridge no longer taught theology and only began to do so again when complaints were made that their curriculums had lost their Christian personality and the institutions were not being proactive in preserving their root character.[169]

When the Reformation took place in England, most of the major cultural institutions were appropriated by the crown, and most traces of Catholicism at an official level disappeared. The exclusionary statutes were eventually revoked in the 19th century. However, the Divinity Faculty of Oxford University was excluded from the revocations, meaning that faculty members had to remain members of the Anglican Church. This rule remained in place right up to the twentieth century.

It is worth highlighting at this point that although there are many similarities in the situations affecting Christian higher education institutions in the UK and the U.S., there are also some significant differences. One such example is that in the U.S., the State and Church are separated clearly via the First Amendment of the Constitution. This is not mirrored in England, where the crown is both the head of state and the head of the Anglican Church and Church of England.

In the 1850s, an effort to create further separation between Church and State at the ancient universities influenced the way in which other new

---

[166] Staff of Catholic University of America, *New Catholic Encyclopedia* (Palatine: McGraw-Hill, 1981).

[167] V.H. Green, *Religion at Oxford and Cambridge* (London: SCM, 1964).

[168] S. Rothblatt, *The Revolution of the Dons: Cambridge and Society in Victorian England* (London: Faber, 1968).

[169] G. Marsden and B. J. Longfield, *The Secularization of The Academy* (New York: Oxford University Press, 1992), 266.

higher education institutions were founded. In the decades following, there was the historic establishment of a "second wave" of universities in England.[170] In efforts to follow this trend of increasing the separation of Church and State, many of these new universities opted out of teaching theology altogether. In others where theology departments were formed, many were intentionally established to be non-denominational, and the focus was not specifically to cater for ordinands or those with a primary interest to enter Christian vocation. One of the results of this change in direction was that a great stride was made towards making the study of theology solely an academic discipline. The head of the Theology and Religious Studies Department at the University of Bristol highlights that this led to "historical critical studies of the Bible and early Church history" flourishing, while other core theological disciplines, such as systematic theology, became neglected.[171]

Another increasing trend seen from that point onwards and even up to today is that theology departments in UK universities have often been merged with other secular departments, such as those in the humanities and other Arts sectors. The effect of this is a clear secularization of the theology departments, with key decisions and wider policies being made by those leading the secular department, rather than by the theological departments themselves. This trend has had far-reaching implications on areas such as recruitment, teaching, disciplinary procedures, and even daily Christian worship and other Christian life offerings within the theology department.

Indeed, when it comes to modern-day Oxford and Cambridge, almost all historical roots to their Christian beginnings have been erased. At Cambridge, the university has repealed all canonical requirements for its Divinity Chairs, and after nearly five centuries of existence, the institution installed its first non-clergyman to hold the Regius Chair. Moving away from their institutional foundations, these historic universities have clearly become secularized.

It can be argued that there is very little place for Christian thought or Christian activity in Oxford and Cambridge nowadays, except perhaps within the Divinity faculties. In recent times even some faculty appoint-

---

[170] D. Hempton and H. McLeod, *Secularization and Religious Innovation in the North Atlantic World* (New York: Oxford University Press, 2017), 65-79.

[171] Gavin D'Costa, *Theology In The Public Square: Church, Academy and Nation* (Hoboken: Blackwell Publishing, 2005), 59.

ments have been questioned by scholars analyzing the landscape of Christianity in higher education. The stark reality is that despite their clear faith-inspired origins and a clear history of Christian influence throughout much of their existence, not many in the present day who would call either Oxford or Cambridge University "Christian universities"; instead, they are, to all extents and purposes, institutions with Christian roots that have become overtly secular in the modern era.

The Second Wave of English Universities

Apart from Oxford and Cambridge, it is difficult to identify other institutions that could be considered "Christian universities" upon their initial establishment. Probably the only two founded prior to the 1900s would be Durham University and King's College London.

Following the Reformation, in which Catholicism was driven out of higher education in England, leaving an Anglican monopoly, the first university to invite Catholics and other non-Anglicans back in again was King's College, which is part of the University of London, in 1827; however, King's College has fallen to the same fate as Oxford and Cambridge with regards to its secularization.

When Durham University was established, it was supported strongly by revenues from Durham Cathedral, as well as the local diocese. Today, even though Durham is far from what can be labeled a "Christian university," it still reserves a Chair in its Divinity School for an ordained Anglican and is the Church of England's sole validation partner for ministerial training.

After this period, the universities that followed were established with a purpose to be non-religious and non-denominational. In the second half of the 19th century, nine civic universities were founded in the major industrial cities of England. Manchester University (1851), Leeds University (1874), and Bristol University (1876) were all fundamentally secular in nature from their inception. Some even explicitly prohibited the teaching of religion at their outset, fueled by secularism, as well as even by some Christians who had suffered exclusion at the hands of the older Anglican-dominated institutions. For example, the University of Manchester, also known at the time as Owens College, imposed an outright ban on any "theological subject that shall be reasonably offensive to the conscience of any student."

Other newly established institutions during this period also prohibited any kind of religious tests for recruitment and admissions. Such examples are the University of Sheffield, which was founded in 1879 and at the time was Firth College, as well as the University of Liverpool, which came into existence in 1881. Thus, there was a period where numerous institutions were established that expanded the landscape of higher education greatly, but at the same time created a more secular influence and setting that could be said to have contributed to the more increasingly irreligious environment of universities in England in the twentieth century.

The UK Government's Hand In Secularizing Christian Institutions

One significant factor in the secularization of universities stems from the fact that they are public institutions, so they receive money from the state purse to support their teaching, research, and operations. As a result, the institution is subject to government oversight in regulations, admissions, and even accreditation of courses. Historically, this affected not only the university sector, but also private Church-established institutions that have made the fateful decision to accept government funds, not realizing that doing so could have implications on their long-term operations and ultimate control of their institution and Christian character.

A perfect example of this control can be revealed through a group of Christian colleges that were established by various Church denominations in the mid-19th century. Between 1839 and 1862, a handful of small teacher training colleges were established by Anglican, Methodist, and Catholic churches to train Christian teachers who would pass the faith onto students.[172] Upon their establishment, the staff and faculty were mainly religious, with communal worship and morning prayer ingrained as part of everyday school life. Attending scripture classes and joining Christian services were compulsory. Each college could maintain its denomination's distinct Christian character and influence the faith environment its students would experience and develop in; however, the decision by these institutions to start accepting government funding can now be seen as a significant turning point in their histories, one that would ultimately prove decisive in their change of identity and ultimate secularization.

The receipt of public funds allowed the government to play an increasingly influential role in a number of key decisions over the coming decades that accelerated the secularization process. The curriculum, pedagogy,

---

[172] Perry L. Glanzer, *British Journal of Educational Studies* (Exeter: Taylor & Francis, 2008), 163.

and other elements came under the regulation and oversight of the government. One example of the government's influence came in the early 1900s, when it was mandated that all church schools had to admit 50% non-denominational students. Religious education classes, chapel services, and prayers were gradually given less emphasis, and eventually compulsory Christian life aspects of the curriculum were lifted altogether as these institutions slowly moved towards secularization.

In the 1960s, the government deemed that there was a great need for more teacher education colleges and dictated a huge expansion of the sector. Existing institutions, including church colleges, were forced to greatly increase in size in a relatively short period of time. The rate of expansion of these colleges meant that maintaining their original Christian identity proved even more challenging and difficult. Mandating chapel or theology classes with the growing number of students became problematic. A lack of staff to accommodate the sudden growth of the colleges meant that recruitment criteria for teachers became less stringent with regards to faith. Teachers with any faith, or even no faith at all, were recruited, further eroding the character of these Christian institutions. As one historian notes, "The constant factor was the ultimate complete dependence of college planning on government approval."[173] The result was that there were now many Church-established colleges that to a large extent had lost their original Christian character. Worse was to come!

After the sudden boom of teacher colleges, the government later deemed that the sector was saturated, resulting in a third of teacher education colleges being reduced by the state. All colleges with church affiliations suffered from this move in various ways. For some, the only way to survive the drastic reduction was to expand academic offerings into more secular courses. For others, it meant merging with other institutions with secular identities or different denominational backgrounds, again pushing these establishments further along the road to losing their original identities and becoming more secularized.

Among the institutions that survived this turbulent period, two will be looked at in more depth below to show the effects such developments have had on them. These two Christian teacher training schools merged with other denominational or secular colleges to establish what are now known as the University of Gloucestershire and the University of Roehampton.

---

[173] G.P. McGregor, *Bishop Otter College and Policy for Teacher Education* (London: Pembridge Press, 1981), 201.

Newer 'Christian Universities' Becoming Secularized

The University of Gloucestershire

The University of Gloucestershire is a well-known higher education establishment in the United Kingdom, and it has been highlighted extensively throughout various literature as one of the "new universities" that is—at least in a limited sense—a "Christian university." This label has been attached to the University of Gloucestershire in large part thanks having been founded by evangelical freethinker Francis Close, who initially established the institution as a teacher training college in 1847 with a Church Foundation Trust.

One-third of the governing Council of the University, which consists of 200 members, derives from the Church Foundation Trust, and these representatives are requested to sign a document stating their active agreement with the Trust Deed of 1847, which states as follows: "The Religious Education to be conveyed in the Colleges shall always be strictly scriptural, evangelical and Protestant and in strict accordance with the Articles and liturgy of the Church of England as now established by law."

Despite these underlying roots of Christianity remaining within the historic Trust Deed, it is difficult to find any type of strong Christian identity on the outward face and general operations of the university in the modern day. Instead, a perusal of the university's current promotional and marketing literature reveals a clear non-exclusive Christian identity being promoted. The erosion of the institution's Christian identity and character has taken place over decades, and undoubtedly for many reasons, but one major factor be that the university has felt the pressures of a modern-day society that is becoming increasingly secularized. In its efforts to attract the required student numbers to be financially viable, it has opted to promote a much broader non-exclusive Christian identity.

An examination of the University of Gloucestershire's 2019 promotional and marketing materials as well as its website reveals clearly that the institution has very much continued down a path of secularization away from its original Christian distinctiveness. It is difficult to find anything in the way of any description of the university's Christian origins within the institution's website, and in particular nothing can be found in its About Us, General Information, and Course Information main pages. Hidden away in the "Student Life" and "Student Support" promotional materials, however, there is a "Faith and Spirituality" informational section:

"The University has its roots in the foundation of the Cheltenham Training College in 1847 by Revd Francis Close and others. Today the University warmly welcomes those of all faiths and world views, drawing on our heritage to offer space for exploring values, beliefs and spirituality in an open and inclusive way."

The university seemingly goes to great lengths to tone down its Christian origins, completely leaving out the label "Christian" from its description, while at the same time making efforts to emphasize that it warmly welcomes "all faiths" and even those of all "world views." It even goes further, not boasting of any "Christian" heritage, but rather of a heritage that explores "values, beliefs" and a general "spirituality." Again, it seems by no mistake that the university opts to include the word "inclusive" while describing its "faith and spirituality."

Even in other areas where it appears the university has maintained a distinct Christian identity; it is almost always countered with an assurance of its diverseness and inclusivity to all ideas and faiths. For example, a subcategory about Chaplaincy is included within this same "Faith and Spirituality" section. The university boasts that it "offers chaplaincy across all of its sites."

This statement indicates a clear backbone to its Christian origin identity. Immediately after this, however, it adds that it has "a team of five chaplains including those from the Christian tradition and a Muslim chaplain, and also associate chaplains from the other major world faiths." As part of its resources for student faith, the institution boasts of "Discussion Groups," "Mindfulness Sessions," and "Times of Shared Silence." It is sure to include alongside its description of a weekly Communion Service another gathering for Friday Prayers for Muslim students and staff, and alongside its promotion of the student faith society "The Christian Union," it adds there is also an "Islamic Society" operating on campus.

One of the most historic buildings at the University of Gloucestershire is the beautiful Chapel at Francis Close Hall—surely a clear sign of its retained Christian identity. Following the promotion of this chapel, however, is the statement that the chapel is "a space used for music and art" as well as for "our weekly World Café." It concludes that the historic chapel is "a busy social space" with "sofas and a pool table—a great place to come and chill."

The university boasts that it has set up a so-called "Faith Space" on each of its campuses and promotes them as a space for all students to come and relax, play games, and meet others "over a tea or coffee." The university should be commended for clearly putting significant efforts into its catering for faith and spirituality across its campuses—something that can be argued a majority of other UK higher education institutions don't put as much effort into as Gloucestershire. However, he general rhetoric and the way the institution looks to promote not just its faith spaces, but also its own identity and history, is alarming when looked at in the context of its original strictly evangelical Protestant scriptural outlook.

It can be argued that the University of Gloucestershire has not maintained its original Christian identity, and has indeed become not only more ecumenical, but also inter-religious and even partly secularized. Indeed, a glance at the most recent Twitter posts on the university's own Chaplaincy social media page shows a stream of posts focusing on almost all other major religions, and none at all regarding Christianity or Christian-specific activities. The most recent Twitter post was celebrating the 550th anniversary of the birth of Guru Nanak—a central figure in the Sikh faith.

Figure 1 – *University of Gloucestershire Chaplaincy's Twitter post celebrating Guru Nanak.*

The post prior to that was a celebration of the university's Muslim chaplain receiving an educational certificate.

Figure 2 – A Chaplaincy Twitter post celebrating the university's Muslim chaplain.

Prior to that, it was of a celebration of Rosh Hashanah and a greeting to all Jewish students and staff, and the post before that features an image celebrating Eid ul-Fitr.

Figure 3 – A Chaplaincy Twitter post celebrating Rosh Hashanah.

Figure 4 – A Chaplaincy Twitter post celebrating Eid ul-Fitr.

Among those inter-faith posts, the only other submissions from the chaplaincy that came even close to Christian specific posts were about a painting exhibition and a general music concert taking place at the university chapel and another post inviting people to the chapel for cheesecake and "a chat."

Of course, only so much can be read into a social media stream of posts on the chaplaincy's Twitter page; however, what was recorded on the social media page corresponds to what was indicated on the university's "Faith and Spirituality" materials and certainly does nothing to counter the argument that the university's strong Christian identity as seen in the Church Trust Deed of 1847 has been greatly watered down in modern times. Indeed, one suspects that if a poll were taken of all the University of Gloucestershire's current students, a huge majority would be entirely ignorant of the institution's Christian origins and history.

Adding even further to the evidence of an institution that has lost its Christian identity is the University of Gloucestershire's official "Strategic Plan 2017-2022." Throughout the 55-page document, the university goes to great lengths to highlight its mission and values. The opening three sections of the document present "Our Mission," "Our Vision," "Our Values"—obvious places for the university to underline some of its proud Christian identity and history, yet an examination of these sections reveals no mention of any Christian ethos, inspiration, or connection to the institution's mission, vision, or values or any Christian roots in the university's founding.

The Mission section simply states that the university was founded on "values" without giving any indication of any Christian specific values. The

Vision section expands a little, promoting that the establishment wants to facilitate students to be able to "transform their own lives for the better." Furthermore, it states that its mission is to see each student leave his or her studies to live "for the benefit of society, their families and themselves."[174] One might expect the Values section to be the place where the institution would expand or at least hint at its Christian-inspired origins or roots; however, the Values section simply lists six words: nurture, creativity, sustainability, service, respect, and trust.

A closer examination of the remainder of the document reveals extensive promotion of the fact that the institution was "founded on values," and it also declares that the university is "proud of our heritage," but any specific reference to its Christian origins or faith values is extremely difficult to find. Throughout the first 37 pages of the document, many headlines in large font and in bold text emphasize various things the university wants to promote.

It is not until page 38—a page filled with extensive block text, the smallest font used throughout the document, and dedicated to describing the institution's partnerships—that a reference of anything explicitly Christian is written. Buried towards the end of the page's text, at the end of a section describing the establishment's "international collaborative partners," is written, "The University has a historical affiliation with the Church of England, and with the Diocese of Gloucester in particular, which continues to be reflected in our values, behaviors and relationships."[175] This short statement is the entirety of the institution's promotion of its Christian roots, inspiration, and sustaining values in this important landmark document of its strategic plan for the five-year period.

Although the university stands out among higher education institutions as one that has maintained at least an essence of its Christian origins and indeed does include this in its literature—albeit in a way where it is unlikely to be found by a majority of potential and current students—it would indeed be difficult to label the University of Gloucestershire as a "Christian university" as it stands today. It would clearly fall into the category of institutions in the United Kingdom that have lost the core essence of their original Christian identity.

The University of Gloucestershire's theological and religious offerings have also been highlighted by academics, with some expressing concerns

---

[174] University of Gloucestershire, Strategic Plan 2017-2022 – 2019 Update Document (Gloucestershire: University of Gloucestershire, 2019), 7.

[175] Ibid., 38.

that the distinctiveness and character of the Christian and theological content has started to dissolve. One prominent researcher on the topic of theological studies in the United Kingdom, Gavin D'Costa, highlights in his writing that in 2005 Gloucestershire's School of Theology and Religious Studies had two offerings: an undergraduate pathway in Theology and a separate pathway in Religious Studies. He emphasizes that even at that time, nearly a decade and a half ago, a thorough research of the university's course materials indicated that the Christian heart of the theological courses had been taken out—that is, the heart to know God more as the core reason to study theology. In its place, the core reason to study the theological courses had become purely academic in nature—that is, to analyse mankind's history and thoughts on spirituality and religion in general.

Indeed, D'Costa highlights that the university's undergraduate course in Theology shared much content with the general Religious Studies course. The Theology course also had numerous units on philosophy, and even one on "the religions of India." D'Costa concludes that all the evidence "highlights my point about there being no real difference between the two fields methodologically, and here the distinction in content has begun to dissolve."[176] He also says that at the time of his writing, the university's theology department was proposing a fundamental change to its structure, whereby it would focus on long distance learning and developing a new even more general program called "Religion, Philosophy and Ethics." Overall, his conclusion regarding the University of Gloucestershire was that the institution had become "thinly Christian" but really a "secularized university ... despite its mission statement." He highlights "financial pressures" as one of the core reasons for this once-staunchly Christian university's secularization.

A look at the University of Gloucestershire's present courses in 2019-20 show that since D'Costa's writings in 2005, the institution's theological studies offerings have become fewer in number and their Christian distinctiveness has continued to decline. At the time of writing, the establishment offers just two religious undergraduate courses under the category of "History, Religion, Philosophy and Ethics."[177] The first, "History and Religious Studies," is described as "the exploration of human belief and action to

---

[176] Gavin D'Costa, *Theology In The Public Square: Church, Academy, and Nation (Challenges in Contemporary Theology)*. (Hoboken: Blackwell Publishing, 2005), 63.

[177] University of Gloucestershire, *Glos.ac.uk* (Gloucestershire: University of Gloucestershire, 2019), Undergraduate Degrees.

gain a deep understanding of key forces in the shaping of our world and identities." The course is promoted as targeting "those who want to ask deep questions about what it means to be human." It talks about understanding "the development of individual, social and cultural identities" through looking at "British, European, American and Soviet history, as well as the major world religions of Islam, Judaism, Christianity, Hinduism and Buddhism."[178] Indeed, all promotional material for the course indicates that this is not a theological course to know God or even to search for an understanding of the Christian faith. It does not even specifically highlight Christianity as a unique part of the course study; rather it is placed equally alongside all the other world's major religions, which in turn all seem to be secondary to the primary focus of the course, which appears to be the study of history and history's impact on shaping society and who we are as a global community today.

The second undergraduate course offering that contains a religious element is "Religion, Philosophy and Ethics." The course description highlights how central religion is to people's lives around the world today, but again it does not highlight Christianity but rather religion in general as the focus of the teachings. Indeed, the description highlights that it teaches "Hinduism and Buddhism as well as New and Non-Religious Movements." The "Course Leader" writes in the description that his own "research and publishing to date has focused upon contemporary Hindu movements in the UK and India" and that he has a specific interest in the "current relationship between religion, populism and national identity."

The course description continues by highlighting that students will "examine philosophy as it emerges in ancient traditions" and "the thinkers of Ancient Greece, the advent of Islam, Judaism and Christianity, and the ancient traditions of Hinduism and Buddhism." It notes that there will be the chance to "examine a range of perspectives on the purpose and meaning of life." The conclusion of the description is alarming to say the least, as it goes on to emphasize that students will also look at "UFO cults, popular culture spiritualties, Pagan traditions and North American Satanism."[179]

---

[178] University of Gloucestershire, *Glos.ac.uk* (Gloucestershire: University of Gloucestershire, 2019), History and Religious Studies.

[179] University of Gloucestershire, *Glos.ac.uk* (Gloucestershire: University of Gloucestershire, 2019), Religion, Philosophy and Ethics.

There are surely few who would argue that the University of Gloucestershire, despite its very Christian origins, could now be labelled a Christian university. Rather, it has now become a perfect example of a UK higher education institution that has become very much secularized, to the extent that it is difficult to find even an essence of its original Christian identity in its modern-day marketing and even in its course offerings.

The University of Roehampton

Another example of a UK university often highlighted for its Christian roots is the University of Roehampton. The institution was initially created as a result of a merger between three church colleges, Whitelands (Anglican), Digby Stuart (Catholic), and Southlands (Methodist), with a secular college called Froebel. The four educational bodies united to become the Roehampton Institute of Higher Education in 1975. All four of these institutions were founded in the 19th century and had their roots as women's teacher training colleges.

Founded in 1841, Anglican Whitelands College is known as one of the five oldest institutions for training educators in the UK. Indeed, Whitelands was the Church of England's flagship women's college and was the first college of higher education in the UK to admit women. The Methodist Southlands College was founded more than three decades after Whitelands, in 1872, and historically has promoted a strong Methodist ethos as integral to its character. The Roman Catholic Digby Stuart College was established in 1874 as a teacher training college for Catholic women. The three Christian colleges merged together, along with the secular Froebel College, which was founded in 1892, as an institution to further the values of Friedrich Frobel, the famous German educationalist. The four colleges found synergy in their missions to provide education for poor and disadvantaged children.

What is immediately striking is the danger when four separate educational institutions with such varying theological backgrounds and characters merge into one where each institution has its own distinct characters somewhat diluted.

In the late 1970s, the institution entered into an association with the University of Surrey, and until 1982, awarded through validation degrees issued by the University of Surrey. In 2000, it attained university status as the University of Surrey Roehampton by entering into a partnership with the Federal University of Surrey. Later in August 2004, the University of Surrey Roehampton became the University of Roehampton as we know it today. One of its founding colleges, the Anglican Whitelands College, maintained a degree of independence until 2012, but at this point it too was legally merged with the university, bringing all the colleges into one core management structure. With so many mergers and various partnerships through the decades of its existence, it is no wonder that the University of Roehampton as it stands today finds it difficult to maintain many of the attributes that made the original Christian colleges unique and distinguished.

With 75% of the institution's founding colleges being Christian, great efforts have been made down the years to keep a Christian ethos and mission at the institution's core. However, an analysis of the university's current literature, website, marketing and course materials make for disappointing reading for one who is seeking for a truly "Christian university." Indeed, a review of the University of Roehampton's current undergraduate course offerings reveals that out of 63 programs running, only three of these have any relation at all to religion or theology. Having three might be considered reasonable in the wider context when considering all universities across the United Kingdom. It must be remembered, however, that Roehampton University was initially founded by the merger of four colleges, 75% of which were theological colleges. Thus, with only three out of 63 courses being related to religion in general, let alone being theologically specific, this amounts to less than 5% of the university's current undergraduate course offerings. It becomes apparent how far the institution has fallen from its Christian and theological roots.

One of the 3 religion-related courses on offer at the University of Roehampton is a "Religion, Theology, and Culture" program, which is part of the School of Humanities. The university markets the program by stating that the course "offers you the opportunity to explore religious traditions and ideas with deep historical roots that continue to shape politics, society and culture today." Furthermore, the summary of the course states,

> Our BA Religion, Theology and Culture degree will enable you to develop the skills you need to understand the impact of religion and theology in both contemporary culture and the ancient and classical worlds... you will learn to think about the historical origins of global religions: Judaism, Christianity, Islam, and Indian Religions. You will also explore ethical, cultural, and religious perspectives on human life and what it is to be human.[180]

---

[180] University of Roehampton, *Roehampton.ac.uk – Undergraduate courses* (Roehampton.ac.uk, 2020).

Such a wide description, it could be argued, reveals a clear ethos to try to promote general religious studies as the predominant purpose of the course. It is likely that such a stance is taken to ensure the course is casting the net as far as possible in trying to attract the widest range of potential students to the course. Universities and higher education establishments in modern times are under intense pressure to attract the necessary student numbers to ensure courses remain viable and within budget constraints, and this pressure could be a clear reason for the general direction Roehampton, and indeed many other institutions, have taken with regards to their faith-related courses. In doing this, they clearly reveal that Christian theology is not being given the central role in the courses any longer, but rather a general religious ethos has emerged.

The second religious-related course at the University of Roehampton is the "Philosophy, Religion and Ethics" undergraduate course. Throughout the description of this course it is clear that again, a clear religious ethos is given a high visibility, but Christian theology is more hidden. The summary of the course begins, "What is the relationship between the White House and the African American Freedom Struggle? How has our understanding of gender and sexuality changed? And what can philosophy teach us about how we think about religion?"[181] The description goes on to add:

> You will consider philosophy, religion and ethics as both separate and integrated disciplines, and look at the connections between being human and ethics ... Although Western thought forms a backdrop to this degree, you will also study Islam, Hinduism and Black American and African contexts, to give you a secure sense of how different ethnic and socio-economic groups offer crucial interdisciplinary and intercultural insights.

This "Philosophy, Religion and Ethics" undergraduate course on the surface appears even further away from putting core Christian theology at its core and places the study of religion in general as an academic discipline as its central premise, promoting the study of understanding religion's place in society rather than knowing or understanding God more to deepen one's faith.

One interesting thing that stands out in the institution's description of its "Philosophy, Religion and Ethics" course is that it goes to great pains to emphasize employability and transferable work skills in numerous places.

---

[181] University of Roehampton, *Roehampton.ac.uk – Undergraduate courses* (Roehampton.ac.uk, 2020) Philosophy, Religion and Ethics.

It appears the course creators are acutely aware of the need to address concerns among potential students as to whether they will be employable upon completing the course.

Midway through, the course description states, "As you progress through this course, you will develop highly transferable and employable skills, while tailoring your studies to your own areas of interest." Further on it adds, "Each year this course dedicates time to developing your professional, transferable skills so that by the time you graduate, you will be ready for your career, have built professional contacts and have some work experience." The course description's conclusion reinforces this point once more: "The University offers extensive career support, with a dedicated career service, excellent connections and organisations and businesses, and an annual employability workshop where you will meet former students and employers from various industries."

There appears to be a concerted effort to dilute and diversify the course content away from its historically Christian and theological offerings. There are also clear hints throughout the university's literature that indicate this is in response to the need to attract potential students who are increasingly concerned with—and rightly so—their future career prospects after investing tens of thousands of pounds, and three or four years, into their undergraduate degree.

There remains, however, one ray of light, as the University of Roehampton has retained one core Christian theological course in its undergraduate offerings, an FdA/BTh in "Ministerial Theology." The program is designed for those already working in Christian ministry and mission and provides "the opportunity to develop your intellectual and practical expertise, while continuing to work in your local church or community." The course description does promote that students will "benefit from Roehampton's historical roots as an institution with strong connections to the church." For those who join the course, the university installs students as members of its Whitelands College, which has retained chaplaincy facilities.

This ministerial-specific course is an important spark of light, especially given the strong headwinds in the current UK university market where theological schools are closing or merging with other departments. One does wonder, however, whether it is only a matter of time before Roehampton's course offerings become diluted even further despite important efforts by some at the institution to the contrary. The lines are becoming blurred, and it is becoming increasingly difficult to distinguish between an institution that can rightfully call itself a "Christian university" and only regular secular establishments that offer a few courses related to theology and religion.

One academic who has studied the secularization of religious institutions thoroughly notes,

> Christian institutions in England take great pains to stress that they welcome students of all faiths or none. Indeed, so strongly is this message of inclusiveness purveyed that it is really quite difficult in some cases to discern from prospectuses which are Christian institutions, and which are not. Even within the covers of their prospectuses, some institutions simply mention their Church roots but without indicating what the church affiliation might signify.[182]

Despite the University of Roehampton's staunch Christian beginnings, being formed through Church of England, Methodist, and Catholic theological training colleges, a general review of the university's current marketing literature and course offerings indeed fit perfectly into this description, and it is almost impossible to tell the difference between this once proud Christian institute of higher education and other secularly formed ones.

Over the decades, there has been a clear reduction in staff and students from any particular denomination, which clearly will have a huge impact on the fundamental nature of the institution. Furthermore, there has been a distinct movement away from the teaching of core Christian beliefs and practices towards "academic theology" and away from core Christian biblical teaching to general religious studies. Such changes can be subtle and take place over time, but the results can be severe in that the course curriculums can become detached from the original institution's Christian goals and mission.[183]

Other subtle but obvious signs of a Christian establishment losing its identity can be deeply ingrained in the life of students. A Christian establishment will go far beyond simply the teaching that goes on in classes and lectures, and they will seek to nurture and raise a student's Christian faith through Christian living. The three Christian colleges that went on to form 75% of Roehampton University would originally have had compulsory Christian worship as a regular and standard part of its courses to students.

---

[182] Sinclair Goodlad, *Christian Universities and College: A Conceptual Inquiry* (St Matthias Lecture, 2002), 9.

[183] Ibid., 6.

However, when such standards are loosened and liberalized and Christian worship becomes not compulsory, but optional, there is a clear change in the nature of the communal unity at the institution. Once that liberalization of Christian living standards has started, it can potentially be a very fast and slippery slope downwards, until all hints of Christian community life and unity in Christian brotherhood there-in are eroded completely. Thus, the modern student life at Roehampton University has no signs at all of compulsory worship, nor indeed any compulsory Christian element of living whatsoever.

Obligations and expectations of Christian student behaviour, which would have been implemented firmly at the establishment of the original three separate Church of England, Methodist, and Catholic theological training colleges have been entirely eroded. This would likely have happened gradually over time, but it has now come to a point where Christian morals and religious forms of life have become totally independent of academic teaching activities to the extent that a large majority of students are likely to be oblivious to any Christian worship or other life activities on offer at the institution. To all extents and purposes, Roehampton University has become secularized.

The Alarming Decline (British Academy Statistical Analysis)

What does this all mean for the current state of Christian higher education and theological teaching in the United Kingdom?

Trends in theology higher education across recent years reveal some alarming signs of a continued decline. Undoubtedly, the sector has failed to fully adapt to the changes in UK higher education in general, but more than this, it has struggled to aptly respond to wider changes in society at large.

In the distant past, many university theological departments were closely linked to the Church and reliant on its support. This link is no longer seen in the current higher educational landscape. Many private Christian Bible schools and colleges still have connection to universities to validate their professional training courses; however, the divide between seminaries and public universities has become much wider than it once was. As a much-expanded higher education sector offers a wider range of courses than ever before, University theological departments offer just a tiny percentage of these. The British Academy has warned that theological education is in danger of being drowned out, especially when there are clear indications of many departments losing their original identity and Christian character.

The Alarming Decline of Christian Theological Education in the UK

Statistics collated in the British Academy's report reveal that in 2018, just over 10,000 students in the United Kingdom in the fields of Theology or Religious Studies across both private and public higher education providers overall. At a glance, that figure could appear to be reasonably healthy; however, the overall trend in enrolment is sharply downwards, in contrast to other major humanities subjects such as history and philosophy, which are experiencing an upward or sustained trend in recent years.

A closer look at the statistics reveal alarming data. The figure of approximately 10,000 students in theology and religious studies courses in 2018 is in fact 6,500 fewer than the number in the academic year 2011-2012, a drop of 40% in student numbers in just six years. Moreover, when annual statistics are viewed, they show a year-on-year decline in students enrolled in theology and general religious studies courses through that period. Breaking the figures down further, statistics obtained from the British Academy indicate that enrolment in first degree (i.e. bachelor's degree) programs was 31% lower in 2018 compared to 2012. In the same period, there was a massive 83% drop in the numbers enrolled in foundation degrees related to Theology and Religious Studies. The graph below, compiling the data from the Higher Education Statistics Agency's (HESA) student records, reveals the sharp drop in student numbers between 2012 and 2018.

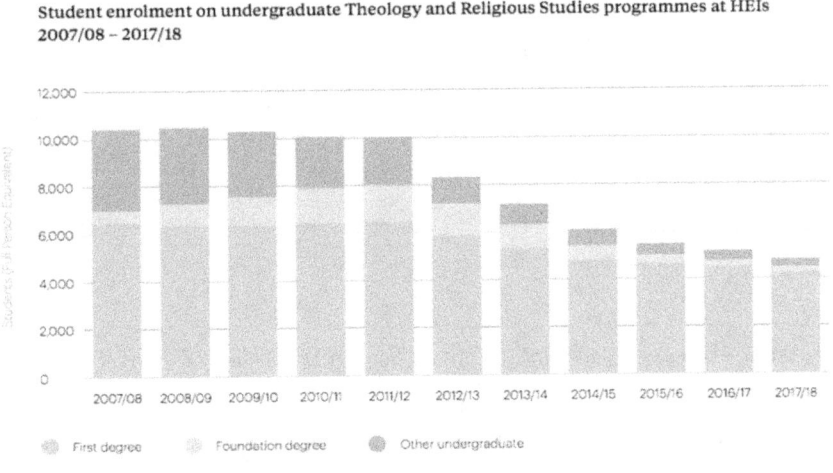

Figure 5 – Student enrollment statistics from HESA (British Academy).

What is particularly concerning is that other humanities subjects that also declined sharply after 2012 experienced a significant and constant bounce-back in enrolment figures over the next five years while the number taking Theology and Religious Studies has continued to drop year-on-year.

The Higher Education Statistics Agency's (HESA) statistics for higher education enrolment for Theology and Religious Studies can be compared to other historical and philosophical subjects. Using these figures, one can compare the first-year degree enrolment numbers to Theology and Religious Studies, against Philosophy. As shown by the graph below, both suffered alarming declines from 2012.

Philosophy, however, was able to quickly recover and even increase its enrolment figures by 2018. The numbers for Theology and Religious Studies, on the other hand, have continued to decline. This graph by the British Academy was compiled using HESA's student records statistics using data for the higher education admissions course code V6 (Theology and Religious Studies), and V5 (Philosophy):

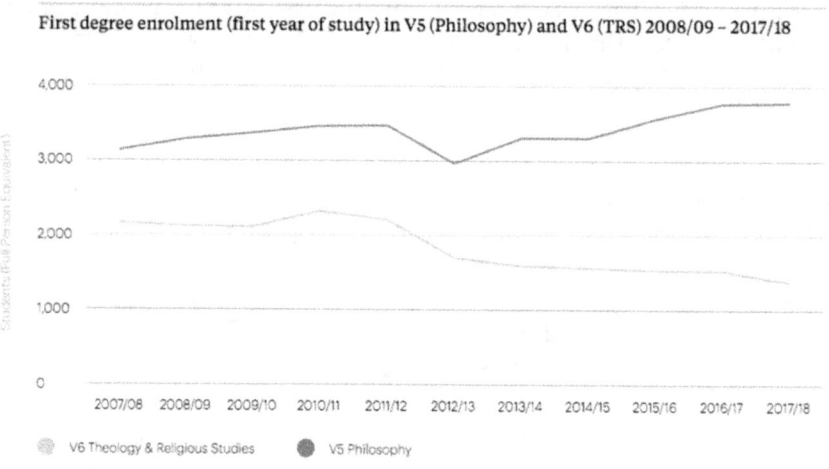

Figure 6 – *First degree enrollment statistics from HESA: Theology & RS vs. Philosophy (British Academy).*

A similar trend is observed when comparing Theology and Religious Studies numbers to other degree courses in History, as well as Archaeology. Both History and Archaeology suffered a drop after 2012, but then bounced back year-on-year until eventually by the end of the period in 2018, they had even seen a small increase in student enrolment rather than any overall decline.

Observing the wider trends in higher education in the UK, the report notes a sharp drop in university enrolment figures across the board in almost all degree courses in the 2012-2013 academic year. This decrease coincided with the year that university tuition in the United Kingdom increased drastically to £9,000 annual fees for a full-time undergraduate degree program. This rise in cost apparently resulted in a collapse in enrolment figures in the year or two after the higher fees were introduced; however, most other mainstream university subjects experienced a bounce-back and recovery after that initial drop, but theology has continued to struggle. There is strong evidence to suggest that the major factor in the drop in overall student enrolment in 2013 was the introduction of higher annual fees.

The report observes that student enrolment fell mainly among English-based students, whereas numbers for overseas international students remained much more consistent throughout this period. These statistics again support the logical thought that the big decline seen in 2013 was largely due to higher student fees. Fees for international students taking degree courses have always been much higher, and the fee increases did not affect these students as much; therefore, the number of incoming international students remained more consistent.

Enrolment figures even within the United Kingdom itself would seem to indicate fees were the major contributing factor. HESA's statistics show that student enrolment in degree courses in Scotland remained consistent through the period. Scottish-based students do not pay any tuition fees in Scotland.

Another factor in the decline of enrolment in Theology and Religious Studies higher education courses could be finances, namely the availability of funding for potential students. With the fees for courses ever-increasing, external support in the funding of course fees has become more important than ever. Sadly, statistics reveal a dramatic drop in monetary support for students, particularly when it comes to foundation degrees.

Foundation degrees are an important stepping-stone for many potential students to begin their pathway towards a full degree and their continued higher education studies. This is particularly important for some who do not have the funding needed to confidently rush into a full three- or four-year degree course. Others may feel uncertain about whether they truly want to commit the many years needed to obtain a theology degree and may feel more comfortable starting with a foundation program or degree, which would hold a far less commitment of time—a single year to begin with—and then they could move onwards to a full degree in this specialism if they chose. As mentioned above, however, foundation degrees have seen a massive fall in external funding. According to the British Academy, as many as 40% of students seeking foundation degrees in theology and other religious studies courses in the year 2007/08 received funding from charities or international organizations. The global financial crisis in 2008 may have had a critical impact on this support system, as funding support for theology foundation degrees plummeted.

The situation deteriorated rapidly, and no UK-based students on theology foundation degree courses had their fees funded by charities or international organizations in the 2016-2017 academic year. As a result, many of these foundation courses are no longer offered to potential students. Thus, there is a worrying gap in the higher education market, and any potential student not yet fully convinced that he or she wants to commit to the numerous years and finances that a full undergraduate degree course entails are left with greatly reduced options.

Overall, there has been a very alarming downward trend in both applications for and enrolment in theology courses, especially from 2013 onwards. This trend is sharply contrasted with other humanities subjects, such as philosophy and history, both of which have seen a strong and continued resurgence after an initial plunge in 2013 following the rise in annual fees. This trend has had, and will have, an unrelenting devastating effect on the theological education landscape across the United Kingdom.

Evidence suggests that the historical changes to theological colleges and institutions, and in many cases their loss of core Christian character as well as ministry and mission purpose, have contributed to the decline over recent decades. In the most recent decade, however, these underlying problems have been exacerbated greatly by financial pressures imposed on the higher education sector. The increase in tuition fees has played a large part in deterring prospective students. It has also pressured institutions to change the courses they offer to accommodate financial burdens. Many theology courses have been merged with more general religious studies topics, and indeed many theological departments have merged with other departments within the humanities sector. Furthermore, the disappearance of many bursaries and scholarships for students, especially for foundation theology degrees, have likely had a larger impact than many realize.

The Alarming Decline (Case Study Examples)

Statistics can only reveal the decline to a certain extent; however, these statistics are a harsh reality, and they feel very real when specific examples of theological departments and Bible schools being closed are examined. An analysis of the current landscape of theology in higher education in the United Kingdom quickly reveals the very real devastating and long-term affect the current decline in student enrollments is having. The facts also reveal that it is not just university theological departments that have had to close or merge with other humanities departments. Private Bible schools and theological colleges that have stood for decades are also being forced to close for good due to financial problems or shuttered under the guise that a re-structuring or re-strategizing of theological training is needed. Even observing the very recent history of Bible schools in the United Kingdom reveal some very alarming examples.

St Michael's College

In 2016, St Michael's College, an Anglican theological institution in Cardiff and the final residential theological college in the whole of Wales, closed its doors. The college was founded in 1892 and trained hundreds of ministers and Christians through the decades, being situated in Llandaff from 1904 until its closure in 2016.

The college faced widespread problems in the years prior to its shuttering, but the end came in 2014 with "A Report On The Future Of Theological Training In the Church of Wales" in which the problems of the college were laid bare. Included in the report was a recommendation that residential training at the college should cease to exist. The report was presented at the Governing Body of the Church of Wales later that year, and following that, further recommendations were made to the bench of bishops of the Church of Wales.

Scottish School of Christian Mission

Another theological school that has disappeared in recent years had numerous names throughout its prestigious existence. Initially established and known for most of its existence as the Bible Training Institute in Glasgow, it was founded in 1892 with the noble mission to evangelize the working classes in Scotland. The institution indeed became home to thousands of theologians over the decades and played an important role in higher education theological training and study throughout the 20th century. In

1990, the institution changed its name to the Glasgow Bible College following a move to a former Church of Scotland building in the trendier west side of the city. At this time, the Bible college was going strong and even had to move to larger facilities—a former nursing and midwifery college next to Strathclyde University. The identity of the college was again changed in 1998, this time to the International Christian College in Glasgow, following a merger between the Glasgow Bible College and the Northumbria Bible College.

The next decade and a half were filled with challenges for the International Christian College. Student recruitment was not where it needed to be, and even though many efforts were made to cut costs or carry out initiatives to reverse the decline, the college was forced to announce the sale of its building in 2013, with the intention of moving to a more budget friendly location. The following year, in 2014, the college leadership announced that the college would close in its existing form. The principal at the time, Richard Tiplay, explained that the college had been struggling with falling student numbers since 2007. Cost cutting measures, as well as the sale of its building, had not successfully helped the college reverse its fortunes. Indeed, between 2000 and 2013, the annual intake of new undergraduate students to the International Christian College dropped from 57 to just 16. The alarming decline resulted in student recruitment being halted in 2014, and the focus was switched from fighting the deterioration situation to helping staff move on and managing the transition or exit of the college's current students. Ultimately, efforts were made to investigate other options of how the institution could survive in a different form.

Those investigations led to an announcement in 2015 that a new institution, Scottish School of Christian Mission, would be born from the ashes of the International Christian College. The new form of the college would focus on delivering courses in youth and community work and urban mission, as well as training in pioneer ministry and missional leadership. The move partnered it with the Nazarene Theological College and allowed the college to offer degrees validated through the University of Manchester as well as access to full undergraduate student loan funding. There was hope that the college had turned a corner and the new Scottish School of Christian Mission would make this new beginning at a new location in Parkhead, Glasgow; however, that hope of a new start was short-lived, and in 2018 the school announced that it would be closing its doors permanently. Its students were passed on to the Nazarene Theological College, and some of its staff also moved to that institution. Another historical Christian theological institution was no more.

Heythrop College

Perhaps the most high-profile theological school closure in the United Kingdom in recent years, if not decades, is that of Heythrop College. This closing in 2019, after more than 400 years of teaching, sent shock waves through the Christian higher education community.

Heythrop College was founded in 1614 as a Jesuit seminary and later became a specialist theology and philosophy college. Indeed, it hosted one of the largest Theology and Philosophy faculties in the United Kingdom. It became a member institution of the University of London in 1970 and remained so until its closure at the end of January 2019. The college's rich and extensive history did not make it exempt from the modern problems and challenges facing theology institutions of higher education. The college openly admits that it faced major problems with sustaining recruitment levels following the 2012 university fee reforms. That declining enrolment, coupled with rising administrative and running costs, meant the college's governing board could see no way out of the challenges facing the institution.

In 2013, the college had discussions about a "strategic partnership" with St. Mary's University in Twickenham, London, but they did not bear fruit. The proposed partnership explored ways in which the college could counter its financial difficulties by being "an autonomous college of the University of London." When those talks collapsed, the college made one last effort at survival, exploring a merger with Roehampton University. Those talks also failed, and it was announced that Heythrop College would immediately stop recruiting undergraduates for University of London degrees. The decision was made in 2015 to begin to wind down operations step by step, preparing for its effective closure in 2018—with final graduations taking place in December 2018 and formal closure in 2019.

The devastating impact such high-profile closures have had on the wider Christian higher education scene cannot be underestimated, and the effects are felt spiritually as well as physically. The premium site that Heythrop College occupied in Kensington, London—the UK's richest borough—was sold, and developers made plans to recreate the site as a luxury retirement complex. The college closed without any plans to transfer any departments or continue in a different form elsewhere. Over 400 years of theological education at Heythrop College came to an abrupt and depressing end.

Revd Angela Tilby, an Anglican priest who spent 22 years as a producer in the BBC's Religious Department, called the loss of Heythrop another "grievous step towards the marginalisation of theology from the university and the loss of Christian witness in academia." She commented,

> The loss is great. The cause of ecumenism is set back by losing this shared academic enterprise. The University of London has lost a unique institution, with a matchless library of 250,000 volumes. And, while the Jesuits retain two centres of spiritual renewal and pastoral care, they have less interactions with the academic mainstream. Their tradition has always valued the integration of serious philosophical study with spiritual development.
>
> It is one more grievous step towards the marginalisation of theology from the university and the loss of Christian witness in academia.[184]

Sadly, the decline is even more widespread than this, and in addition to Heythrop College, numerous other schools have followed or are on the verge of following its demise.

St John's College, Nottingham

St John's College in Nottingham announced in December 2019 that after 156 years, it too had decided to close its doors. St John's College was originally founded as the London School of Divinity in 1863—an Evangelical College with a rich history. Former Archbishop of Canterbury, Donald Coggan, was a past principal of St John's and another Archbishop of Canterbury, George Carey, trained at the institution. The college has become another victim in what is becoming a ravaged theological education landscape in the United Kingdom. The college stated as it announced its closure that the institution was "no longer financially viable in the long term."

Although students who are currently studying at the institution will be able to finish their courses, the process of closure has begun. Alarmingly, the principal of the Eastern Region Ministry Course, Revd. Alex Jensen, has said that there is a "great fear" in the Theological Education Institutions sector that other closures will follow: "Hardly any college or course is financially sustainable. I think there is a recognition in the Ministry Council that there is something wrong . . . The question is if changes will be made before the next college or course falls by the wayside."[185]

---

[184] Angela Tilby, "Angela Tilby: Heythrop's Closure Leaves A Gap," *The Church Times*, September 28, 2018.

[185] Madeleine Davies, "St John's College To Close After 156 Years," *The Church Times*, December 6, 2019.

A general look at student numbers at St John's makes for disturbing reading. In June 2016, there were 223 recorded students at St John's College; however, by 2017 this number had plummeted to just 108. In the year prior to its closure announcement, just 60 students were enrolled. How did this happen? In 2014, a restructuring of the strategy and operations of the college occurred. The decision was made to stop recruiting students, including ordinands, to study on campus. At the time, the college promoted this change as a "remodelling of the college to meet the future training needs of the Church." However, further drastic changes indicate that an underlying stream of problems were forcing the hand of the college's management team. In 2015, it was decided that students would study at St. John's for only two days each fortnight. Then in 2016, the college announced that it would be suspending all student recruitment for the following academic year.

Indicating that the financial pressures being placed on the college were overwhelming, the college sold its land in 2017, and the former campus was renovated for a new housing development. Like numerous theological institutions that have closed in recent decades, St John's was unable to find a way to curb the financial decline and decreasing student enrolment figures. Almost certainly St John's College will not be the last to see its rich history brought to an abrupt end.

Other Challenges in the UK Private Higher Education Sector

Some of the major factors that have contributed to the downward spiral that Christian theological education is now experiencing have been highlighted above. In order to stop this decline, a host of other fundamental issues must be addressed in the upper echelons of the Education Department in the British government.

Requirement for Degree Validation for Private Colleges

One major problem specific to private providers in the higher education sector is that these private institutions cannot themselves issue degrees. Rather they must have their degrees validated by partner university institutions—at a high cost. This forces these private institutions to raise their course fees to cover the cost of the degree validations by public universities, which again likely lowers enrollment significantly due to the high course fees being promoted. This is a problem with the overall system of the higher education sector in the United Kingdom.

This system is in place for good reasons: to ensure students and the public at large that a British university degree is of the highest standard and is fully regulated. In its current format, however, it pushes private Bible colleges and seminaries into a corner where a consistent downward spiral of high fees and decreasing enrollment seems impossible to fight. Something must be done in this aspect, but the changes will need to be made in higher education policy or many private sector institutions may not survive.

Office for Students (OfS) Approval A Barrier to Overseas Recruitment and Student Loans

Another area of major concern for Christian institutions currently working in the higher education sector is that of immigration policy. The policies as they stand make it very difficult for smaller private Bible colleges to recruit international students.

To be able to sponsor an overseas student to travel to the UK on a study visa for degree programs, the institution must be OfS (Office for Students) approved. The OfS is a new independent regulator of Higher Education in the UK, and the standards required for approval are rigorous to the extent they are prohibitory for many smaller colleges. In particular, the standards require a certain level of finances that are difficult to achieve for many theological schools. As a result, many private Bible colleges are not OfS approved.

These requirements ultimately mean that those Bible colleges miss out on a huge range of benefits open to other higher education institutions. For example, Bible colleges that are not OfS approved cannot access public grant funding (such as funding to support teaching). They also cannot access student support funding, so students wishing to attend these Bible colleges cannot access low interest government tuition fee loans, which can be a major prohibition for domestic students as they have no way to afford the high course fees. Also, these Bible colleges cannot sponsor overseas students for Tier 4 student visas; therefore, another potential channel to recruit students is blocked. There is little that any Bible college can do to change this situation. Changes like this are fundamental and a matter of higher education policy in the British government; thus, amendments to support smaller private institutions will need to be made at government level.

Conclusion

The tragic demise of several Christian theology institutions has been highlighted above, and at the time of writing, there are ominous signs for numerous other Christian Bible schools and university theology departments, posing a very real threat that over the coming decade, many more may fall victim to the modern-day challenges facing theological higher education in the United Kingdom.

One issue that must be urgently addressed at many universities is that the focus of the study of theology must be to know God more. Many theology courses now offered at universities look to study the subject as a purely academic discipline. Focus is given to historical Biblical studies and to the theory of Christianity and religion; however, when the heart of theology is watered down, it also loses its power. The core of theological study must be the heart and purpose of knowing God more.

Christian institutions are being bombarded with financial challenges, student recruitment problems, and regulatory oversight matters. In many cases, circumstances have conspired to force institutions down the road to secularization. The form of this secularization can be revealed in many different ways: merging with secular departments or institutions, merging with other denominational bodies that could blur identity, recruiting staff and teachers who are fundamentally not in keeping with the original Christian character of the institution, watering down Christian life offerings such as prayer, service, and disciplinary measures, and a loss of the heart of the theology curriculum offered.

Christian institutions and theology departments must fight to maintain their core identities and make fundamental changes to tackle the decline without selling out on their original Christian distinctiveness and character. These characteristics must be maintained when it comes to staff, professors, lecturers, curriculum, and student behavioural and communal prayer/worship standards.

Despite the overwhelming challenges facing the theological higher education sector in the UK, there are glimmers of hope as well. Many private Bible colleges are still running with healthy levels of student enrollment. Most of these are colleges where links to denominations and church networks are still strong.

Churches can help to drive potentially interested theology students to specific institutions that align with their theology and denominational background. More research must be conducted to understand this relationship between church networks, their leaders, and theological institutions. If these relationships can be analyzed and better understood, these connections can be fostered and used to increase student recruitment to theological schools and Bible colleges.

Institutions alone cannot fix these issues that exist within the Christian higher education sector; churches too must be proactive and evangelical in nature. They must bring more people to faith and send them out to theological institutions to raise a new generation of leaders to continue the genealogy of the Christian faith. With new leaders actively church-planting and fulfilling Christ's mission to bring more believers to Jesus, a pathway may be created to reverse this frightening trend. Otherwise, as warned by the British Academy, theological education may eventually be wiped off the British academia landscape. This grim reality could devastate Christianity in the country for centuries and wipe out all traces of Britain's rich Christian heritage.

Chapter 14: What Is Next?

Dr. William Wagner

Creating a Mega Strategy for Christianity

At the turn of the century many Christian missiologists were formulating plans to win the world in the next century. Numerous plans were created, but few have been implemented. During that time, two well-known authors, David B. Barret and James W. Reapsome, wrote a book entitled *Seven Hundred Plans to Evangelize the World*. In this book, they identify 788 plans, proposals, and scenarios developed from AD 30 to 1991. There has never been a lack of desire by the church to carry out the command of Jesus Christ "to make disciples of all nations." Some of these plans have been carried out and have been successful in that today, approximately one third of all humanity claims to be Christians. Our problem is that we continue to use methods and concepts of the past in today's world, which is vastly different from when those plans were developed, and we find that they no longer provide us with the results that we are looking for. Our world is changing, and we need to update our methods in order to achieve worldwide revival.

Three Dangers for the Christian World Today

Several years ago, Dr. Os Guinness gave a speech at a breakfast in Marin County, California. He stated that the three greatest dangers to the Christian world today are (1) China, (2) Islam, and (3) secularism. A study of modern-day strategies for impacting the world reveals that all three of these groups have Mega strategies in place and are being successful. Let us look at these three.

A good book that can be used in understanding the strategy now being used by China for world dominance is *The Hundred Year Marathon—China's Secret Strategy to Replace America as the Global Superpower* by Michael Pillsbuy. In his book, he carefully outlines the plans now in place for China to supplant the United States as the world's dominant power by the year 2049. He claims that they are more than satisfied with their progress thus far. We are aware of the fact that one of the world's greatest revivals is now taking place in China with over 60 million claiming to be Christians, but just recently the government has once again clamped down on the church and they seem ready to destroy Christianity in their country. The final chapter on this conflict between that communist state and the church has not yet been written.

The second danger is Islam. In *How Islam Plans to Change the World*, a book I wrote on their strategy, I describe in detail the four prongs of their strategy. Today we hear less about the threat of Islam because of the defeat of ISIS and other radical groups, but they continue to make great strides forwards in the Western world through immigration and *Da'wah*. Their strategy is very complete and their religion continues to expand rapidly.

The secular world appears not to have a strategy, but the homosexual movement, which is an important part of secularism today, does have one. What they plan on doing can be found in *After the Ball—How America Will Conquer Its Fear and Hatred of Gays in the 90s*, by Marshall Kirk and Hunter Masen. This book was the starting point of a very well-developed strategy now being used not only by the LGBT movement but by secularism in general.

All three groups that Guinness saw as dangers for our Christian civilization have well defined strategies in place that use modern methods of technology, but they are also concentrated on the modern structures of society. Their success is now being seen on the streets of many Western countries, as a small number of their followers can have such a negative effect on Judeo-Christian society as we now know it.

The Need for Strategy Today

As I write this chapter, many cities in the U.S. and other Western nations are faced with demonstrations and riots in their streets. Christian leaders with whom I have spoken have been blind-sided by what is happening, but when we look behind the curtain, we can see that what is taking place is the result of both careful planning and years of waiting for the right moment. A study of what is happening shows three main streams of influence in these riots. I shall look at the three streams and try to identify those who are coordinating these events.

1. <u>Black Lives Matter.</u> Those who support this direction are both anti-police and anti-racism. They do have some valid complaints, but the movement has been taken captive by the more radical side of society, who are using them as ways to cause disruption. In the beginning, the Black Lives Matters movement did not have an observable strategy, but with time the secularists have come in and taken over the movement to cause chaos and to further their political aims.

2. <u>The Homosexual Agenda</u>. At BLM demonstrations we see many rainbow flags since the LGBT movement is agreement with causing disruption. Their well-developed strategy has been adopted by those in the streets to advance their own agenda. One good example is the use of intimidation to obtain their end. It now appears that anyone who opposes what is happening is in danger of being singled out as an enemy of the people, being accused of being both racist and homophobic, and losing his or her position, as has happened with many CEOs.
3. <u>The Cancel Culture Movement</u>. This movement is an offshoot of the previous two. Because of their success in the early stages, many want to go further and change the Judeo-Christian culture of the West to one that will certainly be anti-Christian. Historical statues and monuments have become their target, and recently some in this movement have even called for the destruction of all statues of Jesus Christ and stained-glass windows in churches. Once again, this movement has adopted the Homosexual strategy and combined it with the "Rules for Radicals." Both groups have stated that they need to have an enemy, and increasingly the enemy seems to be both the political system and the Christian church.

What Can We Do?

At this point the Christian church seems to have been taken aback by the rapid changes in thinking, especially among our young people. Their ideology combined with the Corona virus has produced a perfect storm for those who are the enemies of the church. Since the virus has made it difficult to meet together as a church, most pastors are just trying to keep their heads above water. The church seems to be completely on the defensive today.

In football, the players are often told by their coaches that the best defense is a good offense. The church today would do well to work intensively on a new strategy to combat the forces that are now working against them. Since much is the result of well thought out Mega strategies, it is important that we also go into that direction and develop our own Mega strategy. We need to both accept where we are today and realize the need to plan for tomorrow. This can be done when world class Mega thinkers come together and work in unison to plan. Instead of just apologizing for the mistakes of the past, the church needs to find ways to paint the church in a very positive way.

Avoid the Mistakes of the Past

It is no longer possible to just become static in what we do; we must move ahead and at the same time be very careful not to repeat the mistakes of the past.

1. We have placed too much emphasis on the accomplishments of the leaders. We have often developed personality cults in our churches. In evangelical circles we practically worship those who are both leaders and are successful; thus, many who want to climb the ladder of success seek to promote themselves. This focus has been to the detriment of the faith. I always thought that the best foundation for a Mega strategy would be the Lausanne Movement, but after attending all their major meetings and talking with some of their leaders, I am convinced that it places too much emphasis on both the identity of parachurch organizations and their leaders. I have spoken with many of their leaders about the formation of a Mega strategy, and all agree it needs to happen but only when they and their organization takes the leadership. A study of the three good examples of groups with Mega strategies, the Mormons, The Muslims, and the Homosexuals, reveals that it is difficult to identify the leaders. It appears as if the leaders are happy to just make contributions and not be recognized, which is different from evangelicals who often work for more recognition or to advance to a higher position. We must form a body of leaders who remain incognito.
2. We have not thought big enough. Our churches are filled with leaders at the Micro and Meta levels; thus, our work at these two levels is really excellent and in some instances outstanding, but we are not hearing from those who can think big and are in a place where they can influence the church to also think big. I have discovered that we have many leaders at the Mega level, but they are not always appreciated and are set aside as people who do not fit in and who think outside the box. These leaders need to be identified and encouraged to work together to make great plans for the Church in the future.
3. We have not realized that the implementation of a Mega strategy needs to be done in small pieces. A major new strategy presented to the church will not be accepted, which is why we are looking at the Ten Mountains of Culture. If we break the task down into ten smaller units, then we might be better able to bring about change in the smaller area. Even when we do have Mega thinkers, we do

not have structures where they can work. In government, the "Think Tank" method is used often, but in the church, this is practically a lost art. We do better in adapting ourselves to what we have done in the past and then are satisfied with minor corrections and advancements. Those who want to create new structures for Mega thinkers are often looked upon with suspicion. Most existing structures want new ideas to come from within their organization and not from without. New ideas are not always welcomed.

Moving Ahead

Let us realize that we are greatly mistaken when we say that no one else is working on a Mega level. At least three groups have great plans in progress: Campus Crusade, Youth with a Mission, and Rick Warren and his PEACE plan. There are undoubted others, but it seems necessary that new attempts are made to develop plans at that level.

Ten years ago, as I started thinking about doing work on the Mega level, I felt that what I wanted to do was too big and nothing could be accomplished. Only recently have I seen that the need is even greater and that our Lord has provided the necessary resources. I have developed a five-step plan.

1. Create an Institute that can act as the foundation for any future work in this area. Several years ago, I formed the Olivet Institute for Global Strategic Studies. The purpose of this Institute is to gather those working in the academic world on advanced degrees and encourage them to do their research in areas that will help us to form a worldwide Mega strategy. One of those students, Jenny Clark, has written a chapter in the book.
2. Write a small (100) page book that outlines the three levels of strategy development and then promote the book. Someone recommended that the book be short since busy people do not read long books. I have fond this to be the case. This book was written together with my son Mark Wagner and is now in circulation.
3. Expand on the book and find ten outstanding Mega thinkers who can each write a chapter on their mountain of expertise. Thus, this book. I have been amazed as to how the Lord has brought together ten great experts to contribute to this book.
4. Create a commission of approximately twenty outstanding Mega thinkers of the world to form a "Think-Tank" like group that can

visualize the next steps. One person alone does not have the expertise or the wisdom to do this, but a group of twenty could under the leadership of the Holy Spirit.
5. After this group comes up with recommendations, then another group needs to be created that can best implement the ideas given by the first commission.

We are already way into the five-step plan and my prayers are that in the future we can help the church to do a better job in winning the world to Christ.

Continue to Climb the Mountain

When I moved to Innsbruck, I had many students in my church who were experienced mountain climbers who spent many days climbing to the top of various peaks in the area. I discovered that mountain climbing is a very popular sport in Austria, much like football and basketball in the U.S.

When I asked the students why they climbed mountains, they gave two answers. First, they would say, "because they are there." They saw a challenge in conquering the majestic peaks of the Alps. Second, they would describe what it was like to go to the top, depicting the climb in three stages. In most cases the start of the climb would be in a forest, and it was often difficult to see the top of the mountain or even the path going up. Then about halfway up, they would reach the tree line, where there was no more forest and no more clouded vision. They could then see the goal, the top, very clearly, but they often encountered new problems: snow and cold, difficulty breathing due to the thinness of the air, and exhaustion from the earlier parts of the climb. Good climbers made sure that every move conserved valuable oxygen as well as their remaining strength. Also, they stated that halfway up the mountain, they would become somewhat discouraged and begin to ask why they had undertaken such a task, but they said that most of the time they would continue. The third phase of the climb was convincing themselves that they could do it. To be sure the last half was difficult, but the closer they got to the top, the more exhilarated they felt over accomplishing something. At the top, they could see all the surrounding landscape, especially the valleys and the other peaks. The students would then tell me how exciting it was to conquer the mountain, but they assured me the only way to really know that feeling was to experience it.

In Christianity today we have some mountains to climb. Because of the excellent work by many before us, we find ourselves halfway up the mountain. Now it is time to endure the cold and lack of oxygen and discouragement and continue upward until we develop new methods of making the Gospel of our Lord Jesus Christ known to a lost and dying world. I pray that each of us will be willing to continue to follow the path up the mountain to carry out the command of Jesus Christ to make disciples of all peoples on earth.

World Evangelical Alliance

World Evangelical Alliance is a global ministry working with local churches around the world to join in common concern to live and proclaim the Good News of Jesus in their communities. WEA is a network of churches in 129 nations that have each formed an evangelical alliance and over 100 international organizations joining together to give a worldwide identity, voice and platform to more than 600 million evangelical Christians. Seeking holiness, justice and renewal at every level of society – individual, family, community and culture, God is glorified and the nations of the earth are forever transformed.

Christians from ten countries met in London in 1846 for the purpose of launching, in their own words, "a new thing in church history, a definite organization for the expression of unity amongst Christian individuals belonging to different churches." This was the beginning of a vision that was fulfilled in 1951 when believers from 21 countries officially formed the World Evangelical Fellowship. Today, 150 years after the London gathering, WEA is a dynamic global structure for unity and action that embraces 600 million evangelicals in 129 countries. It is a unity based on the historic Christian faith expressed in the evangelical tradition. And it looks to the future with vision to accomplish God's purposes in discipling the nations for Jesus Christ.

Commissions:

- Theology
- Missions
- Religious Liberty
- Women's Concerns
- Youth
- Information Technology

Initiatives and Activities

- Ambassador for Human Rights
- Ambassador for Refugees
- Creation Care Task Force
- Global Generosity Network
- International Institute for Religious Freedom
- International Institute for Islamic Studies
- Leadership Institute
- Micah Challenge
- Global Human Trafficking Task Force
- Peace and Reconciliation Initiative
- UN-Team

Church Street Station
P.O. Box 3402
New York, NY 10008-3402
Phone +[1] 212 233 3046
Fax +[1] 646-957-9218
www.worldea.org

Giving Hands

GIVING HANDS GERMANY (GH) was established in 1995 and is officially recognized as a nonprofit foreign aid organization. It is an international operating charity that – up to now – has been supporting projects in about 40 countries on four continents. In particular we care for orphans and street children. Our major focus is on Africa and Central America. GIVING HANDS always mainly provides assistance for self-help and furthers human rights thinking.

The charity itself is not bound to any church, but on the spot we are co-operating with churches of all denominations. Naturally we also cooperate with other charities as well as governmental organizations to provide assistance as effective as possible under the given circumstances.

The work of GIVING HANDS GERMANY is controlled by a supervisory board. Members of this board are Manfred Feldmann, Colonel V. Doner and Kathleen McCall. Dr. Christine Schirrmacher is registered as legal manager of GIVING HANDS at the local district court. The local office and work of the charity are coordinated by Rev. Horst J. Kreie as executive manager. Dr. theol. Thomas Schirrmacher serves as a special consultant for all projects.

Thanks to our international contacts companies and organizations from many countries time and again provide containers with gifts in kind which we send to the different destinations where these goods help to satisfy elementary needs. This statutory purpose is put into practice by granting nutrition, clothing, education, construction and maintenance of training centers at home and abroad, construction of wells and operation of water treatment systems, guidance for self-help and transportation of goods and gifts to areas and countries where needy people live.

GIVING HANDS has a publishing arm under the leadership of Titus Vogt, that publishes human rights and other books in English, Spanish, Swahili and other languages.

These aims are aspired to the glory of the Lord according to the basic Christian principles put down in the Holy Bible.

Baumschulallee 3a • D-53115 Bonn • Germany
Phone: +49 / 228 / 695531 • Fax +49 / 228 / 695532
www.gebende-haende.de • info@gebende-haende.de

Martin Bucer Seminary

Faithful to biblical truth
Cooperating with the Evangelical Alliance
Reformed

Solid training for the Kingdom of God
- Alternative theological education
- Study while serving a church or working another job
- Enables students to remain in their own churches
- Encourages independent thinking
- Learning from the growth of the universal church.

Academic
- For the Bachelor's degree: 180 Bologna-Credits
- For the Master's degree: 120 additional Credits
- Both old and new teaching methods: All day seminars, independent study, term papers, etc.

Our Orientation:
- Complete trust in the reliability of the Bible
- Building on reformation theology
- Based on the confession of the German Evangelical Alliance
- Open for innovations in the Kingdom of God

Our Emphasis:
- The Bible
- Ethics and Basic Theology
- Missions
- The Church

Our Style:
- Innovative
- Relevant to society
- International
- Research oriented
- Interdisciplinary

Structure
- 15 study centers in 7 countries with local partners
- 5 research institutes
- President: Prof. Dr. Thomas Schirrmacher
  Vice President: Prof. Dr. Thomas K. Johnson
- Deans: Thomas Kinker, Th.D.;
  Titus Vogt, lic. theol., Carsten Friedrich, M.Th.

Missions through research
- Institute for Religious Freedom
- Institute for Islamic Studies
- Institute for Life and Family Studies
- Institute for Crisis, Dying, and Grief Counseling
- Institute for Pastoral Care

www.bucer.eu • info@bucer.eu

Berlin I Bielefeld I Bonn I Chemnitz I Hamburg I Munich I Pforzheim
Innsbruck I Istanbul I Izmir I Linz I Prague I São Paulo I Tirana I Zurich

www.ingramcontent.com/pod-product-compliance
Lightning Source LLC
Chambersburg PA
CBHW071237230426
43668CB00011B/1482